INLAND TRIPS FROM THE
Costa Blanca

Discover a Countryside
of Stunning Scenery
and Timeless Pueblos

DEREK WORKMAN

INLAND TRIPS FROM THE COSTA BLANCA
Published by Ediciones Santana S.L.
Apartado 41, 29650 Mijas Pueblo(Málaga)Spain
Tel: (0034) 952 485 838. Fax: (0034) 952 485 367
info@santanabooks.com

First Publiahed in October 2003.
Second Edition in November 2006.

Copyright © Derek Workman
Design by Chris Fajardo
Photography by the author
General map courtesy of Generalitat Valenciana

Printed in Spain by Gráficas San Pancracio S.L.
Depósito Legal: MA-1.712/2006
ISBN 13: 978-84-89954-56-4
ISBN   84-89954-56-9

CONTENTS

INTRODUCTION

Since the Scandinavians began their sun-seeking forays into eastern Spain in the early 1960s, the Costa Blanca has become synonymous with miles of golden beaches, almost year-round sun and the relaxed lifestyle that epitomises Mediterranean Spain.

Most of the early visitors never ventured more than a few kilometres from the Mediterranean shore. Those who did were well rewarded. They discovered a region of glorious diversity, from rugged mountains to almost lunar landscapes, and vast areas of natural beauty where the scent of aromatic herbs filled the air and wild flower-lined walks meandered through pine forests.

They stumbled across Neolithic rock paintings, majestic waterfalls, soaring rock faces and deep caves formed over millions of years, and explored picturesque villages where recipes were handed down from generation to generation and the rhythm of life was dictated by the seasons.

Incredibly, this wondrous inland region still exists — and this book is a guide for those who want to experience more of Spanish life than sun, sea and sangría and are ready to jump into a car and visit places where a foreign accent is still a rarity, to explore the narrow cobbled streets of historic mountain villages where the past is in the present, and witness bizarre rural fiestas whose roots go back to pagan times.

The 22 excursions cover the Valencian Community, with a dip into Teruel and Murcia, and are arranged in such a way that you link excursions to create itineraries for a day, a weekend or longer. Each excursion includes a map and route details as well as information on sights to see, overnight accommodation, where to eat and local specialities. The book also has general information on driving, a basic vocabulary and hints on the use of the Valencia language.

REGIONAL INFORMATION
Valencia is one of Spain's 17 autonomous regions. Known as the Comunidad de Valencia in *castellano* (Spanish) and as the Comunitat Valenciana in *valenciano* (see Language below), it is made up of three provinces, Castellón in the north, Valencia in the middle, and Alicante in the south.

Each capital city takes its name from the province, which can be confusing, but when we mention Castellón, Valencia or Alicante we make it clear whether we are referring to the province or the capital city. The Valencia region is variously referred to in this book as the Comunitat Valenciana or the País de Valencia (its original name from the time of the Reconquista) or the Valencia Community. The Generalitat Valenciana is the governing body that provides services within the region.

LANGUAGE

The use of *valenciano*, which is not a true language but a derivative of Catalan, is the subject of debate throughout the Comunitat Valenciana. The regional Valencia government has adopted *valenciano* as the dominant language in all official documents and much of the information it provides, including tourist information, is in both *valenciano* and *castellano* or, as we would know it, Spanish. Fortunately, much of it is also in English.

Anyone with a reasonable command of Spanish should get the drift of *valenciano* in its written form and, as almost everyone in the region understands Spanish, should have no problems communicating with the locals.

This book has been based on the excellent Mapa Turístico (Tourist Map) provided by the Generalitat Tourist Office which uses the *valenciano* version of the place names (sometimes with its Spanish translation). Nearly all other maps use the Spanish version of the name.

Some of the place names we mention could be slightly different from those seen on road signs. In most cases the names used are those seen while actually on the road at the time of researching the book, although these are subject to change as many towns are replacing signs with the *valenciano* version of their name.

Thus, the names of Jijona, Játiva and Jalón can become Xixona, Xàtiva and Xaló, while the *ayuntamiento* (town hall) can be called the *ajuntament*. We have tried our best to avoid any confusion by making our route directions as clear as possible. If the name on a sign is slightly different from that on the map or in the book, it's most likely to be the same place.

INFORMATION

In each excursion, addresses are given of tourist offices or town halls where information can be found. The Generalitat Valenciana produces excellent maps and information leaflets, as does each province and many of the individual town halls. It is always worth asking at both the *ayuntamiento* and the tourist office if the town has both. Many small towns have no information office, but you can usually pick up leaflets from hotels, restaurants and visitor venues. The main website for the region is www.comunitatvalenciana.com. Information about Spain in general, including useful addresses and telephone numbers, can be had by calling 901 300 600 between 8am-9pm seven days a week.

VISITING HOURS
Most national monuments and museums are closed on Mondays. Unless specific opening times are given, it is safest to assume that churches are open only during the times of religious services, usually in the evenings, although if you ask around you may find someone who has a key.

If you are making a special trip to see something, always check opening times beforehand as they can vary from those published, particularly during the summer months when they usually open later in the afternoon and stay open later. Some town halls close at 2pm during the peak summer months of July and August, but no fixed rules apply and it is usually at the individual councils' discretion. *Festivos* are holidays, whether national ones or associated with each town's fiestas, and normally have the same opening times as Sundays.

TRANSPORT
This book is mainly designed for those travelling by car or motorcycle. Public transport, both bus and train, between major towns is usually good although occasionally arrival and departure times can be erratic. Travel between villages is usually by bus, which often runs only once a day.

ON THE ROAD
The Comunitat Valenciana is experiencing a boom in road construction and it is possible to drive to places that 10 years ago were difficult to get to. The road numbers given in the excursions refer to those actually seen while researching the book, but be warned that some of these numbers could be changed in the near future. Thus, you may well find that the road number mentioned in this book is not the one on your map. In some places the road signs display both the old and the new numbers. Take heart: if the road sign says you are travelling in the direction of Dos Aguas and the road is numbered VV3081 while your Michelin tells you it's the CV425, Dos Aguas is still going to be the place you arrive at.

At the time of reviewing the book for the second edition a few of the more rural roads were closed for improvement. Where this occurs it is mentioned, but most are only closed for a few months and may well be open by the time you visit.

Most roads in these excursions are in good condition and even the few that are not are perfectly passable. It is unwise to calculate travelling time by the number of kilometres indicated, especially on mountain roads where progress can be slower than expected.

Driving in Spain is on the right, but be cautious on country roads as some drivers tend to hog the middle of the road. Be especially alert in the early evening, at the time of the *paseo*, when couples and family groups leave their villages to stroll along the country lanes, seemingly unaware of passing traffic.

Drivers and passengers are required to use seat-belts and motorcyclists must wear crash helmets. Though these laws are not always strictly adhered to, fines can be given if offenders are stopped by the police. Drink driving laws, similar to those in the UK, are being much more rigorously enforced. Be prepared for youngsters on scooters and motorcycles riding though red traffic lights or overtaking you on the inside.

The Spanish have taken to "sleeping policemen", or speed control bumps, in a big way. They are sometimes signposted and sometimes not, and can vary from a narrow plastic strip (*banda sonora*) to a wide, raised tarmac band (*paso elevado*). The latter are usually, but not always, alternate red-and-white stripes with the white stripes coming to a point. Approach them with caution as some are dangerously high and there may be a second bump a short distance after the first.

Parking in most Spanish towns and villages can be difficult, especially in the small mountain villages where narrow streets were designed for nothing wider than a donkey with two laden panniers. When visiting these smaller villages, it is advisable to park your car before trying to negotiate the twisting alleyways.

It is wise to observe speed restrictions as speed traps are common and the Guardia Civil highway patrols can impose heavy on-the-spot fines for driving offences. Spain has introduced a stiff penalty for anyone caught using a mobile phone while driving. Be polite with the Guardia Civil and never argue. Accept the situation with as much humour as you can and, if you accept you have committed an offence, pay the fine. Unless you can prove you are a resident of the country, you will be expected to pay the fine on the spot.

Petrol stations are becoming more numerous in the coastal areas but it is advisable not to let your tank get too low when touring as they can be few and far between in country areas and usually close quite early in the evening.

If you are touring with your own vehicle, make sure you carry your documents in the car as this is required by Spanish law, though you can take photocopies of your car documents to your local police station and get them stamped and these will be acceptable on the road.

If you are visiting from another country, these documents should include international insurance, a bail bond in case of accident (Green Card) and an international driving licence, although for short stays by EEC visitors the national licence is usually sufficient. You are also required to carry spare light bulbs and fan belt and each car must have two plastic reflective warning triangles to be placed in front of and behind any vehicle immobilised because of a breakdown or accident. By law all drivers must wear reflective waistcoats outside the vehicle when it is stationary because of an accident or breakdown. If your hire car does not include these, ask for them. You may have to pay a small hire charge, but it will undoubtedly be cheaper than the fine incurred if you are caught without one should a breakdown or accident occur.

MAPS

While the maps in the book should prove sufficient it is always best to have a detailed map of the area to be on the safe side. Campsa produces an annually updated guide with detailed, fold-out maps covering the whole of Spain and tourist and gastronomic information. While in a tourism office, try to get copies of the cream-coloured illustrated leaflets that cover the region's various *comarcas* (areas). There are 18 in all and you can get them in English. Not all offices have them so, when you find one that does, it's worth getting the set. The maps are totally out of scale but provide a lot of information and show some of the smaller roads that the smaller-scale maps don't include.

SECURITY

The rural areas of Spain suffer lower levels of crime than the coastal resorts but it is still wise to take precautions. Always make sure nothing is left in view in an unattended car. If you are staying in a hotel, leave your luggage there. Spanish law requires that your car documents are always with the vehicle, so make sure the glove compartment is locked. When parking, try to use a guarded car park, though these may be difficult to find outside large towns. Sometimes you will be waved into a parking space by unofficial parking attendants, known to the locals as "gorillas", who will expect a small payment. It's advisable to pay them as they will usually keep an eye on your car.

Make photocopies of your passport and other personal documents and leave the originals in the hotel safe, except for your driving licence, the original of which is required if stopped by the police or Guardia Civil (you may also need the original of your passport when cashing traveller's checks). Driving licences, if the new credit-card-sized type with a photo, are usually accepted as proof of identity when using a credit card.

Spain has three main police forces. They are: the Policía Local, or *"los municipales"*, who are the local police and carry out most of the minor tasks; the Policía Nacional, the national police who are responsible for crime prevention and investigation (both these forces wear blue uniforms); and the Guardia Civil, conspicuous by their olive-green uniforms, who are mainly concerned with traffic duties and crime prevention in small towns and rural areas. Do not attempt to photograph any building labelled a "Casa Cuartel". This is a Guardia Civil barracks, which is regarded as a military post, and it is strictly forbidden to photograph them. If you need to go to a police station, ask for the *comisaría*.

EATING OUT

Anyone who thinks Spanish cuisine is restricted to *paella* will be considerably surprised when they venture into the restaurants of the interior. The menu is often dictated by the seasons or produce that is grown in that particular area. Many local dishes are robust and full of flavours derived from local herbs. Locally bred Spanish lamb has no peer and it is quite common to see such rarities to the British palate as *jabalí* (wild boar) on the menu. But don't spurn the *paella* because, as everyone knows, it originated in Valencia and is only one of many excellent rice dishes that will be found on most menus.

The Comunitat Valenciana has excellent restaurants to suit every pocket and a number of associations promote regional cuisine. One to look out for is Parlant Menjant (Talking and Eating), Associació Gastronòmica Muntaya d'Alicant, to be found in the towns around the Sierra Mariola, the area to the west of Alcoi. The restaurants in this association specialise in the mountain cuisine of the Sierra Mariola and can be recognised by a small blue and white plaque.

The *menú del día* is a splendid Spanish institution. For around €8 you will get a three-course meal including bread, wine and dessert. This is usually only available at lunchtimes, but in some of the smaller towns and villages you can find the same good-value *menú* available in the evenings. If you wish to eat *a la carte* ask for *la carta* because *menú* only refers to the *menú del día*, although there will sometimes be a *menú degustación* which is a sampling menu and gives a taste of some of the restaurant's best dishes at a fixed price.

If the restaurant appears to be a little more upmarket and doesn't display a *menú del día*, ask for it anyway as most restaurants offer one even if all of them do not promote it. *Tapas* are usually available at all hours. They are of course a very Spanish way of having a snack but they can work out quite expensive if you try to make a meal out of them.

Don't forget that Spaniards eat late, between 2 and 4pm for lunch and from 9pm onwards for dinner. Most restaurants these days, excepting cheaper establishments, accept credit cards, nearly always Visa and Mastercard and less frequently Diners and American Express. The price for one person for a three-course meal with wine is indicated by a euro symbol (€):

€ under 15 euros

€€ 15–25 euros

€€€ more than 25 euros

WHERE TO STAY

The image of rural Spain as a backwoods of flea-bitten hostelries with holes in the ground for toilets is part of the dim and distant past. Many beautiful old mansions and farmhouses have been turned into delightful rural hotels and it is rare to be offered a room in even the smallest *casa rural* that isn't en-suite.

In rural areas, accommodation is mainly divided into *hoteles rurales* and *casas rurales*, country hotels and country houses. It isn't easy to define the exact difference but a rule of thumb is to assume that a *hotel rural* will have all the amenities of a hotel, including restaurant, bar and lounges, and a *casa rural* is usually a bed-and-breakfast place, sometimes with a restaurant or offering dinner by arrangement. *Casa rural* also applies to a rural house that is let out complete. To confuse matters, a *hospedería* is a *casa rural* with a restaurant open to the public. *Pensión* and *hostal* usually indicate simple accommodation in towns. It is difficult to judge the quality of a place by the star ratings as these only take into account the amenities offered and not the quality of service or atmosphere.

The rates listed here are meant only as a guide as they can vary depending on season and can go up during local fiestas. The price for two people staying in a double room, including taxes, is indicated by the € symbol. Breakfast is usually included in the price.

€ under 40 euros

€€ 40-60 euros

€€€ 60-90 euros

€€€€ over 90 euros

The Generalitat publishes a guide (available from tourist offices) of most of the rural accommodation in the Valencian Community as part of the series of illustrated maps mentioned above.

WORTH KNOWING

Spaniards love their weekend trips to the *campo,* especially to dine *en familia* on Sundays, and if you can go on your trips on weekdays, where possible avoiding peak holiday periods, you will find hotels, restaurants and roads less crowded. If you can only travel at weekends and peak periods and want to make an overnight stay, it is best to book a hotel, particularly during Easter week.

If you don't want to be tied to restaurants, stock up on a few select items for a picnic. Even the smallest village store will usually have a good selection of ham, cheese, fruit, wine and soft drinks, but don't forget to take drinking cups, a corkscrew and a knife. Remember that these shops will normally close for lunch between 2 and 5pm.

The best months for touring are April to June and September to November. During July and August temperatures can make spending hours in a car an uncomfortable experience and it is not advisable to undertake any long walks in these months. During winter months it can be much colder and wetter than most people expect, especially in the mountain areas, so take along warm, waterproof clothing. Whatever time of the year you are walking, make sure you carry plenty of water.

Spaniards in general are very tolerant and casual dress is accepted almost everywhere. But, whereas wandering the streets in nothing but flip-flops and a pair of shorts may be acceptable in coastal resorts, it will not be appreciated in many inland towns and villages — and will be especially frowned upon in places of worship. Also bear in mind that churches in smaller towns and villages often only open during services and you should be very discreet while visiting churches at these times.

LET US KNOW

We welcome your help in keeping this guidebook as up to date as possible. If you come across any changes or discover a restaurant worth recommending or a hotel with a special appeal, please let us know. We shall take it into account when preparing the next edition.

Send your suggestions to: Ediciones Santana S.L., Apartado 41, 29650 Mijas Pueblo, (Málaga), Spain.

If you intend touring the region it would be worthwhile obtaining a copy of *Small Hotels and Inns of Eastern Spain*, also published by Santana Books.

Morella Castle from the Convent of San Francisco

TRIP 1

A HIDDEN GEM

> **AREA:** Northern Castellón province
> **ROUTE:** Vinarós - Traiguera - Sant Mateu - Morella
> **DISTANCE:** 75 kilometres

*Discover a hidden delight on the edge
of the Valencia region, meet an angel and roam
colonnaded streets rich in medieval history.*

At the northernmost reaches of the province of Castellón the road from Vinarós passes through open countryside decorated with ranks of orange, lemon and almond groves before it twists up the slope to the hilltop town of Morella. While there is no doubting the beauty of this historic city, few visitors realise that only 20 minutes after leaving the coastline they pass one of the many gems to be found in the Valencia region, the Reíal Santuari Verge Font de la Salut.

The first thing you see are four stone pillars supporting a square canopy over a stone cross. Then, as you turn down towards them, the cleft in the valley opens up to reveal a chronology of architectural styles from the 15th-century to the present day. Gothic, Renaissance, baroque and neoclassical, interweave with the popular architecture of the Maestrazgo, a scenic region of rugged terrain and medieval villages north of Castellón and including areas of Teruel and Valencia. It's known as the Maestrat in *valenciano*.

The story goes that two young goatherds, Anastasio and Jaime Sorlí, were tending their flock in the mountains where the sanctuary is now built, a dry and sterile land. One of them (history does not record which) was extremely thirsty but had no water. He saw one of the goats rummaging through the thick grass of a ravine, and when it brought its head up its beard was soaked with water. The boy rushed to where the goat was drinking and saw a small fountain gushing from the earth. After drinking his fill, he looked up and saw a vision of the Virgin Mary. The boy had been unable to speak from birth, but when he saw the vision he thanked her, in *valenciano*, for the refreshing drink.

Historians seem unable to agree on the exact date of the miracle, citing a 50-year span from 1384 to 1434, but on September 8, 1439, the day of the festival of the Virgin, the first stone of the Gothic temple was laid. Kings, cardinals, archbishops and civic authorities visited "la Font de la Salut de Triaguera", and by the 16th-century it was one of the four or five most important sanctuaries in Spain, and certainly the most important in the kingdom of Valencia.

As you enter the sanctuary grounds you are struck by the benign mix of architectural styles: painted façades next to Gothic arches, next to rustic Maestrazgo stonework, next to a run of barbecues built into a long stone wall to keep visitors happy.

A saunter down the side of the baroque entrance to the temple, under low stone arches, brings you to a small courtyard, in the cobbled centre of which is located, curiously, the off-set stones of a game of hop-scotch. Ornate paintwork surrounds the door and window frames. To the left, three curved stone steps lead you through a modest doorway, and a short flight of stairs polished by centuries of passing feet brings you to a small landing. Should you turn right, your first sight will be of some ghastly floor tiles, but as you step into the church you witness some of the most stunning ecclesiastical decoration.

The paintwork is that of Vinarós baroque master Eugenio Guilló Barceló who, at the time of its completion in 1736, was Spain's foremost artist of ecclesiastic painting. Almost every inch is covered with symbolic imagery glorifying the Virgin Mary and anywhere that isn't painted is intricately carved, attributed to the Valencia sculptors Francisco Esteve and Antonio Salvador, who completed the work in the mid-1720s.

Almost six centuries since the miracle that created it, after living through fame and fortune, development and destruction, the Font de la Salut is being restored to its former glory.

Rejoin the N232 Vinarós-Morella road, turning right after La Jana on to the CV10 for Sant Mateu. Sant Mateu is typical of a small medieval town. Everything radiates off a central square, the Plaza Mayor or, as it is sometimes known locally, the Plaza Ángel because of the angel that tops the fountain in the square.

The plaza is one of those lovely arcaded squares with little streets running off from its corners and, thankfully, still has some proper village-type shops, although it is mainly taken up with cafes and even the odd estate agent is sneaking in. The pretty 18th-century Fuente del

A colonnaded street in Morella

Ángel, symbolising San Mateo Evangelista, keeps serene watch over the square, but if you want to see the original 14th-century version, minus odd bits and pieces, you will have to visit the Museo Histórico-Etnológico Municipal on Calle Historiador Betí.

Historiador Betí was originally the "posh" part of town and has some excellent examples of the architecture of the Maestrazgo from the 14th and 15th centuries, including the Corta Nova, where the local court is now held, and the Museo. The museum houses a model of a 14th-century stately home and a small collection of local artefacts, including the originals of the Fuente del Ángel and the Fuente de

21

The beautiful Font de Salut

Santa María de Montesa, originally documented in 1365 and named after the soldier-monk Order of Montesa, once as famous as the Knights Templar. The tourist office is in the same building.

Sant Mateu isn't short of grand buildings although unfortunately most are closed to the public. The sheer Gothic magnificence of the 16th-century Palau del Marqués de Villores is worth a stroll up Calle Vols for a gander at its façade, and the Convento de las Monjas Agustinas

(16th-18th-century) just up the street from the Palau, like the famed Windmill club in London, never closes.

Just off the Plaza Mayor, but nonetheless dominating it and the whole of Sant Mateu with its majestic presence, is the Iglesia Arciprestal, built by the military order San Juan del Hospital in the 13th century (religion could be a pretty war-like affair in those days). The church corresponds to the type known as *de conquista*, built during the fight to re-claim Spanish territory for Christianity and drive out the Moors. It was extended during the 14th-century when the Order of Montesa took over the town. An urn is said to contain a reliquary of Saint Clement the Martyr (also said to be that of an anonymous martyr but he can't have been that anonymous if they call him Saint Clement).

Leave Sant Mateu by the CV132 for Chert (Xert), once again joining the N332 to the splendid walled town of Morella.

From its Iberian beginnings Morella has always been seen as a strategic point and been fortified to a greater or lesser degree. Archaeological research has shown remains of Iberian, Greek, Phoenician, Roman, and Moorish civilisations, but it was the Moors who were responsible for the first high medieval walls, built before the 10th-century and partially destroyed when El Cid conquered the city in 1084. The present city walls, more than 1.5 kilometres long, were built in 1330 and have had various modifications over the centuries so that now almost every element of military architectural style is represented.

Architectural grandiosity aside, it's the medieval town within the city walls that makes Morella such a joy to visit. Very few towns have the same sense of history that you experience wandering through the narrow cobbled alleyways, and it takes no great leap of fancy to imagine yourself back in the times when only horses and carts rattled through the streets.

The centre stage of Morella social life is the porticoed Calle Blasco de Alagón. Below those colonnaded walkways much of the city's life

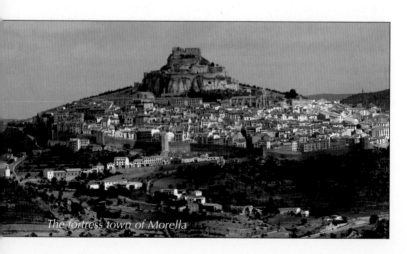

The fortress town of Morella

Sant Mateu´s medieval Plaza Angel

has flowed since it was built in the 13th-century. In 1257 Jaime I authorised the building of 50 workshops and, were he to saunter along the street today, he would recognise the original structure and layout. But where once stood workshops are now restaurants and some of the many delis and fabric shops the town is famous for.

As you wander up the street a glance at the stone columns will show you that they don't follow any specific architectural order, almost as if they were picked up at a local store's "historical stone pillar" department. There are square ones, round ones, octagonal ones, fat, slim, tall and short, even some Romanesque ones with small carved heads. Where they aren't exactly the same height, to keep the floor level the builder has simply stuck in an extra piece of wood or hacked a chunk out to make them fit — and we think we invented reclamation.

One of Morella's most important buildings sits almost at the end of the street, the Palace of Cardinal Ram, now the Hotel Cardinal Ram. Originally the home of an illustrious family, it was the residence of the said cardinal in the late 14th-century, during Morella's period of maximum splendour. Apart from the cacophony of 21st -century life, nothing has changed much in the view from the hotel's windows down Calle Blasco de Alagón.

Wander up the steep, twisting streets and you eventually come to the Basílica de Santa María la Mayor, the splendid 14th-century centre of

Font Angel in Sant Mateu

religious life, with its twin Gothic doors opening off a peaceful small plaza. Described by the Marquis de Lozoya, in his *Historia del Arte Hispánico* as "the most beautiful Gothic church in the entire ancient reign of Valencia", it certainly comes up to scratch for those interested in ecclesiastical history.

Further uphill you come to the Royal Convent of San Francisco — or at least what's left of it — through whose beautiful cloistered arches you can see the castle. It's very impressive from a distance but, after struggling up the steep slope on a steaming afternoon following a good lunch, you may wonder why you bothered. There's nothing to see except some restored stonework and signs telling you that what buildings are left are actually from the mid-1850s. Still, the stunning views over the Sierras de Ares are worth the €1.50 entrance fee.

You can really only do so much history, though, before succumbing to the hearty grub that is the real delight of any visit to Morella and the Maestrazgo. Truffle is king, and the town is full of wonderful delis where you can pick up small jars of the little black gems to titivate your taste-buds when you get back home. In February the town hosts the *Jornadas Gastronómicas de la Trufa* when the restaurants try to outdo each other with culinary delights based on the expensive tuber. You could well get the opportunity to try truffle brandy, made by leaving a half kilo of truffles in five litres of brandy for two years, which results in a very peculiar, but pleasant, flavour that bears no resemblance to anything you've ever drunk before.

It's also worth trying *tronchón*, a hard ewe's milk cheese which originated in a small village just over the border in Teruel province. It has an excellent strong flavour and is served in razor-thin slices that melt on the tongue. *Cecina* or *jamón ternera*, made from beef, has a slightly richer flavour and darker colour than *jamón serrano*. It is also stringier and oozes juice, if that's possible with a dried meat. Vegetarians or otherwise should try the *setas de cerdo silvestres*, chopped mushrooms cooked with *ajos tiernos*, garlic shoots, which, apart from truffles, are probably nature's best fungi friends. Thick and juicy, they have the texture of a good steak.

To round off a meal you will inevitably be offered *cuajada*, a dessert of milk, sugar and sheep's cheese flavoured with artichoke flowers. Soft and creamy with a yoghurt-like texture, it is a delightful culmination of to a robust mountain meal.

To complete the excursion return to the coast by way of the N232 to Vinarós, or experience the beauty of the Maestrazgo by taking the CV12/CV15 via Ares de Maestre to reach the coastal motorway at Castellón de la Plana.

WHAT TO SEE

TRAIGUERA:
Reíal Santuari Verge Font de la Salut. The Font Salut is being restored by the Escuela Taller, a government-funded body that provides training in specialised building and restoration work, and has no fixed opening hours, depending on the work being done.

SANT MATEU:
Iglesia Arciprestal, 13th-15th-century Gothic, national monument.
Museo Histórico-Etnológico Municipal, Calle Historiador Betí. Tel. 96 441 66 58. Open Tues-Sat 10am-2pm and 4pm-6pm, Sun 10am-2pm.
Museo de Cárceles (Prison Museum), Calle La Cort 28. Tel. 96 441 61 02. Open daily 10am-2pm and 4pm-6pm

MORELLA:
Calle Blasco de Alagón, colonnaded 13th-century street.
Basílica de Santa María la Mayor.
Sexenal, the major fiesta held every six years.

The cross of
the Font de
Salut

WHERE TO STAY

SANT MATEU:
Hotel La Pardi, Calle Historiador Betí. Tel. 96 441 60 82.
Basic pension. €

MORELLA:
Hotel El Pastor, Calle San Julián 12. Tel. 96 416 10 16.
Attractive hotel that looks part of the historic architecture but
is brand new. €€€
Hotel Cardinal Ram, Cuesta Suñer 1. Tel. 96 417 30 85.
Housed in a 13th-century palace, the hotel was completely
refurbished in 2005. €€

WHERE TO EAT

SANT MATEU:
Restaurant La Pardi, Calle Historiador Betí. Tel. 96 441 60 82.
Good local cuisine at reasonable prices. €
Plenty of bars serve tapas and light meals.

MORELLA:
El Pastor, Cuesta Jovani 5-7. Tel. 96 416 02 49.
Well-established restaurant serving traditional local recipes.
Recommended. €€
Many bars serve tapas. Some excellent delis if you wish to
dine *al fresco*.
Restaurant Casa Roque, Costa del Sant Joan 1. Tel. 96 416 03 36.
Good local cuisine. Part of the annual Jornadas
Gastronómicas de la Trufa. €€

MORE INFORMATION

Sant Mateu: Tourist Information Office, Calle Historiador
Betí 6. Tel. 96 441 66 58.
Morella: Tourist Information Office. Plaza de San Miguel 3.
Tel. 96 417 30 32.

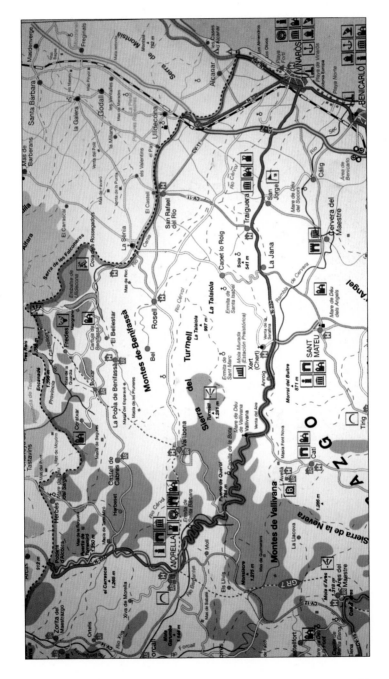

Rooftops and castle wall of Albarracín

TRIP 2

DISNEY'S MOUNTAIN - TOP VILLAGE

> **AREA:** Southern Teruel
> **ROUTE:** Teruel-Albarracín-Rubielos de Mora
> **DISTANCE:** 310 kilometres

Glory at the sparkling architecture of Spain's coldest city and wander the narrow streets of a picture-postcard village that could have been designed by Walt Disney.

In the southernmost province of Aragon, Teruel city is only a couple of hours away from bustling Valencia and the shimmering beaches of the Costa Azahar, but a world away in temperament. As you toil up from the coast (N234) in a queue of traffic wishing the new motorway were finished (by mid-2007 with luck), take pleasure in the fact that once off the major roads all is vast open spaces. And there, within a few kilometres, the landscape can change from rolling Cotswold Downs to ragged Lake District peaks – with a lot of non-British equivalents in between.

Architecturally Teruel is a little gem, renowned for having some of Spain's most beautiful examples of Mudejar structures. Mudejar emerged as an architectural style on the Iberian peninsula in the 12th-century as a result of the Jewish, Muslim and Christian cultures living side by side. It is characterised by the use of brick as the main material. Unlike Gothic or Romanesque, Mudejar did not involve the creation of new shapes or structures but rather reinterpreting Western styles through Muslim influences. It is accepted that the style was born in Toledo, as an adaptation of architectural and ornamental motifs, although it became most highly developed in Aragon, especially in Teruel.

It is characterised by an extremely refined and inventive use of brick and glazed tiles, especially in belfries. Tiles are often cobalt blue and

A village church in rural Teruel

white, although a lustrous green predominates in Teruel. Look for airy patios with a fountain or tiled, reflecting pool and repeated motifs like square flowers and eight-pointed stars rather than faces and images. Teruel's most glorious examples are the towers of San Pedro, San Martín, El Salvador and the Cathedral. El Salvador's is the only tower that can be ascended. From the first floor of the Café El Torre next door you get an unusual, wonderful view of the tile-work glistening above.

Santa María Cathedral has a beautiful belfry but it's worth paying the couple of euros entrance fee to have a gander at the ceiling of carved panels painted in polychrome wood with images that represent Teruel life in the Middle Ages. You need to get there just as the guide

begins her description (in Spanish) when the ceiling is illuminated – the light goes out when she moves on to the next part of her tour. If you want a quick chat with the man upstairs, it's free before 11am.

The gloriously rich brick-and-tile designs are the jewels in the city's crown, enhanced in their settings by the delightfully florid examples of *modernista* art, the Catalan equivalent of Art Nouveau.

On top of a pillar in the historic centre, the Plaza Torico, sits the symbol of Teruel, El Torico, a statue of a bull atop a fluted column. Given the Spanish propensity for big and bold in public sculpture, it comes as a shock to see how small the "little bull" actually is (the suffix "-ico" is a common diminutive).

The buildings that surround the triangular plaza are a mix of architectural styles, with stout columns and tiny narrow streets leading off, enticing you to discover more hidden corners.

Legend has it that in the 13th-century two young people, Diego de Marcilla and Isabel de Segura, fell in love and wanted to marry. Isabel came from wealthy stock, but Diego was skint and her parents forbade the match. In a magnanimous gesture of a sort, Isabel's father gave Diego five years in which to make his fortune and establish a name for himself. At the end of this time he returned to Teruel a wealthy man, only to find his bride-to-be already married to a local nobleman. Poor young Diego died of a broken heart and Isabel, full of despair at his death, snuffed it the following day. You can see the couple, forever linked by alabaster hands, in the cloisters of the church of San Pedro. Sadly, the Plaza de los Amantes alongside the church that dedicates their love must be one of the ugliest in Spain. In true fairy-tale style, the story of the Spanish Romeo and Juliet has been made into a film.

If you want to take something home, pick up a couple of bottles of the cheap but excellent Campo de Borja wine from the Aragon region, but for a real bit of giddy gastronomy nip into Martín Martín, just opposite the defunct Mercado Municipal at the top of Calle Joaquín Costa. In one of the strangest combinations you will come across, it's a pickle, cake and sweet shop. The former are sold loose from about 50 big ceramic pots, or in tins and jars from a mouth-watering selection on shelves behind the counter. On the other side of the shop are containers of lollipops, liquorice sticks, jelly things, crunchy what-nots, twists and twirls of all sorts. Plus a nifty selection of dried fruits, biscuits, cakes and nuts. An adult and children's edible heaven.

Instead of taking the road direct from Teruel to Albarracín, make the slight detour into the Sierra de Jabalón via Bezas (A1513) and the Espacio Protegido Pinares de Rodeno and its Neolithic rock paintings. (Teruel province makes much of its prehistoric heritage and, if you can't see the dinosaurs in real life, you can at least visit a whole theme park designed around their existence on the edge of Teruel.) Rodeno takes its name from the reddish rock in the area that contorts into strange formations.

The road through the Espacio is a delightful wander through pine trees with long vistas of cornfields snaking off into the distance. Nothing prepares you for Albarracín though, with its narrow streets terracing up the hillside and the *casas colgadas*, houses with wooden balconies precariously hanging over the streets below.

When Walt Disney had Mickey Mouse running around medieval

El Torico, Teruel

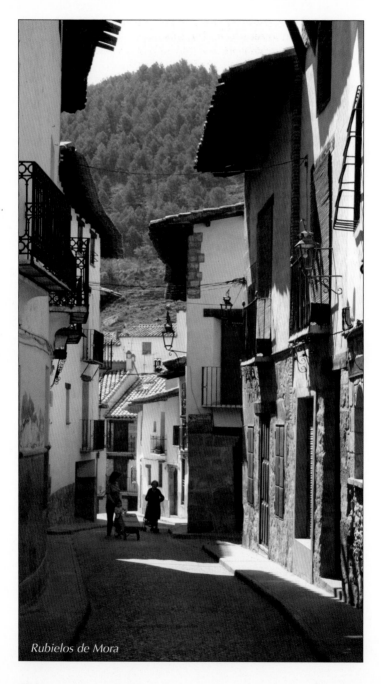

Rubielos de Mora

streets in *The Sorcerer's Apprentice,* he must have conjured up the idea after a visit to Albarracín. This mountain-top village's streets are so narrow that neighbours can not only shake hands from their windows but probably share the same curtains.

Albarracín, on a rocky outcrop above a meander of the river Guadalaviar, has been classified by UNESCO as a monument of world interest. Stand in the centre of the Plaza Mayor and in a 360-degrees turn you'll see a town square almost as it would have looked in the 16th and 17th centuries — without the cars of course. The buildings have been tidied but not tarted up and the streets that radiate off at odd angles are like cobbled, stone-and-iron canyons, up steps, around sharp bends, down tiny alleyways, where even in the height of summer the sun never reaches.

The magnificent mansions — and there are a surprisingly large number of them — date from the 17th-century, when the town experienced rapid economic growth thanks to the raising of cattle and wool exports. That faded during the 18th-century, leaving the town virtually moribund until a few years ago when the tourist industry brought a new lease of life.

If you are a fisherman you may like to chance your line in the Guadalaviar, one of Spain's richest trout rivers, where the national fishing championships are held every year. The surrounding Sierra de Albarracín is a walkers' and naturalists' paradise, while you can hunt wild boar in the Montes Universales National Game Reserve.

If you want to see "genuine Spain" as distinct from the purple-prose "real Spain" beloved by travel and estate agents, take a slight detour through Cella on your way back to Teruel. In a complete contrast to Albarracín, the village wins no prizes for beauty. Half-finished houses are scattered among disreputable-looking farm buildings surrounded by ancient equipment and newly laid-out patios share ground space with half-heartedly cultivated plots, with the pulping factory on the outskirts belching out fumes. It sounds totally anti-touristic, and it is, but it's worth passing through just for the fun of it.

Skirt Teruel and take the road for Corbalán and Allepuz, the A226, which wends its way through beautiful rolling countryside, interrupted only by scattered farmhouses, many in ruins but some still with the curious steeple-like towers seen on early buildings in the region. After Allepuz (blink and you'll miss it) you can stay on the main road to Cantavieja or Mirambel, another couple of must-see mountain villages. This excursion takes a right just after you leave the village on a country road pointing towards Valdelinares, one of the two ski centres in Teruel, the other being Alcalá de la Selva.

Rubielos town hall patio

You feel as if you are driving through somewhere untouched since Noah was a lad. On the outskirts of the few villages you pass are rows of *pajares*, one-storey stone sheds the villagers use to store grain and keep rabbits in. Some are being bought up to make rural homes, although you'll need a lot of building experience and a good bank balance to tackle them.

You begin to realise just how cold Teruel province can get when you see the *pistes* at Valdelinares where, even in mid-April when coastal types are having their first tentative toe-dipping in the Med, the mountainsides are covered in snow and villagers are scarved-up when they nip out for a loaf.

Drift on, past Linares de Mora, with its ancient arched entrance to the village and the church spire rising over the narrow streets, down to Rubielos de Mora, not to be confused with Mora de Rubielos, its next-door neighbour and poor relation in the architecture stakes, bonny as it might be in its own right.

Some claim Rubielos de Mora is as lovely as Albarracín. It is one of those wonderful Spanish villages that seem forever set in Sunday afternoon mode. In the narrow, twisting medieval streets within the walls of the historic centre you may see the occasional granny pulling a wheelie basket and you know it's rush-hour when a cat gets up to stretch its legs after a doze in the sun.

The size of the village belies the fact that it was once one of the most important religious centres in Aragon, with not just one but two convents, one of which is still home to five *monjas clausuradas*, elderly nuns who never leave the confines of the convent.

Enter through either of the 14th-century portals, of Carmen or of San Antonio, and you enter a time warp where grand mansions and stunning *casas señoriales* (noble houses) fill the squares. Not all past visitors are held in high regard to judge by the red paint daubed on a plaque on a *modernista* façade in the Plaza del Carmen — the lettering commemorates the visit of Generalísimo Franco.

An amusing detail on a couple of large houses, long corrugated plaster ribs, isn't a regional architectural oddity. It was a way wily householders stopped the local lads using their walls for an impromptu local handball game that left marks all over a nicely painted house front.

If you feel in need of relaxation after all this beauty, you can nip over the border into Valencia, to Montenejos, and soak in the natural hot water springs or while away an hour in its famous spa. Take the CV20 to return to Valencia from Montenejos or A515 from Rubielos, which joins the N234.

WHAT TO SEE

TERUEL
Mudejar towers of San Pedro, San Martín, El Salvador.
Cathedral.
Dinópolis, Polígono Los Planos, s/n Tel. 90 244 80 00.
Dinosaur park. Open daily 10am-8pm (last ticket 6pm) €18,
children under 11 and pensioners €14.

ALBARRACÍN:
Whole town has been declared of International Tourism
Interest.

RUBIELOS DE MORA:
Ayuntamiento, in 16th-century nobleman's house.
Santa María la Mayor, parish church consecrated in 1620.

WHERE TO STAY

TERUEL:
Hostal Serruchi, Calle Ollerías del Calvario, 4. Tel. 97 860 54
51/675 8089 653. Recently opened *hostal* has all the
amenities of a three-star hotel at budget prices. €€
Fonda del Tozal, Calle del Rincón, said to be the oldest
hostelry in Spain. €

ALBARRACÍN:
Casón del Ajimez, San Juan 2. Tel. 97 871 03 21 or 655 843
207. Unusual hotel in historic house decorated, supposedly,
to celebrate the Christian, Jewish and Arabic faiths. €€€
Hotel Casa de Santiago, Subida de las Torres 11. Tel. 97 870
0316. Set in 16th-century ex-priest's house. Bright, colourful
and idiosyncratic. €€€
Hospedería El Batán, Ctra Comarcal 1512, km43,
Tramacastilla.
Tel. 97 870 6070. Charming country hotel with highly rated
restaurant, 15-minute drive from Albarracín. €€€

RUBIELOS DE MORA:
Casa del Irlandés, Calle Virgen del Carmen 18.
Tel. 97 880 44 62 or 649 612 635. Owned by Irish/Spanish
couple. House and owners are equally delightful. €
Hotel Los Leones, Plaza Igual y Gil 3. Tel. 97 880 44 77.
Elegant historic home of local gentry. €€€

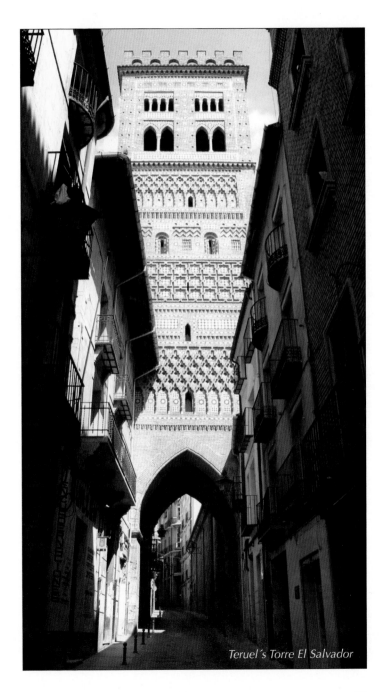

Teruel´s Torre El Salvador

WHERE TO EAT

TERUEL:
La Parrilla, Calle San Sebastián. Serves good portions of local cuisine, heavy stews, excellent *chorizo* and beautiful local lamb. €€
Bar Gregory and **Gregory Plus**, Paseo del Ovelo, for *tapas*, either as a nibble or full dining experience. €€
Bar Serruchi, Calle Ollerías del Calvario. Neighbourhood bar serving excellent local sausages, meats and grilled veg at bargain prices. €

ALBARRACÍN:
Hotel Casa de Santiago, Subida de las Torres 11. Tel. 97 870 03 16. €€
Hospedería El Batán, Ctra Comarcal 1512, km43, Tramacastilla.
Tel. 97 870 60 70. Highly rated restaurant serving local dishes and own highly inventive cuisine. €€€

RUBIELOS DE MORA:
Hotel Los Leones, Plaza Igual y Gil 3. Tel. 97 880 44 77. €€-€€
Hotel de la Villa, Plaza Carmen 2. Tel. 97 880 46 40. Restaurant specialises in local game. €€-€€€

MORE INFORMATION

TERUEL:
Tourist Information Office, Tomas Nogues 1.
Tel. 97 860 22 79.

ALBARRACÍN:
Tourist Information Office, Plaza Mayor 1,
Tel. 97 8 71 02 51.

RUBIELOS DE MORA:
Tourist information Office. Ayuntamiento, Plaza Hispano América. Tel. 97 880 40 01. Open Apr-Oct daily 10am-2pm and 5-8pm. Nov-Feb Mon-Fri 10am-2pm and 5-7pm.

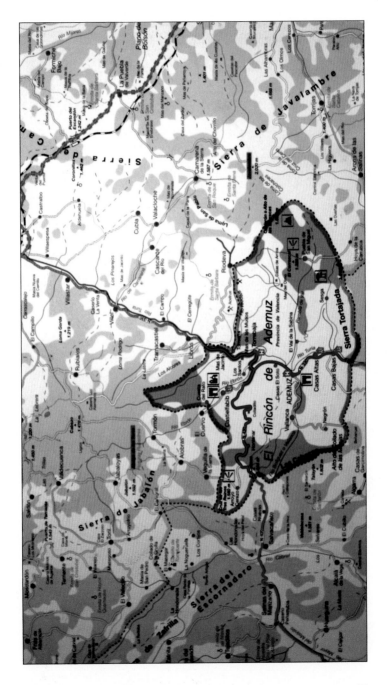

45

MEDIEVAL BYWAYS

> **AREA:** Alta Mijares (inland from Castellón city)
> **ROUTE:** Vilafamés – L'Alcora – Onda – Vall d'Uixo
> **DISTANCE:** 105 kilometres

Drive over a rust-red landscape, explore Valencia's pottery past and underground wonders, and enjoy one of the province's most important collections of contemporary art in a Gothic palace.

Exit from the A7 coastal motorway at junction 47 and take the CV16 in the direction of L'Alcora and Tarragona. Keep to the right side of the slip road and follow the signs for L'Alcora, passing a number of roundabouts. Stay on this road for about 10 kilometres until you see a sign to San Juan de Moro and Vilafamés on the CV160. At a roundabout with three tall, multi-coloured tiled pillars take the road to Vilafamés and you enter the Alto Mijares. Water from this area irrigates the crops of the La Plana district far below.

As the road climbs, everywhere is covered in fine red dust, deposited by this area's historic industry, ceramics. Stunted pine, holm oak and carob are interspersed with occasional olive trees and avalanches of deep-red rock and earth from the quarries that supply the ceramic factories. Soon, however, you leave the dust behind and enter a pleasant terrain of undulating hills covered in gorse and the sweet-smelling Spanish juniper.

Rounding a left-hand bend at the km10 marker, you see the castle of Vilafamés perched on the top of a hill, with sunlight shining through the empty window apertures, its circular tower watching over the village clinging to the hillside.

At the roundabout just below the village, take the first right, following the road up the hill. As you enter the village, take the road to the right of the Cooperativa de Crédito Caja Rural, which leads you into the Plaza de la Font. It is advisable to park here and walk up to the old town. Cross the square and turn right up Carrer la Font. A few metres up the street you will see La Roca Grossa, a huge red stone blackened with age, that hangs on a steep slope and looks ready to slide down any moment and carry half the *pueblo* with it.

Vilafamés is a mountain village of narrow winding streets of white houses edged in chunky red stone. Its history goes back to Neolithic times. Human remains, named *Homo erectus vilafamensis*, have been found from this period as well as Bronze Age cave paintings. However, it wasn't until after the conquest of the Moorish leader Beni-Hemez by Jaime I in 1233 that the village began to take its present-day shape.

The oldest part of town is at the foot of the castle, around the 13th-century Iglesia de la Sangre. Built over an Arab *aljibe* (cistern), this tiny church was renovated during the 17th-century, when its original design was altered, but it still contains an interesting baroque *retablo* (altarpiece) and painted frescoes in the presbytery.

Calle Cuarticho, the arms-width alleyway that runs alongside the church, is one of the oldest thoroughfares and could easily win a "prettiest street in Spain" competition.

Just above the church is the castle, from whose ramparts you can look across to the mountain of Penyagolosa, at 1814 metres the highest peak in the Comunitat Valenciana.

One of this small rural town's unexpected delights is that it has one of the region's most important collections of contemporary art. Housed in the beautiful Palau de Batle, an excellent example of Valencia's Gothic civic architecture of the 14th and 15th centuries, the Museo Popular de Arte Contemporáneo displays the work of more than 400 artists from the 1920s to the present day. Sculptures, paintings, etchings, and holograms unfold before you as you wander through baronial halls and out into the sculpture patio with its beautiful views over the village and the valleys beyond.

As you make your way back to Plaza de la Font, passing *La Asunción* parish church with its baroque organ, on your right you will see a corrugated doorway that looks like the entrance to a garage. Here is *El Perol Trencat* (The Broken Cooking Pot), where you can stock up with ceramics and a wide assortment of decorative items.

Return to the roundabout at the entrance to the village and head back in the direction of San Juan de Moro. One and a half kilometres after leaving Vilafamés a small sign on your right indicates the Cami Costur,

Medieval arch in Onda

a narrow country road. You pass a number of low round stone buildings, farmers' huts. Keep an eye out for the carob tree on your right that looks like a large green crown; an inventive farmer has forced the upper branches to grow vertically and the lower ones to spread out horizontally, supported by stout canes. (Be careful on this road after heavy rains as, after 10 kilometres, there is a ford which gets quite high in times of flood.)

The Museo de Ciencias El Carmen

When you reach the next junction (unmarked but it's the CV165), turn left for L'Alcora. Soon you drop down into a pretty valley, marred only by the eyesore of the Euroacra tile factory. Turn left when you reach the CV190 and the signpost indicating four kilometres to L'Alcora. As you approach the town the road bears sharp left, but you take the right turn over the bridge.

In 1727 the ninth Conde de Aranda opened the Real Fábrica de Loza y Porcelana (Royal Tile and Porcelain Factory) and established

L'Alcora as the foremost manufacturer of fine-quality porcelain in Spain and one of the most important in Europe, whose products graced the tables of the wealthy worldwide. The count imported French specialists to oversee design and production. They brought with them many of their country's decorative styles, but eventually the factory created its own distinctive designs, including tableware in fruit and animal shapes.

The factory fell into ruin at the end of the Civil War, when the wooden roof beams were removed by impoverished locals, but the ceramics industry continued to flourish in L'Alcora and the Museo de Cerámica L'Alcora, in a manor house built in 1907, has an excellent collection of historic and contemporary ceramics.

Close by is the Portal de Marco, the town's 14th-century entrance, and beside it is the small palace built in 1740 by the Marco family, a pillar of the local nobility. The house is typical of the time and region, with its ornate entrance of Doric columns surmounted by semi-circular pediments so loved in classical architecture and topped off by the Marco family shield. On a wall in the the Plaça la Sang, the square behind the house, you can see a wonderful example of the corrugated plastering used to discourage local lads from practising a local ball game against the surface. These are usually quite simple but this is glorious in its ecclesiastical design.

As befits a medieval town whose history is based on ceramics, the Ayuntamiento is a testament to the tile maker's art. Ornate scenes on vast plaques adorn its otherwise square and tedious façade. Nearby, at 12 Calle Pintor Ferrer, the grandly named La Muy Noble y Artística Cerámica de Alcora (The Very Noble and Artistic Ceramics Company of Alcora) continues the tradition of handmade and delicately painted ceramics. In the tiny factory's back room, moulds are filled and pots thrown and women, deep in concentration, reproduce with paint the designs for which the town is famous.

Leave L'Alcora on the road which runs in front of the town hall, turning left at the first set of traffic lights, left again at the next set, a T-junction, and right at the roundabout heading in the direction of Onda.

As you enter Onda and drive up the right-hand side of the underpass, a quick glance to your right reveals the wonderful façade of a tiny tile factory. The front wall catalogues some of their stunning designs. Unfortunately the building is now in ruins and many of the original tiles have been torn off, but it is still a little gem.

The historian Ramón Muntaner said the castle of Onda "had as many towers as there are days in the year". Today only the El Moro tower retains its original height. Restoration has been done with a somewhat heavy hand but the monument is impressive all the same.

Below the castle walls the tiny streets zigzag down to the old town, many of them ending in the Plaza de Almudí. This former market place, with its cobbled pavement radiating from the *Font de Dins* at its centre to the Gothic arches that shade its four sides, was an important grain market from 1418 until the 19th-century. The buildings under the oak-beamed porticos housed a slaughterhouse and butchery and, from the middle of the 17th-century, the local lock-up.

Grutas San José, Vall de Uixo

Onda is another ceramic town but one specialising in tiles, as a visit to the newly built Museo Taulelle Manolo Safont, a tile museum, will testify. Take the CV223 in the direction of Tales and, right on the edge of town, take a left at the school in front of the crafts (*artesanía*) centre. The museum is on the next block.

You can see more than 50,000 examples of architectural tiles from 13th-century Moorish to modern day. Ceramic headstones, votive plaques, religious and celebratory images, elaborate floor tiles, and a collection from the workshops of Bernat Segarra, considered the best Modernist tile-maker in Spain during the early years of the 20th-century, make this a must-visit. Displays show the painstaking processes used in making tiles by hand over the past 700 years.

A few minutes further on in the direction of Tales you come across the beautiful monastery and church of the Carmelites, which sadly has a huge, ugly brick building tacked on the side. This unattractive edifice houses the Museo de Ciencias El Carmen. Do not enter if taxidermy is not to your taste.

A modest collection for private study begun by the Carmelite fathers in 1952 grew and grew until, in 1965, it was opened as a museum to the public. Three floors of more than 10,000 specimens from the animal, plant and mineral worlds — from birds, butterflies and insects to a donkey, an elephant and a giraffe — are displayed in a myriad of habitats. A huge shark dangles grinning from the rafters while below Iberian ibex prance before a snow-topped mini-mountain.

After such excitement, you can relax in the calm of the church next to the museum. As you enter there seems nothing unusual about the altar surmounted by a statue of the Virgin with a beautiful stained-glass window on either side. Then you suddenly realise all those coloured stone blocks are hand-painted, all the way up to, and including, the high vaulted ceilings. Every archway, pillar and spandrel is fake white marble. Even the backs of the doors have been carefully grained, which seems to be a pointless effort as their fronts show them to be made of beautiful pitch pine.

Return to Onda and take the CV20 to Vila-Real, turning off on the CV10 in the direction of the A7 Valencia. Take the exit for La Vilavella (Nord) and drive through the village, joining the CV10 at a roundabout directing you to Vall d'Uixo and Valencia. You are returning to the coastal zone and will travel through orange groves with mountains to your right and the occasional sparkle of the Mediterranean to your left.

Leave the CV10 when you see the CV226 to Vall d'Uixo and Soneja. Two kilometres later you come to a roundabout with three large vertical stones. A sign to the right indicates the Coves de Sant Josep, otherwise known as the Grutas San José, in the direction of Segorbe. When you reach the roundabout at the top of this road a large sign indicates the Grutas San José, the entrance of which runs down the left side of a bar called Les Moreles.

The Grutas are Valencia's second largest cave system, extending 2,750 metres, of which 800 are navigable by boat (although if you are a hardy explorer type a lot more can be visited by cave diving). The caves have been known since prehistoric times but were not explored until the early 20th-century.

The caves as seen today are not totally natural as they have been dynamited at various times to "expand the visitable itinerary". When you enter them, a sense of awe immediately overcomes you as a boatman sculls you through an underground wonderland.

At points the ceiling is so low you almost have to lie down. Strategically placed lights make the surface of the water look like a shimmering mirror as you pass through caverns with names such as Boca del Forn (Mouth of the Oven) and the Sala de la Morenata (Hall of the Dark-skinned Girl). The caves really are stunning, though one could do without the fairy music that accompanies the 40-minute ride.

To complete this excursion, return to the CV10 and turn right for Valencia and south or left for Castellón.

WHAT TO SEE

VILAFAMÉS:
Museo de Arte Contemporáneo, Calle Diputación 20.
Tel 96 432 91 52. Works of more than 400 artists from the
1920s to the present day. Open daily Jun-Sep 10.30am-2pm,
4-8pm, and Oct-May, Mon-Fri 10.30am-1pm, 4-6.30pm,
Sat-Sun 11am-2pm, 4-7pm. Entry €1.80.
Web page:http://www.cult.gva.es/museovilafames
Iglesia Parroquial de la Asunción, 16th-century church,
restored in 19th. 17th-century *retablo* by Bernado Monfort,
18th-century baroque organ.
Iglesia de la Sangre, 13th-century church, heavily reformed in
baroque style of 17th. Painted frescoes in presbytery, ceiling
and chapel of Santa Bárbara.
Castillo, castle with Moorish origins, conquered by Jaime
Primero in 1233. Interesting circular keep.
El Quartijo, medieval quarter and narrow streets of original
town.

L'ALCORA:
Museu de Cerámica L'Alcora, Tel. 96 436 23 68. Excellent
collection of historic and contemporary ceramics. Open
Tues-Sun 11am-2pm, 4-8pm (extended opening hours Easter
and summer months, telephone to confirm). Free entry.
Web page www.alcora.org/museu

ONDA:
Castle and castle museum. Tel 96 476 66 88. Unique
collection of Moslem plasterwork in a small palace dating
from early 13th-century. Open Jun-Sept, Tues-Sun 11am-2pm,
5-8pm. Oct-May, Tues-Fri 10am-2pm, Sat, Sun and fiestas
11am-2pm, 3-6pm. Free entry.
Plaza de Almudí, medieval plaza.
Museo de Ciencias El Carmen, Ctra. De Tales s/n. Tel. 96 460
07 30. Three floors of stuffed animals, plant and mineral
specimens. Open Jun-Sep (Tues-Sun 9.30am-2pm, 3.30-8pm)
and Oct-Feb (Tues-Sun, 9.30am-2pm, 3.30-7pm) and Mar-
May (Tues-Sun 9.30am-2pm, 3.30-7.30pm). Entry: adults
€4.30, pensioners and children €3.10. Last tickets sold 1 hour
before closing time.
Museio de Taulell Manolo Safont, Open Tues-Fri 11am-2pm
and 4-8 pm, Sat/Sun 11am-2pm and 5-8pm.

LA VALL D'UIXO:
Grutas San José. Tel 96 469 67 61. Wonderland of caves and

lakes. Open year around. Opening hours depend on the
month. Summer openings: second week in July to second
week in Sep, 10.30am-1.30pm, 3.30-8.00pm. Other months
have reduced opening hours. Best to call to confirm.
Entry: adults €6, pensioners €4.21, children (4-13 years) €3.

WHERE TO STAY

VILAFAMÉS:
Hotel El Rullo, Calle La Fuente 2. Tel. 96 432 93 84. Small
family-run hotel in the old town. €
El Jardín Vertical, Carrer Nou 15. Tel. 96 432 99 38.
Beautifully restored 17th-century house, opened in 2002.
Two suites and 4 double bedrooms. Evening meals for
residents if required. €€€

L'ALCORA:
Hostal L'Alcora, San Vicente 6. Tel. 96 436 24 28. Modern,
simple accommodation. €

ONDA:
Gran Hotel Toledo, Calle Argelita 20. Tel 96 460 09 72.
Comfortable modern hotel. €€

WHERE TO EAT

VILAFAMÉS:
Hotel El Rullo, Calle La Fuente 2. Tel. 96 432 93 84.
Good-value local restaurant serving regional country cuisine.
Open daily. €

Mesón Vilafamés, Calle La Fuente 1. Tel. 96 433 50 05. Closed Mon. Tue-Fri and Sun lunch only, Sat lunch and dinner. Local dishes, including *ollas*, a stew of lamb and vegetables. Low to middle-range prices. €€
El Jardín Vertical, Carrer Nou 15. Tel. 96 432 99 38. €€€

L'ALCORA:
Sant Francesc, Avda. Castelló 19. Tel. 96 436 09 24. High-quality restaurant, local and inventive dishes. Open for lunch only during weekdays, 1pm-4.30pm, Sat lunch and dinner, 8.30pm-midnight. €€

LA VALL D'UIXO:
La Gruta, Paraje San José s/n. Tel. 96 460 00 08. Elegant and expensive cave restaurant beside Cuevas de San José specialising in fish. Closed Mon. Tue-Thu lunch only. €€€
La Cova, next to *Restaurante La Gruta.* Tel 96 469 01 03. Diverse menu, mainly local cuisine with plenty of fish and meat dishes. Slightly lower price than La Gruta. Open daily for lunch except Tues. Also open for dinner Fri and Sat. €€

MORE INFORMATION

VILAFAMÉS:
Tourist Office, Plaza Ayuntamiento, 1. Tel. 96 432 99 70. Open daily 9.30am-1.30pm.

L'ALCORA:
Ayuntamiento, Plaza Sant Francesc, 5. Tel. 96 436 00 02. Open weekdays 9.30am-2pm.

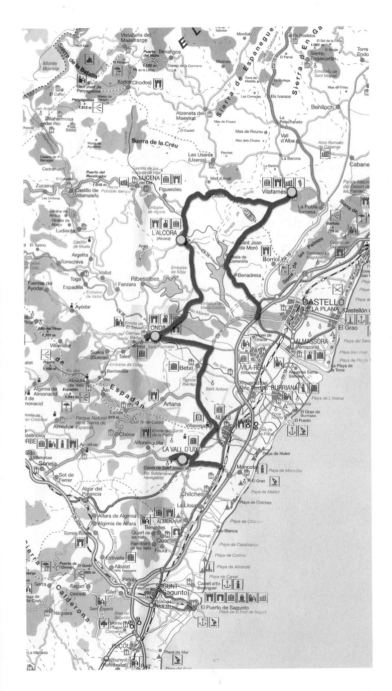

Mountain village in Castellon province

CASTELLÓN'S INLAND BEACH

AREA: Southern Castellón.
ROUTE: Segorbe – Jérica – Montanejes – Onda
DISTANCE: 145 kilometres

Drive through the haunt of fishermen and hunters, delve underground to peer at wax limbs and the "white dove", and soak in thermal pools where Moorish courtesans once bathed.

Take the exit 1A for Sagunto and Teruel from the A7 motorway, a 20-minute drive north from Valencia. Just before Sagunto take the A23 for Teruel and drive 30 kilometres inland to Segorbe. The road follows the Palancia river along the Ruta de los Manantiales (Route of the Springs), snaking through valleys and gorges decorated with poplar, aspen and willow. Tributaries and springs feed the orchards of the Alto Palancia.

The river is the haunt of fishermen after trout, barbel, pike and carp, while hunters scour the forested mountains and broad plains for wild boar, hare, partridge and quail. The valley was for centuries the major link between the region of Aragon and the Mediterranean.

Exit at junction 27 for Geldo and Segorbe, taking the road to the left for Segorbe. At the roundabout take the first exit for Segorbe (with a small railway station sign) and follow the road through a small industrial estate. You pass under a blue railway bridge (you will come back to this to continue the excursion) and continue on the road into town. Shortly after the Guardia Civil barracks a sign, on the right, directs you to the tourist information office. Turn left here on to Calle de Castellón, turn right at the first set of traffic lights and this takes you directly to the tourist office and car park.

The former bishop's seat of Segorbe is now the regional capital and the name of its principal square, Plaza Agua Limpia (Clean Water Square), symbolises the historical importance of the area's springs and rivers. Many streets in the old town have plaques describing their history which is often reflected in their names. Calle Foro Romano, Calle Mezquita and Plaza Almudín are reminders of the city's Roman and Moorish past, while Calle Los Silleros (Chairmakers' Street) recalls the time when each trade could be found in a specific area within the city walls.

A plaque in Plaza del Ángel informs you that it was formerly known as the Plaza de los Cerdos, where every Thursday for centuries the most important pig market in Valencia and lower Aragon was held and only pigs of the highest quality were sold.

The Arco de la Verónica on Calle Argen is thought to be part of the original Roman wall, and on the edge of the old town there are two cylindrical towers that also formed part of the fortifications. Torre Cárcel housed the prison and Torre Botxi was home to the town's executioner (Botxi being the Catalan name for that grim occupation). The city's history as a religious centre is reflected in the abundance of its churches, the most prominent of which is the 12th-century catedral-basílica. Its inherent Gothic style has been considerably modified, like those of most churches in Valencia province. It houses a small museum of art from the 15th to 18th-century, including work by Donatello.

Segorbe's main fiesta, held during the last week of August, incorporates the homage to the city's patron saint, la Santísima Virgen, and a week of bullfights. The high point of the taurine week is the Entrada de Toros y Caballos (Entry of the Bulls and Horses) when horse riders drive bulls down the main street between two densely packed rows of unprotected bystanders who rely on the skill of the horsemen to prevent them from being gored.

To leave Segorbe, retrace your route and take the road to the right just before the main road passes under the blue railway bridge. You join a dual carriageway. A couple of kilometres out of Segorbe (having bypassed Altura) you pass under an arbour of pines with a hotel on the right and arrive at a roundabout. Go straight over, where you will see a sign for La Cueva Santa. The road twists and turns as it rises through pretty countryside sprinkled with ancient farmhouses and ruined mills and, after about 13 kilometres, you see an enormous white building, once a convent but now home to only a handful of nuns.

Retrace your route and, just after you leave Altura, pick up the A23 once more and head for Jérica. A few minutes up the motorway take the exit for Navajas and follow the road under the railway bridge into the village centre.

The White Dove in an underground cave

The Santuario Cueva Santa is dedicated to the Virgin of the Holy Cave, known as the White Dove, and her image is portrayed in bas-relief stucco about 20 centimetres high. The legend goes that Bonifacio Ferrer, a Carthusian prior, gave the image to a shepherd who hid it in a niche in the cave, where it was found by another shepherd in 1503.

At a later date a glorious Doric-style temple was built in the cave, 20 metres below ground, where the image now sits, surrounded by jade and gold. As you descend the stairway lined with tile votive plaques giving thanks for prayers answered and ailments miraculously cured, you pass small side niches and diminutive altars.

Half-way down, a flight of steps to the left leads you to a spine-tingling grotto full of votive offerings dangling from hooks in the rock face or laid in piles on the floor, including wax limbs tied in bundles, suits, wedding dresses, boys' first communion sailor suits, crutches, body supports, a girl's white lace dress now grey with age and dust — the physical reminders of decades of prayers and devotion.

A wall plaque of the "White Dove".

Nothing quite prepares you for your first sight of the temple, with its ornate scroll plasterwork topped by a pair of cavorting cherubim. The tiny stucco image of the Virgin glows in its gold mount and it comes as no surprise to hear that she is the patron saint of Spanish speleologists (cavers).

It is said that, if a drop of water lands on you from the ceiling and you rub it over the part of your body that is ailing, you will be cured. Drops taken from the puddles on the floor will also work but without the same efficacy. You will also be cured if you hear the tinkling of a bell when visiting the cave by night.

This otherwise nondescript little village must have one of the largest stocks of the delightful *modernista* architectural style in the whole of the Valencian Community. Towers, pillars, porticoes and promenades are everywhere, mostly surrounded by beautifully kept gardens abundant with statuary. Most of the houses are in excellent condition, although some have such a spooky dilapidated air that you can imagine opening an ornate front door to find Dickens' Miss Haversham sitting before her spider-webbed wedding feast.

Drive back under the railway bridge and turn right, following the road for the Embalse de Regajo, with occasional glimpses through the trees of the sun sparkling off the water of the reservoir. Keep following the signs for Jérica. The roadside olive trees are not for harvesting but intended for sale to restock other olive groves.

Almost the first view you get of Jérica is the imposing Mudejar bell tower, unique in Valencia and forming an unmistakable silhouette as it overlooks the town. The Muslim-influenced Mudejar style is characterised by an extremely refined and inventive use of brick and glazed tiles, especially in belfries.

Also eye-catching is the Torre del Homenaje, the strong central tower of Jérica castle, which is almost all that is left of the original fortifications standing guard over the river Palancia from the heights of the Peña Tajada (cleft rock).

With its round Moorish towers, Gothic arches and narrow cobbled streets, Jérica is a beautiful little town. As in many such pueblos that have little room for gardens, most of the countless balconies and walls are covered with colourful plants, especially off the prettily named Calle del Pequeño Horno, the Street of the Little Oven.

In the tourist information office on Calle del Río you can pick up a town map that describes a tour around the main points of interest, but Jérica is the sort of place where when you get lost the locals will usually walk you to where you want to go. When you get tired of strolling around town, you can relax by watching the world go by as you sit outside a café on the small square in front of the rather grand Fuente de Santa Águeda.

To continue the excursion, take the road to the right of the fountain for Teruel, CV195. The road rises up through pine-covered mountains and orchards of almonds, carob and figs, to pass between the Sierras of Pina and Espadán.

You pass Montán. Abandoned after the expulsion of the Moriscos (Moors converted to Christianity) in 1609, it was settled later in the

Boy jumping into a mountain pool

A village market

century by 28 families from Provence and a group of Servite monks who built the monastery. It still stands and part has been converted, badly, into apartments. Neither the monastery nor the haphazard village is worth a second glance so it is on to the main destination on this leg of the excursion, Montanejos, six kilometres further on.

Visitors flock to Montanejos for two reasons: walls and water. The walls are the precipitous rock faces of the Garganta de la Maimona and Los Estrechos that have made Montanejos one of the most important centres for free-climbing in Europe. The sheer cliffs rise more than 100 metres high and there are 1,100 climbing routes in the three-kilometre stretch of the Barranco de la Maimona.

The beautiful gorges and pine forests that rise from the River Mijares as it gouges its way through the limestone mountains are a magnet for cavers and walkers, but water is the main reason Montenejos is busy year-round. It has two kilometres of thermal pools naturally heated to a constant temperature of 25 degrees. The salutary effect of its mineral springs has been known for millennia. The water is high in sulphate, magnesium and bicarbonate and does wonders for a wide range of ailments.

At Fuente de los Baños, the largest of the thermal pools and with a beach, the 13th-century Moorish king, Abu-ceit, built a bathhouse to help "keep his favourites always young and beautiful". A sign directs you to the ruin of the *baños árabes*, but little remains now except for a fragment of wall and a pile of rubble.

Although the Fuente de los Baños was recognised as a public utility as far back as 1863, it was only recently, with the opening of the Balneario de Montanejos, that the health-giving waters were utilised for more than a quick dip and drink. Now visitors can choose from a wide range of hydrothermal treatments designed to help physical, respiratorial and circulatory problems as well as those delicately referred to as *enfermedades de la civilización*, or stress.

Montanejos has little else to offer other than the recently restored 17th-century church of Santiago Apóstel and a few narrow cobbled streets in the old town that still have small shops and cafes undisturbed by the booming water business.

Leaving Montanejos and taking the CV20 to Onda, you drive though deep, green pine forests covering rugged mountains. You pass a series of small villages, including Cirat, Torrechiva, Toga and Espadilla, consisting of nothing more than a plaza and a few narrow streets clustered around a church but offering somewhere to stop and enjoy a coffee and stretch your legs.

Eventually you wind down to the suburbs and orange groves of Onda, where you can either take a tour of the town (see Trip 1) or stay on the CV20 and rejoin the coastal roads at Vila-real.

The water spout at Montanejos

WHAT TO SEE

SEGORBE:
Catedral-Basílica. 13th-century cathedral with Gothic cloister and museum of 15th and 16th-century art.
Torre Cárcel, Torre Botxi, and **Arco de la Verónica**. Old town walls.
Santuario Cueva Santa, Ctra. Altura-Alcublas.
Open during daylight hours. Ornate chapel built 20 metres underground.

JÉRICA:
Torre de las Campanas, Mudejar bell tower.
Municipal Museum. Examples of 14 to19th-century ceramics, religious artifacts, local archeological finds and gravestones. Mon-Fri opening by arrangement with the town hall (next to the museum). Tel. 96 412 91 77.
Sat 12noon-2pm and 7-9pm, Sun 12noon-2pm.
Free entry.
Iglesia de Santa Águeda, Originally Gothic church, rebuilt in the baroque style in 1749.

MONTANEJOS:
Barranco de la Maimona and **Los Estrechos.** Two main rock-climbing faces a short distance from the town centre, signposted.
Fuente de los Baños. Natural thermal pool, part of a 2km stretch of thermal waters. The main pool is a five-minute walk from the town centre.
Balneario de Montanejos, Carretera de Tales, s/n. Treatment centre and public indoor swimming pool. Call 964 131 275 for details of treatments and to make reservations. Open every day 9.30am-2pm and 4.30-8pm. Closed Jan.

WHERE TO STAY

SEGORBE:
Hospedería Tasca el Palén, Calle Franco Ricart. Tel. 96 471 07 40. Delightful small hotel converted from 18th-century bakery and oil press. Filled with owner Florentine Sales's collection of everything from doll's houses to ornate tiles. The barrel-vaulted restaurant's walls display enough weaponry to arm a modest insurrection. €
Masía Ferrer, Partida Ferrer, s/n (approx 7km from Segorbe) Tel. 607 473 844. Newly restored rustic house with restaurant using produce from their own gardens. €€

JÉRICA:
El Doncel, Avenida Constitución, 29. Tel. 96 412 80 08. Attractive modern hotel in large restored house. €

MONTANEJOS:
Most of the accommodation in Montanejos caters to people taking the waters, especially large groups. It can be difficult to find a room, so it is advisable to book in advance.

Casa Palacio Apartamentos, Calle San Vicente, 40. Tel. 96 413 12 93. Recently opened serviced apartments partly built into an Arabic tower. Minimum stay a weekend. €-€€
Hostal Gil, Avenida Fuente de Baños, 28. Tel. 96 413 10 63. Small hotel with basic accommodation. €
Hotel Rosaleda de los Mijares, Carretera de Tales, 28. Tel. 96 413 10 79. Modern hotel with small fitness suite. Price includes use of indoor pool. €€

WHERE TO EAT

SEGORBE:
Hospedería Tasca El Palén, Calle Franco Ricart.
Tel. 96 471 07 40. Comfortable rustic style restaurant with open
wood -fire grill. Good range of grilled meats, fish and tapas.
Open 1.30-5pm and 8.30-11pm. Closed Mon. Good-value *menú
del día*. Highly recommended. €
Casino, Plaza Agua Limpia, 1. Tel. 96 471 00 81. Part of the
Palacio Ducal of the Duque de Medinaceli that became the
Ayuntamiento. Basic local food menu at decent prices. Open
daily for lunch and dinner. €
Bernini, Calle Obispo Canubio 15. Tel. 96 471 34 16. Highly
regarded, if expensive, restaurant with inventive menu and wine
list. Open daily for lunch, Fri-Sat for dinner. €€€

JÉRICA:
Restaurante Randurías, beside the river on the edge of town.
Tel. 96 412 97 12. Modestly priced village food. Open daily
lunch and dinner. €

MONTANEJOS:
Casa Ovidio, Avenida Elvira Peiró, 41. Tel. 96 413 13 09.
Spartan but popular restaurant. Local cuisine at modest prices. €

MORE INFORMATION

SEGORBE:
Tourist Information Office, Calle Marcelino Blasco, 3 (beside
municipal car park). Open 10am-2pm and 4-7pm, Tue-Sun.

JÉRICA:
Tourist Information Office, Calle Río, 2. Tel. 96 412 80 04.
Web page www.jerica.com. Open 10.30am-1.30pm Sat and Sun.
At other times ask in Ayuntamiento, Calle Historiador Vayo, 19.
Tel. 96 412 91 77.

MONTANEJOS
Tourist Information Office, inside the Balneario de Montanejos,
Carretera de Tales, s/n. Open every day 9.30am-2pm and 4.30-
8pm. Closed Jan.
Asociación Escuela de Escalada de Montanejos,
Carretera de Tales, 27.
Centro Ecuestre la Garrocha. Tel. 600 535 180. Does 45-minute
pony and trap rides, also hires out horses.

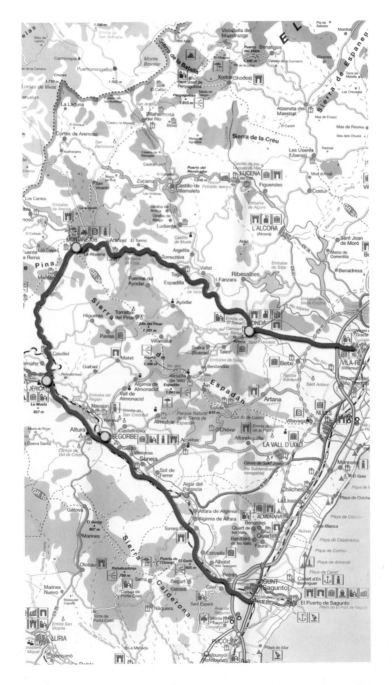

71

Benisanó Castle

TRIP 5
CHILDHOOD CASTLES AND SWEET STONES

AREA: West of Valencia city
ROUTE: Benisanó – Benaguasil – Pedralba – Casino – Llíria
DISTANCE: 75 kilometres

From the semi-industrial suburbs of Valencia, a mere hop takes you to one of the prettiest castles in the region, the sugared-almond village and the town with the oldest musical history in Spain.

From the autoroute that bypasses Valencia, take the exit for the CV35, to the north of the city, in the direction of Llíria. After 17 kilometres, leave the CV35 at exit 15 on the road signposted to Benisanó and Benaguasil. Leaving the semi-industrial suburbs of Valencia behind, you enter an area of olive groves, with a view of Llíria's white-and-cream Monasterio de Sant Miguel nestled in the hills to your right.

At a T-junction 1.5 kilometres from the motorway at exit 15, follow the sign for Benisanó, half a kilometre further on. Go directly over the roundabout at the beginning of the town and, after five sets of traffic lights (very close together), you will see a castle on your left. A small road runs uphill to the Plaça Comte de Sástago, directly in front of the castle gate.

The Castillo de Benisanó is one of the most delightful in the region, with a central keep, small circular tower and proper crennellations, just like all toy castles have. It even has slits to shoot arrows through. Built during the second half of the 15th-century, the castle-cum-palace was the home of the Cavanilles-Villarrasa family, governors of Benisanó. With its stout beams, twisted pillars and beautiful stained- glass windows, it has a cosier feeling than most castles. On the ground floor is a ceiling designed by one of the Vatican architects (a similar one can be found in the papal city).

A few metres' walk from the castle entrance is the Iglesia de los Santos Reyes. The church looks ancient but is actually little more than 80 years old. Seriously damaged during the Civil War, it was restored in 1945 but didn't receive its final lick of exterior paint until 1983.

Though the church is simple compared to many in the region, its *trompe l'oeil* side chapels are glorious in their own way. It houses a number of artworks from the original 15th-century building, including La Adoración de los Reyes Magos attributed to Claudio de San Leocadio, set high in the *retablo* behind the altar, and Jesús el Nazareno by Juan de Juanes in the sacristy. As you leave the church, light pours through a modern but pleasing stained-glass rose window above the entrance, depicting the Three Kings.

The old part of town retains much of the shape of the original walls that surrounded it and the narrow streets are entered by the three arched portals of Valencia, Bétera and Llíria.

To continue the excursion, drive back through Benisanó to the roundabout at the town entrance and turn right on the CV373 to Benaguasil, just 1.5 kilometres away. At a sharp left-hand bend as you enter the town (just after a telephone and post box on your left) take the right alongside the Bar/Restaurant Pelotari, then a left a few moments later signposted Ntra. Sra. Montiel Santuario. At the end of this road, turn right following the signs for the Santuario. Stay on this road to take you through the town.

Benaguasil doesn't have a lot to offer the tourist, but the locals are inordinately proud of their new town hall, opened in early 2003 and said to be the finest in the locality. It is rather impressive as modern architecture goes. You can locate it by following the signs for Ayuntamiento as you drive through town.

Feeling peckish? The Bar Palau, just opposite the town hall, offers a *bocadillo de sobresado y queso*, an enormous toasted sandwich of local sausage meat and cheese.

Leaving the town, the road takes you in the direction of Pedralba 12 kilometres away, although it isn't signposted until you reach a roundabout almost two kilometres after Benaguasil. Go straight across the roundabout on to the VV6124.

After five kilometres, you crest a rise to view a wide valley of orange groves with a scattering of houses and farms. If you fancy a paddle or a picnic, take the left turn immediately after you cross a newly restored concrete bridge signposted Rambla Primera, in front of a sign for Parque Natural la Fenosa. The road zigzags through orange groves to a small park in the bend of a narrow river where you can sit at

Almond trees can be seen all over the region

Parc Sant Vicente in Llíria

wooden benches to eat lunch cooked at the large barbecues provided.

Continuing on the VV6124, a couple of kilometres later you will notice some odd-looking red piles of earth. On closer inspection they prove to be mounds that supported pylons for electricity cables that once criss-crossed a quarry, now abandoned and flooded and raucous with the croaking of frogs. As the quarry got deeper, the diggers worked their way around the pylons, leaving the strange mounds.

While not outstandingly scenic, the road to Pedralba is a pleasant drive through orange groves and gently sloping hillsides. At the junction with the VV6122, turn left to Pedralba. Two kilometres later you reach the VV6123 where you turn left again (you will be returning past this junction to continue the excursion). As you descend into Pedralba, the ancient cemetery is to your right, with a red cliff surmounted by a cross behind it.

At a Y-junction, with a building directly in front, bear left (you will see a pale blue house on your left). Follow the sign for Villamarxant until you reach the main road with a Petronor filling station ahead and turn right. Take the next right for Casinos and Llíria and park because you will be leaving by this road.

Walk back to the T-junction and turn right onto Calle Acequia (you will see a beautiful blue-and-white tiled sign for the Fábrica Harina de Salvador Civerá Peiro). The street is named after the narrow canal that runs along a row of beautiful *modernista* (Art Nouveau) houses, now in a poor state of repair. Arched stairways pass over the canal to the houses and narrow channels run between them to irrigate the orange groves behind. The town hall planned to demolish these former homes of the Pedralba wealthy and build new apartment blocks. Fortunately, they have seen the light and plan to restore them instead.

Halfway up Calle Acequia, a tiny alleyway on the right called Calle Iglesia takes you through narrow streets to the 18th-century parish church. The splendid late baroque façade and graceful fluted columns either side of the impressive doorway are decorated with images of the sun and moon. Unfortunately, you can't stand back for a full view of its ecclesiastical magnificence as it is completely boxed in on all sides by tiny alleyways.

Atop the church's bell-tower, a loudspeaker keeps the local populace informed and up to date with public announcements and advertisements, including one listing the day's best buys at a local supermarket. The passageway facing the church leads to the Plaza de la Constitución and the old town hall, whose façade frames a green painted panel where the locals can chalk up their own announcements. To the right of the town hall on Calle Mayor are a number of attractive examples of Art Nouveau architecture, particularly the curved bay window at number 13, now sadly in need of restoration.

Retrace your steps to Calle Acequia and reverse the directions to take you back out of town in the direction of Casinos, 11 kilometres away on the VV6123.

In Moorish times, Valencia was known as the most fertile and productive region in the known world and until recently was the world's biggest producer of rice. Home of the famous *paella,* it still supplies much of the rice consumed in Spain.

The region has been given a new lease of life by the miracle of drip-feed irrigation. On this trip, you pass through great swathes of once-abandoned land that is being cultivated again thanks to the thousands of metres of thin black plastic tubing that is replacing the old concrete channels and carrying water to the rows of newly-planted orange trees.

As you approach Casinos, you see the groves of almond trees, the source of this small rural town's fame. At the junction of CV35, turn right and enter the town. Just after the bridge and a set of traffic lights is a small square where it is usually possible to park.

Packaging peladillas

The home of sugared almonds

Casinos is the centre of sugared almond production and at Fábrica Carmela on Avenida Valencia (just beside the traffic lights), the fourth generation of the Jarrin family serve various versions of these crunchy delicacies as well as their own make of *turrón* in their shop-cum-cafe.

Peladillas (sugared almonds) are made by revolving toasted almonds in a drum that slowly coats them with sugar that is then allowed to harden. Fábrica Carmela make a version for kids called La Piedra (The Stone) that looks like a dappled bird's egg and is a real tooth-cracker. *Garrapiñadas* are given their roughness and soft texture by being stirred in caramelised sugar, and *piñones* are pine nuts that have been given the same treatment as sugared almonds.

A detail of the Iglesia Parroquial in Pedralba

Two ladies chatting in Pedralba

Stay on the CV35 as you leave Casinos and head towards Lliria 12 kilometres away. As you approach the town, ignore the first exit for Llíria (oeste) and Pedralba, and take the second, the CV25, two kilometres further on, signposted Marines, Olocau and Llíria.

When you reach the roundabout at the bottom of the slip road, look for the indication to Centro Ciudad and a small sign for Turismo Llíria. A few metres after leaving the roundabout, another sign for Turismo Llíria directs you to the left. At the next stop sign turn right and immediately left, down the side of a carwash.

At the junction with the main road turn right where you will immediately see the new building of the Mancomunitat Campo de Turia on your left, below which is one of Llíria's two tourist offices. This one, which has information about the town and the region, is a long walk from the centre of town, so it's best to visit it first. The second one, the town hall information office, is in La Forn de la Vila, one of the two 15th-century bakeries that stood by the entrance to La Vila Vella, the medieval part of the town.

A statue of a Grecian maid complete with lyre in the Plaza Mayor proclaims "Llíria a la Música", supporting the local claim that the town is known world-wide as La Ciutat de la Música (the City of Music), though a number of other towns in the Valencia Community claim the same. Llíria was the first town in Spain to have a town band, formed in the 19th-century, and now has two, La Primitiva and La Unión Musical, regarded as two of the best in the region.

The precursor of modern-day Llíria was Edeta, an important provincial settlement during the fourth century. Its remains can be found at the foot of the hill on which sits the Sant Miguel monastery. During excavation of the site, important remains of coloured Iberian pottery were discovered and can now be seen in the Museo de la Prehistoria in Valencia city's La Beneficencia.

The tiny church on the hilltop Monasterio Sant Miguel will steal your heart. Its baroque ostentation, culminating in the winged and silver-armoured Sant Miguel ramming his spear down the throat of a black demonic creature, could overwhelm if it wasn't for the serenity that wraps around you as you sit in a pew, hearing nothing but birdsong. You want to close your eyes and hang a "Do Not Disturb" sign around your neck.

The view from the hilltop alone is worth the ride through the higgledy-piggledy streets, with views across rustic and cultivated land to the Sierra Calderona to the north and the blue Mediterranean to the east.

Llíria is a bustling modern town but still has some excellent examples of the architecture and culture of times past. Santa María de la Sangre church is a superb example of an *iglesia de la Reconquista,* the kind of churches built during the Christian re-conquest of Spain combining elements of the Romanesque and Gothic. The structure is simple but has a glorious wooden ceiling painted with colourful scenes showing knights and ladies, mythical beasts and decorative patterns based on plants and heraldry.

On Plaza Mayor, the imposing 16th-century ayuntamiento, officially known as Ca la Vila, has been functioning as a town hall for more than 400 years. The building was reopened in early 2003 after a three-year restoration, which included the cleaning and repairing of a stained-glass window commemorating those who died in the Carlist Wars.

Just a few metres away is the Asunción church, a magnificent baroque edifice that took more than 50 years to build, being completed in 1672. The Doric columns of its façade flank sculptures by Raimundo Capuz, whose monumental San Miguel vanquishing the Devil rides high above a central niche.

Feeling spiritually replete? Time to feed the inner man — and there is no better place to go than the Pastissería Ca Susi at Calle Sant Vicent 1. It is said to be the best bakery in town, which the number of customers crowding the tiny triangular shop appears to confirm. Sra. Susi herself presides over trays of *besitos de Llíria* (Kisses of Llíra, an almond biscuit), *torta de mazapán* (marzipan cake sprinkled with chopped almonds) and *torta de aceite con sardina* (long flat loaves baked with sardines on top).

To complete the excursion, return to the CV35 for Valencia and rejoin the *autovía* that bypasses the city.

Restaurante Barbacoa Lafuente in Casinos

WHAT TO SEE

BENISANÓ:
Castillo de Benisanó, 15th-century castle/palace on Plaça
Comte de Sástago. Open Sun 11am-2pm. Entry €1.80.
Iglesia Santos Reyes, Plaça Comte de Sástago. Built 80
years ago on site of a 15th-century church, houses
artwork from the original building.

PEDRALBA:
Calle Acequia, houses in the *modernista* style with arched
steps over a canal.
Iglesia Parroquial, 18th-century late-baroque church.
Casa-Museo Pedralba 2000, Calle Bugara. Modern art
museum. Open Sat/Sun noon-2pm, 5-7pm. Entry €2

LLÍRIA:
Ca la Vila, Plaza Mayor. Original 17th-century town hall.
Nuestra Señora de la Asunción, Plaza Mayor. 18th-
century parish church with rich baroque ornamentation.

Santa María de La Sangre, 13th-century church in the old town, decorated in the Mudéjar style.
Monasterio de San Miguel,16th-century monastery. Closed to the public but you can visit the chapel. Locals say that it houses a feather from the wings of Archangel Gabriel. Open mornings Mon-Sat 9am-1pm, Sunday 7am-2pm, afternoons 3pm-8pm every day.
Edeta, remains of the Iberian town on hillside below the monastery.
Forn de la Vila, restored medieval bakery on Calle de la Sang, Vila Vella, that now houses the town's tourist office.
Museo Arqueológico, Plaza Trinquet Vell, Vila Vella. Attractively laid-out archeological museum housed in

modern building in the old town. Open May-Sep, Tues-Fri
8am-2pm and 5-8.30pm, Sat 11am-2pm and 5-8.30pm,
Sun 11am-2pm; Oct-Apr, Tues-Fri 10am-2pm and 5-7pm,
Sat 11am-2pm and 5-8pm, Sun 11am-2pm. Entry €1.20.
Parc Sant Vicent. Pleasant park with playground, 2km from
town centre in the direction of Olocau.

WHERE TO STAY

BENISANÓ:
Hotel Restaurant Rioja, Eixida Portal de Bétera 10 (in the
centre of town). Tel. 96 279 21 58. Pleasant modern hotel,
charming lounge for residents. €€

LLÍRIA:
Residencia La Salle, Partida Carraccec, s/n, Urbanización San
Miguel. Tel. 96 279 06 42. Modern stopover in countryside
5km from town. €€
Pension Siglo 21, Avda Delec Furc, 16. Tel. 96 279 37 35.
Small pension above bar. €
Hostal Les Reixec, Pla de l'Arc, 77. Tel. 96 278 07 87.
Comfortable basic accommodation. €

WHERE TO EAT

BENISANÓ:
Hotel Restaurant Rioja, Eixida Portal de Bétera, 10.
Tel. 96 279 21 58. High quality, reasonable prices.
Established in 1924, run by the same family for four
generations. Recently refurbished. Specialises in made-to-
order *paella de Valencia de leña* (*paella* cooked over a wood
fire). Also available *avestruz con salsa frambuesa* (ostrich in
raspberry sauce). Open Mon-Sat for lunch and dinner, and
Sun for lunch only. €€

BENAGUASIL:
Montemio-Bori, Ctra. Benaguasil-Llíria, km1.
Tel 96 273 01 20. Medium-priced restaurant offering
Mediterranean/Basque/French cuisine, especially with roast
meats. Open daily for lunch, also for Sat dinner. €€

CASINOS:
Barbacoa Lafuente, Avenida de Valencia, 46. Tel. 96 164 70
81. Unusual, amusing restaurant with a live fig tree growing

in the middle. Diners sit on plastic garden furniture with red gingham tablecloths to eat dishes of the owner's choice. When the restaurant is full, he shuts the doors and won't allow anyone else in. He says it is *muy peligroso* (very dangerous) to expect a table on Sunday if you don't book. Mainly barbecued meat and fish. Open daily for lunch only. €€

LLÍRIA:

Casa Segundo, Calle San Vicente, 30. Tel. 96 279 36 06. Unpretentious. Good basic food in modern surroundings. Open daily for lunch and dinner. Closed Wed. €€
Porta de L'Aigua, Parc Sant Vicent, Ctra Llíria-Marines, km3.2. Open daily for lunch. Large cafeteria and restaurant. Excellent value *menú del día* at €7 in cafeteria or a slightly enhanced version in the restaurant for €18. Bargain help-yourself buffet on Sundays and fiesta days with more than 35 dishes to choose from for only €12.90. €–€€

MORE INFORMATION

BENISANÓ:

Ayuntamiento, Plaza del Ayuntamiento, 1. Tel 96 278 07 01. Open Mon-Fri 8am-3pm.

BENAQUASIL:

Ayuntamiento, Plaça Mayor de la Vila, 17. Tel. 96 273 00 11. Open Mon-Fri 8am-3pm.

PEDRALBA:

Ayuntamiento, Calle Ismael Quiles, 6. Tel. 96 270 70 01. Open Mon-Fri 8am-3pm.

LLÍRIA:

Tourist Office (Generalitat), Edificio Sede de la Mancomunidad de Camp de Turia, Pla de l'Arc, s/n. Tel. 96 279 36 19. Open Mon-Fri 9.30am-1.30pm and 3-7.30pm, Sat 10am-1pm. Tourist Office (Llíria), Calle de la Sang, 8 (in the old town). Tel. 96 279 15 22. Open Tues-Fri 10am-2pm, 4-7pm, Sat 10am-2pm. Closed Sunday. Offers free guided walks around the historical parts of the city on Sunday mornings at 11. Contact office for programme (in Spanish only).

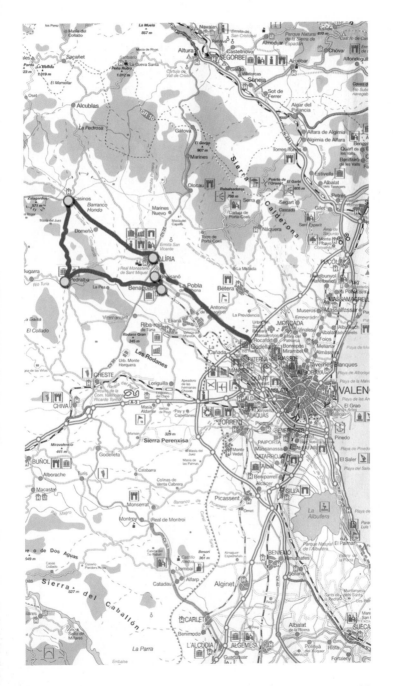

Bizarre chimney pots in Casa de Medina

TRIP 6

EXPLORE THE MORISCO MAZE

AREA: Alto Turia region, west of Valencia city
ROUTE: Villar de Arzobispo – Chulilla – Chelva – Tuéjar - Utiel
DISTANCE: 205 kilometres

Wander a medieval maze to a symphony of swirling water, marvel at a Moorish village clinging to the side of a cliff, and pray for a miraculous cure in a mountain sanctuary.

From the autoroute bypassing Valencia city, the CV35 dual-carriageway to Adamuz wends its way through a light industrial landscape. After it passes Llíria 11 kilometres later, take the road to Casinos, where it becomes a two-lane country road (still the CV35). The land is flat and dry, with long stretches of irrigation channels running alongside the road, but a more attractive drive awaits you in the rolling hills ahead.

At 39 kilometres, you drive into Casinos, the sugared-almond centre of Valencia and, as you cross a bridge leaving the town, a sign to your right directs you to Villar de Arzobispo (VV6206), a further 10 kilometres.

The road begins to climb slowly through the almond groves that supply the sweet factories of Casinos. Just after the 5km mark, the road dips into a valley and in the distance you see Villar de Arzobispo and the scarred mountains that provide the marble and stone for local industry.

Less than one kilometre from Villar, you skirt a roundabout to which you will return to continue the excursion.

The story goes that during medieval times a knight returned home to Villar after fighting the infidels and discovered his wife *en flagrante delito* with a chap who had stayed at home. He punished them by building two houses facing each other and imprisoning one lover in each, so that they could see one other but never have physical contact.

The town describes itself as "a dynamic centre of regional services", but what the visitor finds is a sleepy little place of shady narrow alleys. The Plaza de la Iglesia has a pleasant array of architecture, from the 16th-century parish church and archbishop's palace (the town was formerly linked with the Archbishopric of Valencia) to the grand *modernista* mansion on the opposite side of the square and the arched portico of the town hall.

The museum, the Casa Museo de los Cinteros, on Calle Hospital, is housed in a traditional village house of the type constructed in the late 19th-century. It displays life in a typical village home around the 1850s and in it you will find a large collection of agricultural tools, furniture, kitchen utensils, ceramics and clothing typical of this era.

The town's main commerce is wine, a selection of which can be tasted at the Cooperativa Agrícola el Villar on Avenida Ingeniero Tamarit, and at the privately owned Bodegas Comeche next door.

Return to the roundabout at the entry to Villar and take the C234 to Chulilla 11 kilometres away. The flat road takes you through vineyards laid out in military precision. A couple of kilometres later you cross the CV35 Llíria to Adamuz road and join the CV395/VV6241.

This is a pleasant, cultivated lowlying landscape of grapes and almonds and after four kilometres you pass through Vanacloig, little more than a scattering of houses most of which seem to be falling down. Shortly after leaving the village, you drive through a shallow valley of varied cultivation offering a wonderful changing palette of greenery.

At the km42 marker, you see on your left the Instalación Recreativa de Pelma, a picnic area with barbecues and walks beneath the shady pines. A short while later on the outskirts of Chulilla, as you round a bend by La Rueda restaurant, you see the village hanging on the cliff face ahead with the walls of the castle suspended above. As you get closer it comes as no surprise to see that some of the houses have actually tumbled into the canyon below.

Stay on the road through the village and, as you exit the main square, parking signs direct you to a short track off the main road with parking on either side.

The narrow streets of white-painted houses are full of twists and turns, steep curving stairways and dead ends. The high elegance of the

A typical street in Chelva

parish church, Nuestra Señora de los Ángeles, suddenly becomes a low wall as you wander up the little alleyway behind it.

Follow the signs to the castle and you come to a metal-barred gate in a breeze-block wall with no announcement that you have arrived at

One of the many waterfalls in the area

the entrance. Despite a hand-painted sign that says "Prohibido el paso", the gate is unlocked and you are free to wander in.

A very rough stone path runs up the high wall that obliterates any view except for occasional niches that give a narrow perspective of life in the village below. The castle is Moorish in origin but underwent rebuilding in the 14th to 16th centuries. During its lifetime it served as the residence of the local nobility and as an ecclesiastical prison. Not much of the structure is left but the views across the valley and the weathered orange tiles of the village rooftops are splendid.

The cuisine of the region is represented by ollas, thick stews rich in beans, vegetables, meat and mountain herbs. You might try cocotes, small pastry parcels filled with spicy sausage. At the Cafetería Baronia, tucked in the corner opposite the town hall on the Plaza Baronia, you can buy locally produced honey.

Leave the car park and turn right at the main road at the bottom of the short track. The road immediately begins to rise and takes you through a landscape of rugged hills and broken terrain with rough-textured mountain slopes of creamy earth and spiky scrub. Seven kilometres later you see the blue-tiled dome of the Ermita Virgen de los Dolores at Losa del Obispo, peeping out of the pine trees that guard the village cemetery.

You join the CV35 once more, heading for Chelva 16 kilometres away. If you wish to take a pleasant break by a dam, after three kilometres a sign to your left directs you to the Embalse de Loriguilla, 4.9 kilometres away. Otherwise, continue on the road to Chelva.

Just after the km59 marker, you get a glimpse of a beautiful waterfall. To get a closer view, take the next left that sends you briefly back in the direction you have come. After a few moments, a sharp right leads you to an old stone bridge, after which you see a rough track to your left. Follow this for a couple of hundred metres, taking a left fork that brings you to open ground where you can park, picnic and take a paddle in the river Tuéjar, just behind a screen of spindly trees.

To continue the excursion, you can either rejoin the CV35 or turn left on the road at the end of the track (with yellow lines, bridge to your right) that joins the CV35 one kilometre further on.

As you enter Chelva, look out for signs for the Ayuntamiento, which is in the Plaza Mayor at the bottom of Calle Mártires. The parking is limited in the plaza, both in the number of spaces available and the time allowed to park, so it may be best to park on the main road and take the short walk to the square.

Chelva is unusual in that it still has, more or less intact, the original Morisco and Jewish quarters (although you would be hard pushed to tell which is which without a map). As you walk the higgledy-piggledy streets, you are accompanied by the sound of water either gushing from the dozens of fountains from which you can slake your thirst or surging below the metal gratings that cover the channels taking the water down to the river. The village sounds as if it is in permanent flood.

Twisted houses tumble down narrow alleyways, some of them quite literally, and it's like walking through a medieval maze without ever being sure you will reach the centre. The fading designs painted on the streets are renewed each year to celebrate the fiesta of the Virgen del Remedio held from August 15 to 20.

The Plaza Mayor is dominated by the imposing bulk of the 17th-century Los Ángeles church, which has a series of shell-fluted niches once ornamented by a profusion of statuary, now long gone. Above the main entrance, the angels supporting the town's coat of arms are chipped and broken, some limbless and headless, and one poor cherub has had a totally inappropriate face of a different design, size and material stuck on what is left of its head.

The interior decoration is credited to Juan Bautista Pérez Castiel, the master of works for Valencia cathedral. The saving grace of the church is its unique clock set high on the painted bell-tower that tells you not only the time but the days and months as well.

The fine *modernista* houses that surround the square give the impression of a once-elegant provincial town. Now, sadly, they are mostly cracked and peeling. The original Renaissance town hall on Calle Caballeros in the Jewish quarter is altogether more beautiful.

Before you leave Chelva you might want to visit Embutidos de Chelva, a sumptuous shop of locally made sausages and bottled meats. Here you can be tempted by *longanizas* (spicy pork sausages), *lomo en aceite* (pork fillets in olive oil), and *blanquettes* and *morcadillos* (white and black puddings).

Return to your car and take the road opposite Calle Mártires that has lots of signs on it, one of which directs you to Ahillas. After a two-minute drive, you will see an ancient bullring to your right. Opposite this, a short track to your left leads you to a car park. Take the flight of stairs to the side and you enter a small square where the 20 spouts of the Fuente de Gitana sparkle in the sunshine. It's a surprise to find such a beautiful and ornate fountain in the middle of nowhere. There's a café at the side of the plaza if you need refreshment.

Chelva´s unusual clock

Continue on the road uphill that rises steeply for five kilometres. A sign directs you left to the Santuario del Remedio. This sanctuary sits 850 metres above sea level and has been a pilgrims' destination for centuries. (Note the low walls that support footpaths through the hillsides, once the only routes through this terrain.)

The sanctuary is a pleasant, cool chapel, though the peaceful ambience is somewhat marred by the noise from the television in the café next door. A side chapel displays bundles of wax limbs, artificial hairpieces, a rack of fancy dresses - all votive offerings calling for the Virgin to cure a loved one.

The tiered terraces here with their benches are a delightful spot to rest or picnic. If you want a meal, the Santuario has a restaurant.

Retrace your route back to the Chelva. As you descend, you will see an olive grove cut out of the top of a hill and surrounded by pine trees, a secret garden that can only be seen from above.

When you reach the main road (CV35), turn right for Tuéjar five kilometres away. After passing the tourist office on the outskirts of Tuéjar, turn into the village.

Tuéjar doesn't offer much to justify a visit. As you reach the old town, follow the sharp bend that sends you in the direction of Utiel and the Embalse de Benalgéber. The road climbs upwards through pine-covered hillsides before levelling out at 850 metres. It is a beautiful drive on a summer's evening, as the haze softens the blues and greys of the distant mountains and the pine trees dapple the road with their elongated shadows.

At the km11 marker, you catch your first glimpse of the reservoir in the valley to your right, twinkling like frosted glass. It's worth stopping here for a few moments to breathe in the fresh air and listen to the breeze rustling through the pines. It's a curious sensation to stand on the cobbled road halfway across the dam and look up at the massive bulk of the power station built almost into the rock. Now in ruin, it looks like the stone skeleton of a deserted space station.

Cross over the dam and pass some derelict buildings and deserted workshops that serviced the power complex. Shortly after this a sign to your right directs you to a recreation area by the reservoir, three kilometres away. Stay on the main road and a strange sight awaits you a couple of hundred metres further on.

When the Confederación Hidrográfica del Júcar constructed the dam in the 1950s to hold back the River Tuéjar, the residents of the soon-to-be-flooded Benagéber village at the bottom of the valley were given the choice of being relocated to the outskirts of Valencia city or rehoused higher up the valley.

At the new village of Benagéber the rows of one-storey terraced houses — they look like holiday camp chalets, charmless and identical — became home to those who didn't fancy city life. Many are still lived in, but the more substantial buildings that housed the offices and management of the dam now lie shuttered and derelict. The village church has its rose window smashed and jars of dead flowers sit forlornly in front of its weathered door. The stunning vistas aren't wasted though, as a holiday centre has recently been built to allow teenagers to enjoy all manner of rural pastimes.

Upward and onward is the only way to go, in the direction of Utiel 29 kilometres away, a beautiful drive through the Sierras Atalaya and

Twenty spouts of the Fuente Gitana, Chelva

Negrete, with the occasional cornfield among the pines. Small vineyards set in the red earth become more frequent as you approach Utiel. Requena is one of Valencia's biggest wine-producing regions with its own Denominación de Origen.

At km39, you enter a strange little village called Casa de Medina, a scattering of houses around an unruly village green. At the T-junction, turn right and follow the CV390 to Utiel, eight kilometres further on. In front of you as you turn you'll see a curious *bodega* with two conical chimneys resembling dove cots.

When you reach Utiel, turn left at the junction with the N330 to Valencia, passing under a bridge. The road takes you through the town and, just as you cross over a bridge by the Guardia Civil post, look out for the small sign that directs you to Valencia to your left. This takes you to the E901/A3 autoroute to return to Valencia (76 kilometres away).

WHAT TO SEE

VILLAR DE ARZOBISPO:

Casa Museo de los Cinteros, Museo Etnología, Calle Hospital, 2. Tel. 96 164 64 19. Open Mon-Fri 7-9pm, Sat-Sun noon-2pm. Household ephemera and agricultural equipment of the mid-19th-century.

Cooperativa Agrícola el Villar, Avenida Ingeniero Tamarit, 8-12. Tel. 96 272 00 50. Open Mon-Sat 9am-1pm & 4-7.30pm, Sun 9am-1pm.

Bodegas Comeche, Ingeniero Tamarit, 10. Tel. 96 272 00 78. Open Mon-Fri 8.30am-2pm & 4-7pm. Sat-Sun 9am-2pm.

Granja-Escuela La Serranía, off Avenida Jorge de Austria. Working farm near the Convento Carmelita, where you can feed livestock, go horse riding (€9 an hour) or hire mountain bikes (€2.40 per hour).

CHULILLA:

Castillo de Chulilla, castle of Moorish origin overlooking the town.

Hotel Balneario de Chulilla, Afueras, s/n. Tel 96 165 79 13. Open Mar-mid-Dec. 4km from Chulilla on the CV6241 Sot de Chera/Requena road (turn at junction beside La Rueda restaurant). The hotel is also a health spa with water rich in lime, magnesium and sulphates. Naturally heated swimming pools, and a range of treatments. Prices from €6-27.

Chelva Town Hall

CHELVA:

Barrio Antiguo, original Morisco, Arab and Jewish quarter, behind the town hall on Plaza Mayor.

Nuestra Señora de los Ángeles, 17th-century church in Plaza Mayor.

Fuente Gitano, one of the dozens of fountains in town, on the road to Santuario del Remedio.

Santuario del Remedio, pleasant, cool sanctuary full of votive offerings, 5km outside town on the Chelva-Ahillas road.

Acueducto Peña Cortada, Valencia's best-preserved Roman aqueduct, a 6km walk from

Chelva. Map and route obtainable from the town hall.
Embutido de Chelva, shop selling locally made sausages and
potted meats on Avenida Mancomunidad Alto Turia, 21.

WHERE TO STAY

VILLAR DE ARZOBISPO:
Hostal La Posá, Avenida Ingeniero Tamarit, 9. Comfortably
basic accommodation. €

CHULILLA:
Casa Serena, Calle Turia, 39. Tel. 96 165 7083 or 696 832
445. Pleasant, colourful casa rural with lovely views from its
terrace. €€
Hotel Balneario de Chulilla, Afueras, s/n. Tel. 96 165 79 13.
Open Mar-mid-Dec. Attractive hotel in Victorian building,
surrounded by pools, river and walks. €€-€€€ depending on
season.

CHELVA:
La Posada, Avenida Mancomunidad Alto Turia, 20,
Tel. 96 210 01 24. Functional hostal at modest prices. €

TUÉJAR:
Hotel Álvarez, Avenida Ramón Villanueva 26.
Tel. 96 163 52 82. Modern hotel/restaurant. €€

WHERE TO EAT

VILLAR DE ARZOBISPO:
La Posá, Avenida Ingeniero Tamarit, 9. Tel. 96 272 07 19.
Inexpensive local food. Open lunch and dinner daily. €

CHULILLA:
La Rueda, Calle Ermita, 10. Tel. 96 165 70 25. Open lunch
and dinner daily except Tues. Closed mid-Sept to mid-Oct.
Pleasant rustic restaurant, modestly priced menu of local
cuisine and chef's inspirations. €-€€
El Pozo, Calle Arrabal, 7. Tel. 96 165 72 72. Open Fri/Sat/Sun
for lunch and dinner. Well-priced local cuisine. €-€€
Hotel Balneario de Chulilla, Afueras, s/n. Tel. 96 165 79 13.
Three restaurants, from the upmarket to (in summer) a
riverside barbecue, with imaginative menus to suit all
pockets. €-€€€

CHELVA:
Rincón de los Pasos, Avenida Mancomunidad Alto Turia, 20.
Tel. 96 210 92 12. Open daily lunch and dinner. Closed
Friday night and Sunday night. Very modest prices, good
home cooking. €-€€
Ermita del Remedio, Ctra Chelva-Ahillas, Km 5.
Tel. 96 210 0410 or 637 29 69 71. Open for lunch week-
ends only. Beamed restaurant serving own specialities
including a mix of four types of squid, *paletilla cordero al
horno* (roast shoulder of lamb), and *trucha con salsa de
jamón y almendras* (trout in ham and almond sauce).
You need to book. €€

MORE INFORMATION

VILLAR DE ARZOBISPO:
Leader Office, Calle de los Cruces, 52. Tel. 96 272 07 68.
Open Mon-Fri 8am-3pm, 4-7pm.

CHULILLA:
Ayuntamiento, Plaza Baronia, 1. Tel. 96 165 70 01.
Open Mon-Fri 8.30am-2.30pm.

CHELVA:
Ayuntamiento, Plaza Mayor. Tel. 96 210 00 11.
Open Mon-Fri 9am-2pm.

TUÉJAR:
Tourist Information Office, Ctra Chelva-Tuéjar, km73.
Tel. 96 163 50 84. Open Jul-Sept 10am-2pm, 4-8pm Mon-
Sat, 10am-2pm Sun. Rest of year 10am-1pm Mon-Fri,
10am-2pm, 4-8pm Sat, 10am-2pm Sun. The main tourist
office for the five villages of the Alto Turia region.

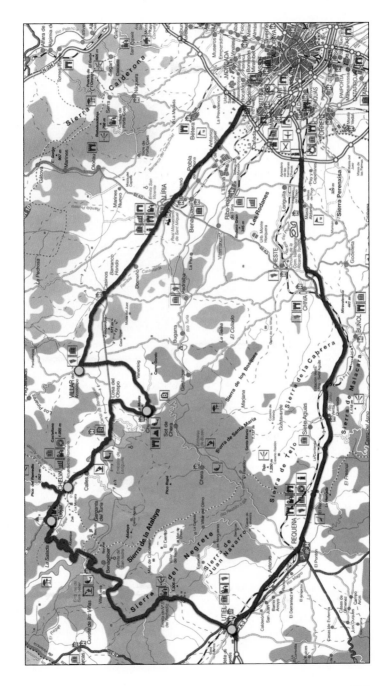

Stark scenery in the Sierra de Dos Aguas

TRIP 7
THE ROUTE OF THE SQUASHED TOMATOES

AREA: Hoya de Buñol and Chiva, west of Valencia city.
ROUTE: Cheste – Chiva – Buñol – Dos Aguas
DISTANCE: 114 kilometres

Drive through the green and pleasant land of Hoya de Buñol, where bubbling springs and spectacular cascades once fed a vast savannah roamed by giant rhinoceros, elephants, wolves and bears.

From the A7 autoroute that bypasses Valencia, take the E901/A3 to Madrid and the Aeropuerto. After 12 kilometres, take exit 332 for Cheste and Godelleta. Stay on this road for two kilometres. As you enter Cheste, you cross a metal bridge over a rail track, followed immediately by a roundabout. Turn left off the roundabout and almost immediately right on Calle de La Ribera. This leads into the square in front of San Lucas Evangelista church.

The *chestanos* are said to be very proud of San Lucas's hexagonal bell tower. At 51 metres, it matches that of the Micalet tower of Valencia cathedral. In 1982, the church was declared a Monument of National Artistic Interest, and has been completely restored, its rich cream stonework glowing as if it were completed last year and not in 1770. High above the main doorway cherubs perch precariously, praying on a pointed pediment, while to the left of the main altar is a mural attributed to the 18th-century artist José Vergara (or one of his students).

Unfortunately, the charm of the church is somewhat marred by the appalling 1970s apartment block beside it, but the *modernista* (Art Nouveau) façade of the building that houses the Salón de Té Verdi opposite helps restore the ambience. You can nip in to try some of the home-made local specialities such as *tortas de toros,* small pastries with raisins and nuts, or *testaminos,* made with sugar, flour, egg yolk and occasionally an assortment of fillings such as chopped almonds. In the Plaza del Dr Cajal, the main square, the Fuente del Ayuntamiento spouts forth in front of the elegant town hall. The fountain was designed in 1802 by Vicente Marzo, president of the Real Academia de Bellas Artes de Valencia. Also on the square are the splendidly ornate Sindicato Agrícola y Caja Rural and the town casino (a kind of gentlemen's club where the town's solid citizens socialise) with its sinuously curving ironwork and colourful tiled panels. Sadly, the interior is rather a letdown — it was slightly modernised in the 1980s but not very well.

Tucked behind the municipal market in Plaza Mercado, the Ermita de la Virgen de la Soledad Gloriosa, named after the town's patron saint, was originally built in 1573, but has been considerably restored since. Numerous plaques advertise various facelifts, most notably a medallion below the twin bells that informs the public in bold lettering that the façade was restored in 1904 at the expense of one José Rodrigo Martínez. In such manner do the rich pave their way to heaven.

To the side of the market the rickety hand-made sign for the long-closed Cine Goya, which looks more like a barn with balconies than an entertainment centre, recalls the time when every tiny village had its own cinema.

As you wander the streets, take a look at some of the tiled side panels framing the front doors of many of the *modernista* houses.

Leave Cheste by returning over the railway bridge you came in on and follow the CV50 signs for Chiva, a couple of kilometres away. When you get there, turn left at a roundabout with half an arch on it, following the one-way sign. At the next Stop sign, turn right and continue into the village.

Chiva is a bustling little town but, apart from a collection of paintings by José Vergara and sculptures by his brother Ignacio in the parish church and the hilltop sanctuary of the Virgen del Castillo, there isn't a great deal for the visitor to see. Its greatest claim to fame is that it is the birthplace of Enrique Ponce, one of Spain's favourite bullfighters.

On the fountain in the Plaza de la Constitución, with its 20 lions' heads spouting constant streams of water, a plaque depicts the Torico de la Cuerda. This is a reference to the fiesta in the last two weeks of August, when brave (or foolhardy) young men try to grab a rope tied around the head of a charging bull to direct its movements.

Plaza de Armas, Buñol Castle

Lion fountain in Alborache

Behind the fountain a large pond is the home of a couple of geese and some large fish, plus (on my last visit) a collection of plastic bags. Houses back directly on the pond, rather like a poor, latter-day Venice.

Leave Chiva via the Valencia road, the way you came in, and at the next roundabout at the bottom of the hill turn right. Moments later at another roundabout turn right again and immediately begin climbing a hill in the direction of Madrid. After one kilometre a footbridge crosses the road with the Restaurante Canario on your right. Almost opposite the restaurant a narrow road on your left twists its way up to the Santuario de la Virgen del Castillo.

The Santuario is only open the hours of Mass but it is worth climbing the hill just to enjoy the panoramic views of the surrounding countryside that varies from rolling olive groves and stately pine-covered hills to industrial estates. On clear days they say you can see the distant Mediterranean. Nearby are the ruins of the castle, said to be of Roman and Moorish origin.

Return to the main road and turn right (the junction is on a long bend, so exit with care). At the roundabout at the bottom of the hill, turn right for Godelleta seven kilometres away, joining the CV50 for Alzira. Continue on this new road and exit at Godelleta Norte. Moments later you see a roundabout with the village's name laid out in bricks.

Godelleta has little to offer other than its sweet Moscatel dessert wine, the best in the region. You can pick up a bottle at a bargain price at the Coarval shop in the front of the San Pedro Apóstol wine cooperative, just as you cross the bridge after the roundabout.

A bend at the edge of Godelleta (just after you cross the bridge) points you in the direction of Buñol, 13 kilometres away (CV3036). A couple of hundred metres up the hill from the main road, a small sign on a right turn points to Buñol. Stay on this pretty country road, crossing over the junction with the VV3034 to Chiva and Turis, and continue in the direction of Buñol. Directly ahead you will see some of the windmills that are doing so much to destroy the visual beauty of Spain.

The first views of Buñol are rather spoilt by the towering chimneys of the cement factory that drives the local economy. As you drop down into the small town you soon lose sight of these behemoths and enter a busy little pueblo that nestles around an ancient castle whose history goes back to the first century BC.

Entering the town, you come to a roundabout with a building bearing a strange yellow-and-green sign for the Diputación Provincial de

Valencia. Take Avenida País Valenciano, the road to the left of this building. Park here if you can because the road narrows as it enters the older part of town (over the bridge) and parking is difficult.

There are more than 300 fountains in the town and its immediate surroundings, with such splendid names as La Alegría (The Happiness), La Umbría (The Shady Place) and La Jarra (The Jar). It was this abundance of water that caused the first Iberian settlers to name the town Bullón, meaning fountain. Roman settlers created irrigation channels and aqueducts to supply the surrounding fields and built the original castle keep, later heightened to 25 metres by the Moors.

Little is known of life under the Visigoths during their stay in this area, but the Moorish conquerors enclosed the *kalaa* (castle) with its high walls and built the Torre de Musa (later known as the Torre del Sur) that led to the first urban development, the narrow streets that ring the castle. Salvador church, built into the castle, sits on the site of a former mosque.

Notable visitors to the castle have included Rodrigo Díaz de Vivar, more widely known as El Cid, but perhaps its most famous resident was Francis, a king of France imprisoned there by Carlos I in 1525. In the early 19th-century, the town formed the dividing line between Aragon and Castilla and the castle served as a prison during the Carlist Wars of 1833-1839 and 1872-1876.

Anyone who likes twisting alleyways and cobbled streets will be in their element in the meandering thoroughfares around the church and castle. Wander behind the Ayuntamiento into the heart of the castle to reach the Plaza de Armas, a medieval square partially inhabited and retaining much of its original appearance.

Lovers of marching music will be interested to know that Buñol boasts two bands, each with more than 120 musicians. One is named La Artística but is known locally as Los Feos (the Ugly Ones).

A short walk out of town along El Cid, the road that goes past the town hall and church, brings you to the pretty little San Luis sanctuary, alongside which are a new open-air auditorium and several restaurants, mainly open during the summer months or when there is a concert at the auditorium. (If you stand right in front of the door of the Santuario, a sensor turns on the light allowing you to see the image of the saint inside).

These days, Buñol is most famous for its annual tomato battle called *La Tomatina* which, in a country known for weird fiestas, must be one of the weirdest.

Buñol's annual tomato battle

One day in the 1940s a resident of Buñol wandered across the square in front of the town hall on market day singing — badly — the song *Amada Mía* from the Rita Hayworth film *Gilda*, using a funnel as a megaphone.

Shoppers and stallholders alike objected to his raucous rendition and began to pelt him with tomatoes, but some of them missed the intended target and hit other bystanders, provoking a tomato battle all over the square.

The following year a local civic dignitary was in the wrong place at the wrong time and found himself the centre of unwanted attention as youths gathered in the square (this time with their own tomatoes) to celebrate what was already becoming known as "the day of the tomato".

The local authorities banned the event, but fines and even prison sentences could not stop the villagers from celebrating the bizarre fiesta. There were public uprisings and even a "funeral of the tomato", when a giant tomato was paraded through the town as a protest against the ban. Now the fiesta is an annual event.

At 11am on the last Wednesday in August, a single shot gives the signal for teams of men in six enormous wagons to heave 140 tons of ripe tomatoes on to the cheering crowd of 30,000 or more cramming the town square.

Intermingled with the locals are visitors who have travelled from all over the world. Drenched in juice, they pelt one another with the tomatoes until, on the chime of 12, a second shot is fired and they sink wearily into the bright red slush that covers the square.

Buñol street

They don't have long to relax, however, as soon a swarm of town hall staff, volunteers and neighbours swoop down with hosepipes, buckets and brooms. While the exhausted revellers drag themselves to the showers in the municipal swimming pool, the square is scrubbed spotless in less than an hour.

For hearty mountain eating you could try Buñol's famous *perdiz en escabeche* (partridge in pickle sauce), *olla podrida* (a thick stew of vegetables and pork), or the simple *patatas en caldo*, a working man's staple of potatoes in broth. You will also find local sausages and plenty of rice dishes, including *arroz con caracoles* (rice with snails). For a picnic you could try the *(bollos con sardines)*, flat loves baked with sardines and bacon laid over them.

Leave Buñol by following the signs for Macastre, five kilometres away. After Macastre, sit back for a relaxed ride to the sierra of Dos Aguas. Beautiful, rolling countryside comes into view as you reach km8. The land is uncultivated apart from a few orange groves, and the hillsides are pockmarked with bright yellow gorse bushes. Here the occasional *algarrobo* (carob) tree sheds its dark brown pods on the roadside in the autumn. Shadowed clefts break the undulating hillside. This sinuous drive is particularly pleasant in late afternoon summer sunshine.

You travel through delightful countryside where arbours of pine trees cast shadows across the road. You are passing through the Sierras Malacara and Martés that together form one of the main nature reserves of the area, as well as being rich in discoveries of the Bronze Age and Iberian cultures.

Sixteen kilometres from Buñol, a sign on your right directs you to the Embalse de Forata. A few minutes' drive further and another right (signposted) takes you to an attractive open area where you can park, have a picnic and take a stroll. The *embalse* (reservoir) is a little further on. A road crosses it, should you want a closer look, but at the other end you have to turn around and come back.

Retrace the route from the reservoir to the main road from Buñol and turn right on CV425. Turn left at the sign on a roundabout for Dos Aguas, just over three kilometres later. The road climbs higher and you see tiny olive groves atop shallow hills surrounded by rough moorland, giving the appearance of monk's tonsures with a few hairs sprouting from bald pates.

A kilometre after the roundabout, you crest a rise and see the dark turquoise water of the Naranjero reservoir along one side of a valley. This must be one of the most beautiful views in the whole of the Valencia region. Park for a few moments; you will hear nothing but the sound of the breeze rustling through the undergrowth and the twittering of birds.

The bright yellow of the gorse mixes with the dark green of rosemary and the deeper green of holm oak. The shades subtly change as they move toward the hazy greyish/green of the mountains in the distance. Through a cleft in two hills you see Dos Aguas dozing in the sun.

Paella in a country restaurant

Stay on this road and eight kilometres further, just after the outskirts of Dos Aguas, you join the VV3081 (CV425 on Michelin maps) which leads to Real de Montroi after a pleasant 22-kilometre drive. Stay on the VV3081 and continue via Montserrat and Colinas de Venta Cabrera to the Valencia bypass and autoroute.

Monument to Cheste motorbike race track

WHAT TO SEE

CHESTE:
San Lucas Evangelista, completely restored Monument of
National Artistic Interest.
Ermita de la Virgen de la Soledad Gloriosa, a 16th-century
hermitage, restored several times.
Circuito de la Comunidad Valenciana Ricardo Tormo,
racetrack opened in 1999 and named after the Valencia
motorcycle champion who died of leukemia in 1998. Has
hosted World and European Superbike championships and
the Spanish Formula 3 championships, as well as regular
Formula 1 races. Spectators get an uninterrupted view over
the whole circuit. Call 96 252 52 12/13 for information
and prices, which vary depending on the event.
La Sárgula, the archery range that is the home of the
Spanish Championship.
Campo de Tiro de la Sociedad Valenciana de Caza y Tiro,
considered one of the best clay pigeon-shooting ranges in
Europe. Contact the Ayuntamiento for information.

CHIVA:
San Juan Bautista, parish church with paintings and
sculptures by artists José and Ignacio Vergara.
Ermita de la Virgen del Castillo, the hilltop sanctuary just
outside the town.

BUÑOL:
Castle and medieval quarters, situated off Calle El Cid, above the Ayuntamiento.
Plaza de Armas, original medieval castle square.
Ermita de San Luis, a pretty little hermitage and fountain 15 minutes' walk from the town centre.
Auditorio al Aire Libre, open-air auditorium. Venue of regular concerts and the Bienal de Música, a bi-annual gathering of some of Europe's most outstanding bands. Contact the town hall for concert details.
Tomatina, tomato-throwing fiesta held on the last Wednesday in August.
Cuevas y cascadas, a number of caves, waterfalls and pools around Buñol can be explored with the aid of a detailed map.

WHERE TO STAY

CHESTE:
Bar Sol, Calle Chiva, 2. Tel. 96 251 07 74.
Local cafeteria with a few basic rooms. €

CHIVA:
La Orza, Dr Carachón, s/n. Tel. 96 252 2194. Closed August. Newly built hotel and restaurant. €€
Restaurant Canario, Avenida Antigua Reino de Valencia, 4. Tel. 96 252 28 66. Basic accommodation. €€€

BUÑOL:
Hotel Condesa Buñol, Calle Blasco Ibáñez, 13. Tel. 96 250 48 52. Pleasant newly refurbished hotel. €€
Posada Venta Pilar, Avda. Pérez Galdós, 5. Tel. 96 250 09 23. Old coaching house recently refurbished. €€
Note: Prices in Buñol can rise considerably during the Tomatina fiesta in August. Advanced booking essential if you intend to stay there during this time.

WHERE TO EAT

CHESTE:
Bar Sol, Calle Chiva, 2. Tel. 96 251 07 74.
Neighbourhood bar/restaurant. Affordable fixed-price menu. €

CHIVA:
La Orza, Dr Carachón, s/n. Tel. 96 252 21 94. Closed
Sundays. Speciality rice with langoustines. Set menu for hotel
guests. Medium to high price. €€–€€€
Restaurant Canario, Avenida Antiguo Reino de Valencia, 4.
Tel. 96 252 24 34. Closed Sunday evening. Local cuisine,
modest fixed price menu for lunch and dinner or affordable
à la carte. €€

BUÑOL:
Condesa Buñol, Calle Blasco Ibáñez, 13. Tel. 96 250 48 52.
Closed Sunday except for hotel residents. Newly opened
restaurant. Regional cuisine and good value *menú del día*,
medium-priced à la carte. €–€€
Las Brasas, Calle Blasco Ibáñez, 53. Tel. 96 250 16 65.
Well-established restaurant offering local specialities.
Medium to high price. €–€€
Posada Venta Pilar, Avda. Pérez Galdós, 5. Tel. 96 250 09
23. Old coaching house recently refurbished serving good
basic local food. Lunchtime menu and dinner (weekends
only). €€

MORE INFORMATION

CHESTE:
Ayuntamiento, Plaza del Dr Cajal. 96 251 00 51.
Open Mon-Fri 8.30am-2.30pm.

CHIVA:
Ayuntamiento, Plaza Gil Escarti s/n Tel. 96 252 00 06.
Open Mon-Fri 8am-3pm.

BUÑOL:
Ayuntamiento, Calle El Cid. Tel. 96 250 01 51.
www.bunyol.es. Open Mon-Fri 8am-3pm.

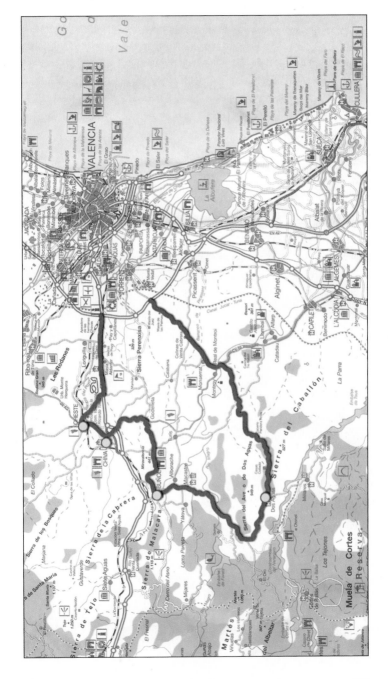

The wines of Requena

THE HIGH WINE COUNTRY

> **AREA:** West of Valencia city
> **ROUTE:** Siete Aguas – Requena – Utiel
> **DISTANCE:** 190 kilometres

Travel to a rust-red plateau where you can wander ancient alleyways above and below ground, enjoy bargain-priced wine and stock up on delicious sausages.

Take the A3 autoroute for Madrid which starts in the centre of Valencia, passing under the autoroute that bypasses the city to the west. You leave the semi-industrialised suburbs quite quickly, then pass Cheste, Chiva and Buñol. Leave the A3 at junction 306 (48 kilometres from Valencia) and take the VV6308 for Siete Aguas. After four kilometres, when you see a playground on your right, turn left into the village.

Siete Aguas has one of the most outrageous fountains you will ever see — a vast affair of ornate tile-work dedicated to San Isidro Labrador, the patron saint of agriculture. In lettering above the image of the hallowed saint, farm labourers exhort the "Celeste Patrono de la Agricultura" to protect them in their battle with the hard soil and to give them wine, oil and bread.

Sharing star billing with San Isidro is a large tiled image of a tranquil village scene with a river meandering through it. Smaller tiles depict agricultural scenes, including such unlikely ones as a woman with a parasol being chased by a bull, a boy in a sailor suit pulling a donkey, and a game of football in full swing.

Villagers gather to fill five-litre containers from the six gargoyles and

Tinajas in the underground caves of Requena

one lion's head that spew forth a constant supply of fresh water, the chatter of the ladies competing with the screeching of the geese in the pond opposite. The geese have been provided with a home, a little white circular house with a blue roof, from which protrudes a metal sculpture of baffling complexity. Siete Aguas itself has little to offer historically, other than that the body of El Cid supposedly rested here en route to Castilla.

Return to the road by the playground and turn left for Madrid and Requena. Rejoin the A3 (direction Madrid) and soon you enter the Altiplano de Requena-Utiel, the highest, most western part of Valencia province on the fringe of the meseta of La Mancha.

You leave the rugged Mediterranean landscape behind and enter a vast plain covered in grapevines, which have replaced the mulberry trees that, in the 18th-century, made Requena the fourth largest producer of silk in Spain. More than 800 looms manufactured this sumptuous fabric for export to the Americas.

Then the vines took over and by the end of the 19th-century the area was widely known for its wine production. The Denominación de Origen Utiel-Requena is respected in particular for its *cava*, which is gaining an international reputation.

From the A3, take the exit 291 for Requena (N111) and follow the signs for the Centro Urbano. At the fourth set of traffic lights after a bridge turn left and at the bottom of the street turn left again on a dual carriageway. This leads to the Plaza del Portal, at the end of the tree-shaded Avenida Arrabal, where you will see the Oficina de Turismo and Casco Histórico alongside one other.

La Vila is the medieval heart of Requena, whose name is said to derive either from the Arabic *rekina* or the Latin *richenna*, meaning "the secure" or "the strong". Some of the original walls of the castle still stand and are in a relatively good state of conservation.

La Vila is full of tucked-away little corners with makeshift gardens. Despite a good deal of tourist promotion, it still has a delightful tumble-down feel about it, partly due to the piles of ancient beams, roof tiles and large stone blocks waiting to be used in restoration work.

Calle Santa María is one of the most important streets in this quarter, where the Knights of the King's Roll built their homes after the Reconquest, forcing the Moors out to the Las Peñas quarter.

Santa María church, two-thirds of the way down the street, has been on the list of national monuments since 1931. Its florid Isabelline

Emilia's award-winning sausages

As you walk up the Cuesta del Castillo, the steep street that takes you from modern Requena into La Vila, with the 10th-century Muslim Torre de Homenaje to your left, you come face-to-face with the Carnicería Emilia.

The sausages that make this butcher's shop worth a visit are at the back. On mouth-watering display are *morcilla de cebolla,* fat black puddings with onion, *perro blanco,* stout haggis-like sausages, and the slim, dark *perro* and the even thinner, spicy *chorizo longa.* All these homemade products are of a sufficiently high standard to have been awarded the Requena Denominación de Origen.

Gothic style is a delight. Begun in the 14th-century, it was redecorated in the baroque style in the 17th-century, but fortunately its awe-inspiring front entrance with saints on pedestals and rich Gothic motifs was left untouched.

There are two other grand churches in La Vila but the 13th-century San Nicolás is in such a bad state of repair that stout metal beams shore up the façade to stop it collapsing. It would take a great deal of divine intervention ever to get it back to a state of grace. The tiny alleyway beside the church is called Calle Paniagua (Water and Bread Street) to signify the two basics of life.

As you wander the streets the buildings constantly remind you of Requena's heritage: the Casa del Arte Mayor de la Seda (House of the Fine Art of Silk Weaving) celebrating the city's silk trade, the 15th-century palace of El Cid (where legend has it he met King Alfonso VI to make arrangements for his daughter's marriage) and the Casa de la Inquisición in the aptly named Calle Cuartel (Jailhouse Street).

Beneath La Vila's warren of streets lies a very different labyrinth, a series of caves dug over centuries to serve as homes, wine cellars, storage areas for oil and grain, sanctuaries for women and children during battle — and even a chapel and ossuary (when the caves were re-discovered and cleaned, more than 20 wagonloads of bones are said to have been removed).

Flights of steps inside houses lead to long-sealed-off trapdoors. Sadly, all traces of cave life have been removed, but you can still see some of the enormous *tinajas*, earthenware jars up to three metres high, that were used to store the wine and olive oil.

Entrance to the caves is in the Plaza de Albornoz but, if you want to see how they would have looked in use, cross the square to Mesón La Vila which has created a small museum in its private cave. It's debatable how many of the original caves would have had a bar, as this one does, and the collection of rusting old farm instruments is more fit for a junkyard than a museum. It's amusing nonetheless and, frankly, more interesting than other caves on view, especially when you learn it was apparently used during the Inquisition to interrogate the locals.

Lively Requena is a pleasant town to explore and enjoy the examples of almost every historical element of Spanish architecture. It also has some excellent little food shops, such as the one at 20 Calle del Peso, just at the end of Avenida Arrabal.

On the Avenida itself, the Mesón del Vino is one of the town's oldest and most respected restaurants. As you enter the bar at the front, you see two large arched paintings, so blackened with age and nicotine that you can't make out what the scene is.

A great bull's head stares down at you. Named Guapito, it met its end in Requena's Plaza de Toros on September 18, 1901. No matter what you think of bullfighting, you have to admit it takes courage to face up to a live bull that size.

To leave Requena, drive back down Avenida Arrabal until you come to a roundabout with a fountain. Cross the roundabout following the signposted N332 for Albacete and one kilometre further on you come to El Pontón. Look for a small sign on your right directing you to the

Torre Oria three kilometres on, just before you get to El Derramador. The first thing you see as you approach the Bodega Torre Oria is the way-out kitsch onion dome and ornate wrought-iron balcony of the tower from which the *bodega* takes its name. A decorative sign on the stunningly tiled front of the main house informs you it was originally known as Finca de Oria de Rueda Bodega San Juan.

The *bodega* buildings, built between 1897 and 1903, are the epitome of the Catalan Art Nouveau style. It comes as no surprise to find that the chap who created this glorious monument to wine production, Valencia architect José Donderis, was also the brain behind the design of Valencia's splendid Estación del Norte, recognised as one of the most emblematic modernist designs in the Valencia region.

Unfortunately, the main house's interior is now in a sad state of repair, having lain empty for decades, but there are plans to restore the building to its former opulence. Visitors are only able to see the entrance hall. The *bodega*'s true value, at least in economic terms, lies in the vast underground cellars, where six million bottles of wine are maturing, of which one million are *cava* (Spanish sparkling wine).

From Bodega Torre Oria, continue on the peaceful country road towards Utiel, 10 kilometres further on. You pass a series of low-lying *pueblos* that barely interrupt the skyline, Barrio Ayoro, San Juan and Calderón, and wineries almost the size of small villages. At the roundabout with three enormous *tinajas* in the centre on the A3, go straight across and, at the junction just beyond, turn right before a row of modern three-storey houses.

Utiel may lack the charm of nearby Requena, but it does have its moments, particularly in the warren of narrow streets around the church. The church itself is magnificent in its simplicity. Barely decorated, in complete contrast to most of the churches in the region, the simple stone walls and barley-sugar-twist pilasters with their gilded capitals have a majesty that outweigh much of the extravagant ornamentation seen elsewhere. Recordings of Gregorian chant enhance the peacefulness and it is the sort of place that encourages you to sit awhile and absorb the tranquillity, even if you're not religiously inclined.

Utiel's Cooperativa Agrícola is the *bodega* to visit for well-priced wines. Grapevines depicted in tiles decorate each side of its arched entrance with a panel above showing an idyllic rural landscape.

The huge metal door looks more appropriate for a prison entrance, but it opens to reveal the work going on around the huge shining vats in which the wine is produced. Large plaques reveal the winery was built between 1949 and 1960 and has a capacity of 30 million litres.

A tiled plaque decorating the front of Siete Aguas

If you want to sample the product, you can do so at the shop next door.

To see how it's all done, visit the Museo del Vino housed in the Bodega Redondo, a circular ex-winery, where tools and equipment used in wine-making for centuries past are on display.

123

A quiet street in La Vila

Unlike the façade of the Cooperativa, the bullring almost opposite is not a thing of beauty. Even so, the locals are inordinately proud of their *plaza de toros,* which was built in 1858 and rivals that of Bocairent as the region's oldest. It is Valencia's second largest, smaller only than the bullring in the capital.

Leave Utiel by the road you came in on, passing the Guardia Civil barracks on your right. When you come to a roundabout with a filling station and a large new hotel on your right, El Tollo, turn right for Madrid. About one kilometre later, this road joins the motorway but you go straight ahead on the N111 in the direction of Caudete de las Fuentes (two kilometres), a sleepy village with a factory that — at least according to the owner — is unique in all Spain.

At Caudete, go across the first roundabout and at the second take the VV5025 to Las Casas, a sharp right that has you almost going back on yourself. The road twists up around the edge of the village and, as you pass a sign that you are leaving Caudete, you see on your right a low cream-coloured factory.

Artesanías Folklóricas España boasts that it is the foremost, if not the only, factory in Spain dedicated to the production of items of folk interest. If mock 17th-century pistols, model galleons, florid fans (almost all Spanish fans are made in the Valencia region), flamenco dresses and clattering castanets are to your liking, this is the place for you. All those little souvenirs of Spain tourists love are here under one roof — and at factory prices

Return to the roundabout and go straight across for Los Isidros, VV8108. You begin a lovely drive through pine forests and vineyards and run-down little villages. Despite consisting of mere handfuls of houses, all have signs directing you to the "Centro Ciudad" and great glittering tanks where thousands of litres of wine are slowly fermenting.

At the next junction turn left for Los Ruices and Requena on the VV8101. Pass Los Ruices and, at the junction two kilometres along, turn right on the N322, once again heading for Los Isidros.

At the junction with the N332, turn left for Requena and after three kilometres turn right for Los Duques (VV8021), shortly after which you arrive at Campo Arcis, a veritable city compared to many of the tiny *pueblos* you have been passing through. If you haven't picked up any wine, you can do so at Bodegas Sebiran where they have been producing it for almost 90 years.

When you reach the N330, turn right for Almansa and, a few minutes later, left at La Portera. There is a large sign for Yátova as you leave the main road, but watch out for another small one moments later on the front of a cream-painted building opposite Bar La Sartén. Turn left here on the CV429. Beyond La Portera relax and enjoy the view and rural serenity as you gradually leave the vineyards behind, passing the small villages of Hortunas and Mijares.

At Yátova, follow the road that skirts the town (VV3037) and head for Buñol through almond, carob and olive groves. When you get close enough to see Buñol cascading down the hillside, just after a sharp left-hand bend you take a very sharp right, opposite a couple of battered road signs, and continue downhill. You pass over an old iron bridge, immediately start to climb again and turn right at the next junction, then follow the motorway signs for Valencia.

WHAT TO SEE

SIETE AGUAS:

La Fuente de San Isidro, an ornate fountain dedicated to Spain's patron saint of agriculture.

Fauna Ibérica, Parque de la Naturaleza, near El Rebollar, just off the autoroute between Siete Aguas and Requena at junction 297. Tel. 96 213 80 76. Nature park where you can see Spanish wildlife, including the rare Iberian lynx, in almost natural surroundings. Open daily 10am-8pm Apr-Oct & 10am-5pm Nov-Mar. Entry €13 adults, €8 children.

REQUENA:

La Vila, walled town of Moorish origin dating from the Caliphate period (8-11th-century).

Cuevas de La Vila. Caves dug under the streets of La Vila. Guided tours (Spanish speaking only) 11am, noon, 1pm, 4.15pm, 5pm & 6pm, Tues and Thurs mornings only, Fri-Sun afternoons only. Entry €3 adults, €2 children and pensioners.

Museo Municipal de Requena, housed in Carmelite convent in Plaza Consistorial. Tel. 96 230 12 00. Open 11am-2pm daily except Mon. Entry €3 adults, €2 children & pensioners. Ethnological museum, reproduction of a rural house with furnishings from the 18th-century, displays of regional costume, and the history of wine production in the locality.

Muestra del Embutido de Artesano. A three-day celebration of locally made sausages held every February (dates vary slightly, check with tourist office).

Fiesta de la Vendimia, annual wine festival held last week in August and first days of September to celebrate end of the grape harvest.

UTIEL:

Museo del Vino, Bodega Redonda, Calle Sevilla, 12. Tel 96 217 10 62. Free entry. Wine museum in circular *bodega*.

Bodega Cooperativa Agrícola de Utiel, Avda. Marín Lázaro 8. Tel 96 217 14 68. Open for sampling and buying weekdays (except Thurs), 4pm-7pm, Thurs 9am-12.30pm, Sat/Sun 9am-12.30pm

CAUDETE DE LAS FUENTES:

Artesanías Folklóricas España, Ctra. de Las Casas, s/n. Tel 96 231 91 88. Manufacturer of Spanish folklore artifacts. Shop open Mon-Fri 9am-2pm, 4pm-8pm, Sat 10am-2pm.

WINERIES:

The area of the Utiel-Requena Denominación de Origen has 108 *bodegas*, some producing more than a million bottles a year, others only tens of thousands. Most offer guided tours and tastings.

Pago de Tharsys, Ctra. Madrid-Valencia, km274, Requena. Tel. 96 230 33 54. Web page www.pagodetharsys.com. Open Mon-Sat from 11am-2pm & 4-7pm. Sun holidays 11am-2pm. Small, family-owned *bodega* that produces a limited range of wines, including *cava* and *petillant* (slightly sparkling) white and rosé, mainly from their own vines. They include a white *vendimia nocturna*, the only one in the area, and a *vino dulce*, also unusual for Requena. English-speaking guide.

Dominio de la Vega, Ctra. Madrid-Valencia km270, San Antonio (on the outskirts of the village). Open to the public Sat March-Dec from 10am-2pm or by prior arrangement. Since starting production in 2002 the *bodega* has won a number of awards, including best *cava* in Spain in 2003 and best *rosada* (rosé) in the Valencia Community in 2004. The four owners principally involved in production have almost a century-and-a-half of wine-making experience. Extremely well-priced wines, even its prize-winners are affordable. English-speaking guide.

Bodega Torre Oria, Ctra Pontón-Utiel, km3. Tel. 96 232 0280 (web page www.torreoria.com). Open Mon-Fri 10.30am-2pm, 4pm-6pm, Sat 10am-2pm. During Nov & Dec, Sat 10am-4pm, 4.30-6.30pm, Sun 10am-2pm.

Bodegas Sebirán, Calle Pérez Galdós, 1, Campo Arcis. Tel. 96 230 33 21. Open Sat 11am-2pm, 4-6pm, Sun 11am-4pm. Web page www.bodegassebiran.com

WHERE TO STAY

SIETE AGUAS:

Casa Rosa, Calle Victorino Sánchez, 7. Tel. 96 234 02 15. Small modern hotel. €€

REQUENA:

Alojamiento Turístico La Vila, Calle Cristo, 21. Tel. 96 230 03 74. Small rustic hotel in Moorish quarter. Some rooms furnished with antique furniture. €€

Hotel La Vila, Plaza de Albornoz. Tel. 96 230 1275 or 96 230 0374. www.hotellavillarestaurante.com. Same owners as above, opened at end of 2005 in splendidly restored historic house. €€

Hotel Doña Anita, Plaza de Albornoz, 15. Tel. 96 230 5347 or 656 341 988, Email casadeanita@tubal.net. Web page www.tubal.net. Looks historic but built from scratch in 2005. Elegant hotel with hydro-massages in each room. €€

SAN ANTONIO DE REQUENA:
Casa Doña Anita, C/Mayor, 13. Tel. 96 232 0676. Email casadeanita@tubal.net. Web page www.tubal.net. Delightful small hotel completely restored from an original modernist family home, furnished with antiques. €€

VENTA DEL MORO:
Casa del Pinar. Tel. 96 213 90 08. Beautifully restored farmhouse, relaxed hotel with two workers' cottages tastefully converted into *casas rurales* let individually. Very highly recommended. Must book. €€€

UTIEL:
Hotel Castillo, Calle Camino, 90. Tel. 96 217 10 84. Modern hotel above restaurant of same name. Closed 15 Sep-15Oct. €

El Tollo, Alto San Agustin s/n. Tel. 96 217 02 31. Stylish hotel opened in 2002. €€€

Entre Viñas (also known as Finca el Renegado). Tel. 96 213 90 71. Beautifully restored former farmhouse set in modern vineyard with bodega. Single and double rooms and two apartments each with two double bedrooms, kitchen and living room. Rooms €€, apartments €€€-€€€€. Owned by small company specialising in rural activities, which can be arranged through the hotel.

WHERE TO EAT

SIETE AGUAS:
Casa Rosa, Calle Victorino Sánchez, 7. Tel. 96 234 02 15. Open daily for lunch and dinner except Mon. Modern restaurant serving Mediterranean cuisine and *cocina casera.* €–€€

REQUENA:
La Posada de Águeda, Ctra. Madrid-Valencia, km283. Tel. 96 230 14 18. Owned by an inventive chef and his

delightful wife after whom the restaurant is named. Open daily for lunch and dinner. Very highly recommended. €€-€€€

Mesón de La Vila, Plaza de Albornoz, 13. Tel. 96 230 21 32. Rustic restaurant in what was once the house of the Inquisition. Good local food, modest prices. Diners get free entry to private caves (€1 for non-diners). Open daily for lunch and dinner except Mon. €– €€

Mesón del Vino, Avenida Arrabal, 11. Tel. 96 230 00 01. Open daily except Mon for lunch and dinner. Closed all September. Rustic style restaurant specialising in local cuisine. €€– €€€

VENTA DEL MORO:

Casa del Pinar, Tel. 96 213 90 08. Excellent country restaurant owned by an English chef and his Spanish wife, the first to open a proper Spanish tapas bar in London. Very highly recommended. Must book. €€- €€€

UTIEL:

Restaurante Castillo, Calle Camino, 90. Tel. 96 217 10 84. Open daily for lunch and dinner except Monday (closed Sep 15-Oct 15). Comfortable, elegant décor, menu of local dishes and own invention. Good robust food, highly recommended. €€

El Carro, Calle Heroes del Tollo, 25. Tel. 96 217 11 31. Open daily lunch and dinner. Well-regarded restaurant. Makes its own ice-cream — try the olive oil or rosemary flavours. €€

El Tollo, Alto San Agustín s/n. Tel. 96 217 02 31. Stylish modern hotel recently opened. Mid-price range Mediterranean cuisine. €€

MORE INFORMATION

SIETE AGUAS:

Ayuntamiento, Arrabal, 2. Tel. 96 234 00 03 Open Mon-Fri 8.30am-3pm

REQUENA:

Tourist Information Office, Calle García Montés, s/n (beside entrance to La Vila). Tel. 96 230 38 51. Web page www.requena.es, email requena@touristinfo.net. Open Tues-Thurs, Sun 9.30am-2pm, Fri/Sat 10am-2pm, 4-7pm.

UTIEL:
Tourist Information Office, Puerta Nueva, 11. Tel. 96 217 11 03. Email touristinfo_utiel@gva.es. Open Wed-Sun 11am-2pm, & Thurs-Sat 4-7pm.
Museo del Vino (Bodega Redondo*)*, Calle Sevilla, 12. Tel. 96 217 10 62. Open Mon-Fri 10am-2pm.
Ayuntamiento, Plaza del Ayuntamiento, 1. Tel. 96 217 05 04. Open Mon-Fri 8.30am-3pm.

Ask at the tourist information offices or the Bodega Redonda in Utiel for a copy of "*Ruta del Vino de la D.O. Utiel-Requena*", an excellent book giving details of *bodegas*, restaurants, museums etc in the area. Not normally on display, but it is free.

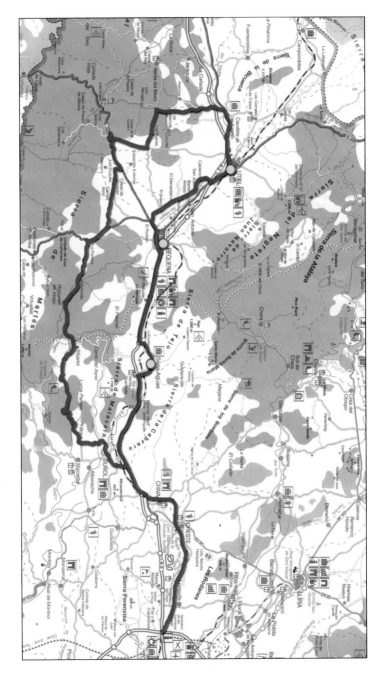

The cupola supposedly designed by Gaudí

LABYRINTH OF THE FULL MOON

AREA: Canal de Navarrés, Macizo del Caroig, north Alicante province
ROUTE: Sumacàrcer – Navarrés – Bicorp – Anna – Enguera – Moixent.
DISTANCE: 120 kilometres

Enter the mountainous heart of the Valencia region where a vast subterranean reservoir feeds verdant forests and a wonderland of lakes, mountain pools and towering cascades.

From the N340, the inland autoroute which passes close to Xàtiva and runs north to Valencia, take exit number 855 for Alcàntera del Xúquer. This is the third exit north of the one for Xátiva (junctions on this road are marked by the kilometre number and not sequentially).

As you leave the motorway, follow the signs for Alcàntera del Xúquer and Sumacàrcer. At the next junction (barely a km further on), turn right on the VP3072 and follow the signs for Càrcer and Sumacàrcer. (Considerable road work was going on at the time of writing so, as you leave the motorway coming from the south, look for a sign for Vidal to your right — you need to go in this direction until you reach the Alcàntera road.)

Almost immediately you enter Alcàntera del Xúquer and just as rapidly find yourself in Càrcer. You pass through the ubiquitous orange groves of Valencia as you travel gently over low-lying hills.

Turn right at the roundabout (VP 3072) just after the km5 mark. Four kilometres later, as you turn a bend, you see ahead on the terraced hillside the pretty cemetery of Sumacàrcer, with its hexagonal turrets and row of cyprus trees. One kilometre further on, you reach the village itself. Follow the signs for Navarrés, 10 kilometres away, on the road snaking up the pine-covered hill behind Sumacàrcer.

The road levels out after two kilometres and you travel through stately, greyish-green olive groves interspersed with the brighter green of almond trees. The earth, when newly turned, is a deep brick red that glows with fecundity.

You are entering the Macizo del Caroig, dubbed with the poetic name of the "labyrinth of the full moon". The rivers Friale, Grande, Cazuma and Ludey flow through a picturesque landscape of lakes, ravines and waterfalls, where water-courses disappear underground, popping up now and again, to finally reappear when they reach the river Escalona.

The diversity of this beautiful region has made it an important centre of rural activities, from climbing, mountainbiking, canoeing, fishing, trekking, horse riding and swimming to leisure walks and studying the profusion of cave paintings that go back to Neolithic times.

The local gastronomy reflects the hardness of life here, with such dishes as *mojete arriero* (spicy cod-and-tomato stew) and *olla con pelotas* (a rich stew with dumplings). You will also find dishes of delicious chantrelle mushrooms, picked from the mountainsides and known locally as *pebrazons*, and savoury tomato, red pepper and bacon *tortas*, a kind of Valencian pizza. For those with a sweet tooth there are *rollets d'aiguardent*, liqueur-filled rolls.

This area is the domain of *los caliqueños*, hand-rolled cigars sold in brown-paper-wrapped bundles of 20 for the ridiculous price of €2.50, if you know where to look. The Canal de Navarrés (the valley in which most of the villages are situated) was historically the centre of tobacco-growing in the Valencian Community, and the workers used to take leaves home to "roll their own".

These days most of the tobacco is brought from Granada, but the *caliqueños* have become a cottage industry and for every small cigar-producing factory there are a thousand homes making these lumpy, slightly curving smokes — totally illegally. However, this contraband trade is largely ignored and, if you ask politely, most of the cafes will sell you a pack, usually from under the counter or from a store cupboard, but never on open display.

The villages of the Canal de Navarrés are rarely beautiful and, apart from the usual church and sanctuary, have little to offer the history

The Albufera park

buff. Visitors to this area usually come for the water, the walks and spectacular scenery.

The town of Navarrés shows its Arab origin in the narrow streets of the old town at the foot of the hill, crowned by the shrine dedicated to the Cristo de la Salud (the Christ of Good Health). From the courtyard

135

19th century circular stone house used by farm workers near Enguera

of the *ermita* you can look over expanses of flowers grown commercially around the town, which have caused Navarrés to be dubbed "the little Spanish Holland".

Leaving Navarrés on VV3071 in the direction of Quesa and Bicorp, the road dips and dives as it enters the mountains, a rough but attractive countryside. You breast a rise at the km14 marker (four kilometres after leaving Navarrés) and Quesa lies in the valley before you. Apart from stopping at the town hall to pick up information (and a good little map of the area) or at the Museum of Contemporary Art if you are there at the weekend, Quesa has little to offer except for Los Charcos (The Ponds), a delightful picnic and camping area, an eight-kilometre drive from the village.

Drive through Quesa and, at the roundabout just outside the village, take the second exit for the Camino los Charcos. After two kilometres, you come to a Y-junction. Take the left fork, uphill. The narrow road soon levels out for a pretty, meandering drive through pine and carob trees. Pocket-sized orange and almond groves grow in the reddish earth of the eroded hillsides.

As you reach Los Charcos, a wooden sign directs you to a campsite to the right and Los Charcos to the left. You drop down into a recreation area with a kiddies playground, picnic areas and barbeques set alongside the clear, tinkling waters and calm shallow pools of "The Ponds", inhabited by shoals of small fish and the occasional fat striped frog.

Way-marked walks guide you through a landscape of lavender, spurge flax, oleanders and mountain ash and past the Abrigo de Voro, a rock shelter where prehistoric Levante rock paintings depict archery scenes.

On your return trip, as you crest a rise two kilometres from Los Charcos, the valley opens out to your left with a beautiful patchwork of cultivation. Back at the roundabout at Quesa, the VV3071 takes you towards Bicorp.

Near the km18 marker, as you drop into a valley, note the curious colour scheme: the deep purplish-red rock of the hillsides graduates into a greyish yellow. You cross a long bridge and climb the other side of the valley. Down to your left among the fruit groves you will see a series of boxes on poles. These are beehives, providing the honey for which the area is renowned.

Three kilometres later, Bicorp appears on your right. Take a look at the row of cottages on the edge of the ravine; you will notice that the backs of two of them have actually tumbled down the precipice. And that's probably the most interesting feature of Bicorp.

However, along a track on your left just before you get to Bicorp is the Cueva de la Araña (Spider's Cave), said to be the most important collection of prehistoric cave paintings in Spain (the last two kilometres are inaccessible by car).

Proclaimed a World Heritage site, the cave paintings show men (or women) collecting honey — the only illustration of prehistoric honey collection in Spain. There are other paintings in caves in the area and expert guides are available to explain their meaning for you.

Retrace your route from Bicorp through Navarrés, following the VV3076 to Bolbaite and Chella. Three kilometres after Navarrés, you come to Playamonte, a recreation area built around a small lake.

Four kilometres further on you reach Chella, where a group of experts are studying the claim that the blue-and-white tiled cupola of the parish church, the Virgen de Gracia, was designed by the famous architect Antoni Gaudí. If it was, it will surprise a lot of people as it looks just like any number of cupolas in the Valencia region. But time, and the experts, will tell.

The waterfall at Chella

Climb to the lookout at the top of the town and you have a glorious view over the surrounding valley, with finely ordered orange groves and vineyards looking like a neatly sewn quilt. The *chellinos*, as the locals are known, have christened this spot Paraíso. There is not a sound except for the water cascading from El Salto, a waterfall that tumbles 30 metres into the deep green pool below.

Mouldering at the bottom of the gorge is the ruin of an old electricity station that generated power from the force of the falls. Now little more than four creeper-covered walls, it is home for a herd of goats whose owner cultivates the fan-shaped garden laid out in front of the main entrance.

Four kilometres down the road (still on the VV3076) lies Anna, a delightful village with a liquid appeal. A multitude of fountains bubble and cascade in the hills and valleys surrounding the *pueblo*. The most important of them, as far as Anna itself is concerned, is the Albufera, a half-kilometre drive from the edge of town. You can find it by taking the right turn just after the Fiat service station, in front of the log cabin Tourist Office.

The Albufera is a spring-fed lake whose water filters underground to irrigate the fields surrounding the village. The island in the middle of the lake, called El Merendero, is home to families of ducks and geese. You can hire a boat for closer inspection. The lake, surrounded by willow and poplar trees, has picnic benches and peaceful areas for a doze in the sun. A delightful spot to while away an hour or two on a balmy summer's day.

Return to the main road and turn right, and, after one kilometre, you come to a roundabout indicating Enguera is five kilometres away on the CV590. Along the arrow-straight road, you pass the modern, elegant Hotel Fuente Lucena, seemingly stuck in the middle of nowhere, next to a factory, but with lovely views over the valley.

Shortly after you enter Enguera, a left turn up the side of a blue Cepsa garage takes you into the centre of town. There's parking in town, but it's probably best to park on the main road and walk the couple of minutes into the centre.

Enguera is a pretty little place of narrow streets and shady squares where elderly gentlemen pass the hours in relaxed conversation. Going as far back as the 11th-century, the castle was incorporated into the Crown of Aragon in 1244. But little more than a century later, in 1365, it was destroyed by the order of Pedro IV, who considered it too much of a threat to the security of his kingdom.

It's still possible to see many fine examples of the houses known locally as *heredades,* two-storey buildings with a corral, the homes of the 18th and 19th-century bourgoisie who made their money in the wool trade. These days the town's fortunes are based on wrought iron, furniture and olive oil. In San Miguel church, part of the Carmelite convent, there are paintings by Carnelo and Segrelles and an anonymous altarpiece attributed to the so-called Maestro de Enguera. Return to the main road and follow the CV590 in the direction of Ayora. It's a peaceful ride through a gently rolling, unirrigated landscape, with the occasional cornfield adding a rich green or golden hue, depending on the time of year you pass through.

As you approach the km36 marker, to your right you will see a stone cairn with a weathered board stuck on a metal pole alongside a rough track. (It's directly opposite a white-and-blue arrowed sign indicating a bend.) The sign reading Cuco Magno (on maps it is sometimes referred to as Cuco Montanyola) directs you to one of the unusual 19th-century circular houses that rural workers used during harvest time to avoid having to trek back to their village. Don't drive up the track as the surface is very bumpy with lots of sharp stones. You can park the car on a small patch of land beside the road. From there it's only a five-minute walk.

As you walk through the dry moorland, the air is filled with the scent of rosemary and wild mountain thyme and you see small bushes of white rock rose. The arched entrance to the *cuco* is through stout walls almost two metres thick and made of layered flat stones. The ceiling is beautifully constructed with thinner stones tapering to a central peak. The only fittings are a dry sink and a small fireplace. Dozens of these *cucos* are scattered throughout the Sierra de Enguera. Returning to your car, carry on for another seven kilometres until, just after the km29 marker, you turn left on the VV3055 (marked as CV589 on Michelin maps) for Navalón. A large yellow sign warns you the narrow road is in bad condition and you should drive carefully (*carretera estrecha, firme en mal estado, circulen con precaución*). Despite the warning, the road is no better or worse than many you will encounter on these trips and is, in fact, a very pretty drive through rolling countryside.

After four kilometres you will pass the tiny village of Navalón de Abajo and, one kilometre further, Navalón de Arriba (Lower and Upper Navalón). Continue towards Moixent. After about four kilometres, as you climb a hill, a sign to your left advertises El Teularet, Centre d'Ecoturisme i Formació. The centre, a little over a kilometre's drive down a metalled road. focuses on environmental training, but also has way-marked walks, a small farm and rest areas. Back on the main road, the road begins to wend its way down to Moixent. To end the excursion, follow the signs for Valencia for the north and Albacete for the south. The latter connects with the N330

The park in the village of Anna

autoroute for Alicante. For Benidorm and the central Costa Blanca, follow the signs for Ontinyent, where you return to the coast via Alcoi and the Guadalest valley.

Home-made cigars from the Canal de Navarrés

WHAT TO SEE

The **Canal de Navarrés** has many rivers, waterfalls and pools usually only accessible by footpaths, many of which are way-marked. Check tourist information offices for details of walks and also for routes to see the many cave paintings (*pinturas rupestres*).

QUESA:
Museo Alberto Hernández y Mercedes Rubio, on the left immediately after the sign for Quesa as you enter the village. Tel. 96 225 60 01. Museum of contemporary/romantic art. Open Sat/Sun 11am-1pm. Entry €1.

Los Charcos, 8km from village. Recreation area with freshwater pools, picnic area, playground and way-marked footpaths to view cave paintings. Open all year. Entry €1.50.
Fiesta La Reserva, the stew festival. In 1690, an epidemic wiped out the whole of Quesa's population except for one family, who lived on stew and slowly repopulated the village. To commemorate the event, on February 14 each year all visitors are served *caldero*, a hearty stew.

BICORP:
Cueva de la Araña. World Heritage site of prehistoric cave paintings. 12 kms from village, last two kilometres only accessible on foot. Two local experts give free guided tours of the caves, in Spanish only. Contact Loli on 657 190 668 or Paco on 670 446 508.

CHELLA:
Mirador del Salto, viewing point for El Salto waterfall and surrounding valley.
La Virgen de Gracia, parish church with cupola allegedly designed by Gaudí.

ANNA:
La Inmaculada, 17th-century parish church with baroque altar-piece and paintings of the same period.
La Albufera, small boating lake with picnic area. Entry €2 Easter-Nov, free other times of the year. Boat hire Easter-Nov only, €6 per hour.

ENGUERA:
Convento de Carmelitas Descalzas, 17th-century convent.
Ruinas del Castillo, ruins of the 13th-century castle.
Cuco de Mago (Montanyola), 19th-century round agricultural worker's house, 11 kms from town in direction Navalón.
(There are a number of caves and relics of Iberian settlements in the area but only accessible on foot).

WHERE TO STAY

NAVARRÉS:
Hotel Oliver, Plaza de la Iglesia, 5. Tel. 96 226 72 03. Modest establishment (despite its two stars) in mid-20th-century building. €

ANNA:
Hostal Lar Galego, Calle Mayor, 181. Tel. 96 221 05 73. Closed
Sept. Small, pleasant *hostal* completely refurbished in 2001. €€

ENGUERA:
Hotel Fuente Lucena, Ctra. Gandia-Ayora, km51 (just outside
Enguera). Tel. 96 222 60 96. Attractive modern hotel with
pleasant views over valley. €€
El Borreguero, Calle Santa Bárbara, 21. Tel. 96 222 41 58.
Comfortable accommodation in simple rooms in large old
town house. If you plan to stay for a few days, El Borreguero
has full cooking facilities. €

NAVALÓN DE ARRIBA:
El Teularet. Tel. 96 225 30 24. Recently completed hotel,
refuge and wooden cabins. The refuge has rooms to sleep
from 2-12 people and the cabins accommodate up to 6,
charges on a per person basis depending on number per
room. Hotel €€

WHERE TO EAT

NAVARRÉS:
Tapas. A number of bars and cafes offer *tapas*.

QUESA:
Bar La Parra, Avenida. Valencia, 1. Tel. 96 225 60 22. Open
daily. Basic village bar/cafeteria. Well-priced lunch and
dinner menus of local food. €

CHELLA:
Restaurante Gavi, Avenida Constitución, 72.
Tel. 96 222 00 26. Open daily. Unpretentious bar/restaurant
that serves excellent grilled local meats and local dishes at
unpretentious prices. €

ANNA:
Restaurant Lar Galego, Calle Mayor, 181. Tel. 96 221 05 73.
Open daily except Monday for lunch and dinner.
Closed Sep. Modest prices. Galician specialities, served
weekends, can be more expensive. For a feast try the *carne
trinchada*, thick slices of meat and steaks from Galicia,
Salamanca and León that you cook to your personal taste
on a *very* hot stone placed on your table.
Bar-Restaurante Marchena, Lago de la Albufera.
Tel. 96 221 01 41. Open daily lunchtimes only, all year.

Large open restaurant with large shaded terrace overlooking the lake. Cheery sisters Loli and Paqui specialise in typical Valencia food, cooking local meats over wood fires. Very modestly priced menu of the day and *menú de degustación* (allowing you to sample many different dishes). €– €€

ENGUERA:
Hotel Fuente Lucena, Carretera Gandia-Ayora, Km 51. Tel. 96 222 60 13. Open daily for lunch, dinner Sat/Sun only (except for residents). Modern hotel restaurant. Well-priced *menú del día* (Mon-Fri only) and interesting, mid-range price *a la carte*. Try *Camembert frito con salsa alarandanos* (fried Camembert with blackberry sauce) followed by *solomillo con virutas de ibérico, gratinado con queso de oveja* (sirloin steak with shavings of Iberian ham and gratineed ewes' cheese). €€
Bar Willy, Plaza Ibáñez Marín, 17. Tel. 96 222 53 09. Open daily for lunch and dinner, closed Monday. Modern restaurant above a bar. Reasonably priced regional food. Popular with the locals. €– €€

NAVALÓN ARRIBA:
El Teularet, a short drive from the village on the Moixent road. Tel. 96 225 30 24. Traditional Valencian cuisine with vegetarian options. Chicken and rabbit have come from El Teularet's own farm and, whenever possible, their vegetables. Good- priced lunch and dinner served daily. €€€€

MORE INFORMATION

NAVARRÉS:
Ayuntamiento, Calle de la Iglesia, 2. Tel. 96 226 60 01. Open Mon-Fri 8am-3pm.

QUESA:
Ayuntamiento, Calle Hernán Cortés, 4. Tel 96 225 60 01. Open Mon-Fri noon- 2pm.

BICORP:
Ayuntamiento, Calle Iglesia, 11. Tel. 96 226 91 10. Open Mon-Fri 8am-2pm.

ANNA:
Tourist Information Office, Calle Mayor, s/n. Tel. 96 221 01 36. Open daily 10am-2pm.

ENGUERA:
Asociación para la Promoción Socio Económica Macizo del Caroig, Casa de Cultura, Plaza Manuel Toslá, s/n.
Tel. 96 222 48 16. Web page www.turcaroig.com
Agencia del Desarrollo Local – Enguera,
Plaza de las Palmeras, Bajo. Tel. 96 222 47 61.

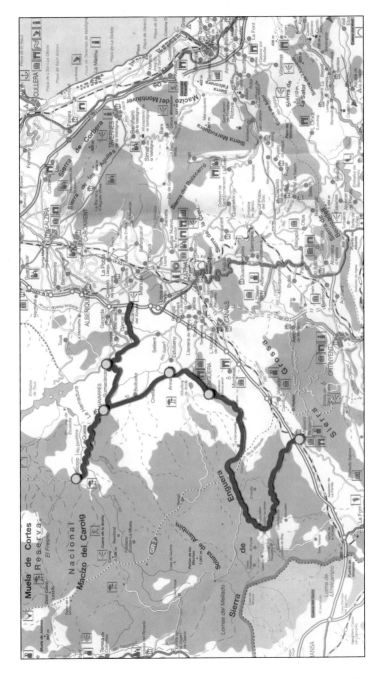

TRIP 10
PITCHFORK CENTRE OF THE WORLD

AREA: Valle de Ayora, western Valencia
ROUTE: Picassent – Dos Aguas – Cofrentes – Jalance – Jarfuel – Ayora – Moixent
DISTANCE: 162 kilometres

Enter the land of honey, hearty country stews and long-pronged wooden pitchforks — and take the waters beside an inactive volcano.

From the A7 autoroute to the south of Valencia, exit at the junction for Silla, Alcacer (Alcàsser on some maps) and Picassent. Ignore a sign for Toris and Picassent to the right on a roundabout and take the second road to Picassent and the centre of town. You will see signs for both Turis and Toris (it's the same place). At the next roundabout turn right and cross a bridge into the town.

By the bridge are small sculptures of an aged man and woman on pedestals. These are probably the most interesting thing you will see in Picassent, apart from a nice church façade, so drive on through orange groves with a scattering of houses and low-lying hills ahead, following the signs for Turis (VP3065).

At the next junction, in front of the Venta Cabrera, take the road for Montserrat and Montroi. Go straight through Montserrat to the next roundabout where you turn left and soon enter Montroi. Follow the signs for Real de Montroi and Tavernes de la Valldigna (CV50).

You leave Montroi by a long bridge at the other end of which Real de Montroi begins. At the first set of traffic lights turn right for Dos Aguas. Almost immediately is a dog-leg, left and right, signposted Dos Aguas (VV3081).

After two kilometres, you begin to leave suburbia behind as you climb through orange groves. There are pleasant views over the cultivated valley to your right, but you soon enter a landscape of softly rolling hills.

Near the km7 marker, you pass the Colonia Fuente Real, a tiny group of whitewashed houses that look all but abandoned, with a miniature church and square.

Broad, beautiful vistas open up as the mountain road rises and you pass between the Sierra del Ave to the right and the Sierra del Caballón to the left. Soon a twist in the road reveals the village of Dos Aguas, set like a disorderly pile of sugar cubes on a hillside. Sadly, close up the village doesn't match its prettiness when seen from a distance.

At Dos Aguas turn right for Buñol, up the right-hand side of Mesón Lepanto. The rickety rural road is perfectly passable and takes you through glorious mountainscapes, along possibly one of the most beautiful valleys in the Valencia region.

After some almond groves, you come to a roundabout. Turn left for Cortes de Pallas along a long straight stretch of well-made road. Head straight across the next junction for Venta de Gaeta (seven kilometres) and the N330 (26 kilometres). Although a large yellow sign warns *carretera estrecha, circular con precaución* (narrow road, drive with care), the road is well made and it's a lovely drive through pine trees with stirring vistas of the Muela de Cortes Nature Reserve to your left. You are almost as high as you can get in the Communitat Valenciana. Gentle hills covered in pine forests sretch as far as the eye can see, broken occasionally by rugged grey crags. This is the Sierra de Martés with typically Mediterranean vegetation: pine trees, rosemary, thyme, rock roses, broom and esparto. In other parts of this mountainous region you can also see juniper and kermes oak.

At Venta Gaeta, a tiny *pueblo*, the view suddenly changes to a shallow valley of cornfields, almond trees and vineyards, where goatherds tend enormous flocks, which provide the delicious roast kid's leg. This area also provides some of the finest peaches in the region.

After Venta Gaeta comes Los Herreros — blink and you'll miss it — followed by more tiny villages. At a T-junction with the N330, turn left for Cofrentes (12 kilometres). You are now in the Valle de Ayora. This road, historically an important north-south communication route, once marked the border between Christian and Muslim territories.

Vineyards become more common but there are beautiful broad vistas of pine forests, marred only by the two vast cooling towers of the nuclear power station at Cofrentes, a mere blip in the otherwise stunning scenery.

The castle town of Ayora

As you drop down to Cofrentes, you see its castle standing four-square on a rocky promontory above the village and, as you get nearer, you pass a large wetland, the confluence of the rivers Júcar and Cabriel. On the opposite side of the valley to the much-restored Arab castle is Mount Agrás, an extinct volcano.

Entering Cofrentes is tricky. As you pass under a narrow stone bridge, the entrance to the village is a sharp left, too tight to make the turn.

Keep going and turn around a little bit further on to come back and take the narrow road which crosses over the bridge. Follow signs for the Ayuntamiento and the Mirador.

The Mirador, a paved area with a fountain, offers splendid views of the valley. At the foot of the castle is a small tourist office. The castle itself is closed for the foreseeable future, undergoing major restoration.

Most people come to Cofrentes to take the waters at the spa of Los Hervideros (The Boilers). Go back to the main road and, just as you are about to leave the village, a sign in front of the Guardia Civil barracks indicates Casa Ibáñez and the Balneario (four kilometres). As you turn right, look to your right for a grand view of the castle. Built in 1908, the Balneario de Los Hervideros is almost a village in *modernista* style, with a hotel, cottages, gardens, swimming pools, sports centre, minigolf, supermarket, chapel, a theatre, hairdresser and gift shop.

The scent of pine trees fills the air and aged ladies and gentlemen sit in the shade playing cards after their treatments in the baths. You can also see them walking along the byways aided by stout bamboo walking sticks.

Volcanic activity keeps the water at a constantly warm temperature (the nearby volcano is extinct). The salts and minerals in the water are said to be beneficial for those suffering from rheumatics and locomotive problems, while taking a tipple will also do your digestive system a power of good. You can even have a top-to-toe beauty treatment of vapourisation, hydro-massage, body peeling and power-shower, among other pamperings.

Back in Cofrentes, turn right for Ayora (25 kilometres). After two kilometres, take a right to Jalance (2.5 kilometres) on the old N330 (you are on the new bypass). As you enter the village, the first thing you see is the tower of the new Hotel La Valle, a grand chateau-like building.

From Jalance's ruined 11th-century castle, you get wonderful views of the Ayora valley. If you are there at a weekend or during August, you can visit the Cueva de Don Juan, a 60,000-cubic-metre cave at the end of a 12-kilometre drive through a ravine that cuts into the Júcar valley.

The village has the main tourist office for the area. Look out for signs as you drive through the town as it is tucked up a narrow street below the castle.

The Ayora valley is well known for its hearty country cuisine and gives its name to the famous *gazpacho ayorinos,* a rabbit and chicken stew with wafer-thin pasta. Each town in the valley has its own version of the dish. *Calducho,* a stew of chicken breast, mushrooms, tomato and cured ham, is a speciality of Jarafuel, while Cofrentes offers *olla cofrentina*, stewed pork, potatoes, pinto beans and cardoons (a vegetable of the thistle family) and in Jalance they serve up *ajotono*, mashed potato, cod and tomatoes. For desert you could be offered *grullos*, honey cakes, or *aguamiel*, baked pumpkin slices with honey. A few minutes after leaving Jalance, you rejoin the new N330, continuing toward Ayora (17 kilometres). Next stop is Jarafuel, whose main claim to fame is that it is the Spanish centre (and therefore probably the world's) for the production of the *horca*, a long-pronged wooden pitchfork

Wooden pitchforks and walking sticks

In the plantations around Jarafuel the *almez* (hackberry), a flexible tree peculiar to this region, is carefully cultivated so that its growth takes on the required shape for the *horca*, a long-pronged wooden pitchfork. Four thinner branches sprout from the main branch which is harvested and baked in an oven to remove the bark. Then it is bound with flat lengths of wood and round stones and left to dry for a couple of months so that it retains the distinctive curved pitchfork shape.

Jarafuel is also a major producer of *bastones* (walking sticks) in every conceivable shape and size, including those made from a tree root whose handles are carved into the shape of lions, elephants, horses and other animals, their heads and limbs following the particular growth of each individual root.

Among several small factories, Bastones Martínez on Calle Juan XXIII has a huge selection. If you can get a glimpse into the factory, you will see a strange assortment of Heath Robinson machinery that bends, strips, straightens, carves and sands the *bastones* and *horcas*.

If you feel like a dip, Jarafuel has a large municipal swimming pool (with a smaller one for children), next to which is El Molino restaurant, whose awnings provide welcome shade from the heat of the sun.

As you travel on down the N330, you are skirting the westward edge of the Valencia region as it rubs shoulders with Castilla-La Mancha. This area is Spain's principal producer of honey, especially those with orange and rosemary flavours. *Uniflora* indicates a honey's flavour is derived from only one flower and *milflores* that the bees have visited a variety of flowers.

Ten kilometres south of Jarafuel is Ayora, with 5,000 inhabitants, half the population of the entire valley. Entering past small cornfields and tall crops of maize, and the first thing you see is the castle keeping a watchful eye over the low-rise town.

The castle, more formally known as the Palacio Fortaleza del Duque del Infantado, can be reached by taking one of the steep streets from the Plaza Mayor, the prettiest route being via Calle San Nicolás, where all the houses are whitewashed and feature a band of blue outlining the door and window frames.

La Asunción parish church has an impressive 16th-century altarpiece, the Tablas de Yáñez de Almedina and the Milagro del Ángel (Angel's Miracle) by Vicente López.

Honey has been produced in the Valle de Ayora since time immemorial. From 1344 to 1747 the quality of its production was governed by the Ordenanzas Municipales del Valle de Ayora. These days the Sociedad Cooperativa Apícola de España watches over the artisan production that still uses many time-honoured methods. If you want to know everything there is to know about honey, visit Ayora during the last two weeks of October for the Corte de La Miel (Honey Festival). Honey and honey products can be bought at shops throughout the valley.

To complete the excursion, you have a delightful drive through the Sierra Enguera. Leaving Ayora in the direction of Almansa, on your left you will see a hermitage on a slight rise with a cross under a cupola in front of it. Turn left here for Enguera (CV590). You pass immediately into a landscape of dark, dusky-pink earth and undulating, almond-clad hills.

At the junction with the CV593 for Navalón and Moixent, turn right. Don't worry about the *carretera estrecha* (narrow road) sign, as this road is perfectly adequate.

Near Moixent you access the A35 autoroute. Follow the signs for Valencia for the north and Albacete for the west. For Benidorm and the central Costa Blanca, follow the signs for Ontinyent, whence you return to the coast via Alcoi and the Guadalest valley. For Alicante you can first head towards Almansa before taking the A31 south.

WHAT TO SEE

COFRENTES:
Castillo. The castle is closed for major restoration.
Balneario de Los Hervideros, s/n. Tel. 96 274 74 01 and
96 189 40 25. Spa offering a wide range of medicinal and
therapeutic water treatments. Open daily.
Closed Dec 19-Feb 24.

JALANCE:
Castillo. 11th-century castle with stunning views of the Ayora
valley. Free entry.
Cueva de Don Juan. Huge cave in the Júcar valley. Open
Sat/Sun 10am-2pm. Open daily during the month of August,
same hours. Entry 3€

JARAFUEL:
Bastones Martínez, Calle Juan XXIII, 12. Tel. 96 219 81 25.
Manufacture of wooden pitchforks and walking sticks.
Large showroom with extensive display.

AYORA:
Nuestra Señora de la Asunción. Parish church.
Palacio Fortaleza del Duque del Infantado. Castle ruins.

The Cofrentes castle

WHERE TO STAY

COFRENTES:
Balneareo de Los Hervideros, Tel. 96 189 40 69.
Accommodation is usually included as part of a treatment
programme but rooms can be booked separately and
treatment paid for on an individual basis. €€€

JALANCE:
Hotel del Valle, Colón, 41. Tel. 96 189 70 00. Elegant newly
built three-star hotel with swimming pool. €€€
Albergue de Jalance, Calle Mayor, 9. Tel. 96 219 60 48.
Basic pension with full board for less than you'd pay for a
meal in most places. €
Casa Ferdi, Calle Iglesia, 12. Tel. 96 219 61 72 or 610 27 67
08. Restored casino (village meeting place) in the old town
below the castle. Décor of agricultural bric-a-brac and
antique furniture. €€

JARAFUEL:
Casa Rural Rufina, Escuela, 11. Tel. 96 219 80 56/ 616 30
72 40. Pleasant newly renovated house in old quarter. €
El Molino, Piscina Municipal, Camino Molino, s/n.
Tel. 96 219 81 53. Has a few simple rooms. €

WHERE TO EAT

COFRENTES:
Balneareo de Los Hervideros. Tel. 96 189 40 69. Restaurant
open lunch and dinner. Reasonably priced local cuisine.
Mainly caters for residents who dine in blocks and on fixed
menu. €–€€

JALANCE:
Albergue de Jalance, Calle Mayor, 9. Tel. 96 219 60 48.
Open for lunch and dinner. Modestly priced local food that
matches the modest décor. €
Hotel del Valle, Colón, 41. Tel. 96 189 70 00. Three-star
hotel with mid-upper price menu of Mediterranean cuisine.
Open daily for lunch and dinner. €€–€€€

JARAFUEL:
El Molino, Piscina Municipal, Camino Molino, s/n. Tel. 96
219 81 53. Open daily lunch and dinner. Simple restaurant

serving local food beside village swimming pool. Large
shaded terrace. €– €€

AYORA:
Plenty of bars and cafeterias serve tapas and lunches.
El Rincón, Calle Parras, 10. Tel. 96 219 17. Open daily lunch
and dinner. Mainly local cuisine. Try their *gazpacho ayorino.*
€–€€

MORE INFORMATION

COFRENTES:
Oficina de Turismo, Plaza la Iglesia. Tel. 96 189 4316.
Open Mon-Fri 10am-1pm.

JALANCE:
Oficina de Turismo, Calle Industria, 11. Tel. 96 189 71 71.
Open Tue-Fri 10am-2pm, Sat 9am-2pm, Sunday 11am-2pm.

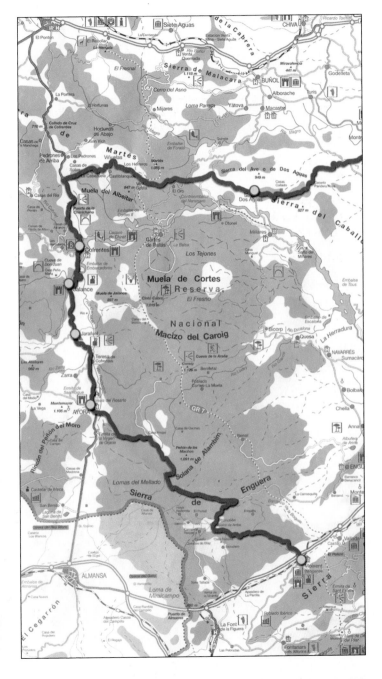

José Segrelles studio, Albaida

PUPPETS, BONFIRES AND CHURCH BELLS

AREA: Sierra Grossa, north-west of Benidorm
ROUTE: Canals – Moixent – Ontinyent – Albaida
DISTANCE: 55 kilometres

Visit the highest church bell tower in Valencia, the town with the biggest bonfire fiesta in Spain and a unique puppet museum that hosts the annual International Puppet Fair.

Approach on the inland Valencia-Albacete autoroute N340/A35 and, where it passes just west of Xàtiva, take the exit for Canals.

Canals is a pleasantly busy little town, a mixture of modern and historical. As you wander the streets of the old town, look out for the tiled plaques high on the walls with dedications to the saints.

Canals has two main claims to fame. It is the birthplace of the Borja Pope Calixto III and the Guinness Book of Records declares it makes Spain's biggest *foguera* (bonfire).

In the early hours of the *Día de la Inmaculada* (December 8) a single pine trunk is erected in the Plaza Mayor and in the days leading up to the *Día de la Foguera* (January 16) a huge, perfectly tapered conical bonfire is built with a circular base 11 metres in diameter. They say 1200 cubic metres of wood are used in its construction and it is covered in green pine boughs. The celebration is dedicated to San Antonio Abad.

A country hermitage near Fontenares

The town is also proud of the huge sycamore called La Lloca that has provided shade for generations of townsfolk in the Plaza Pont del Riu. A few streets away on the Plaça Mercat, the aptly named Casino Gran, a stylish *modernista* building, was erected in 1930, funded by a big win on the lottery. In its great open interior, murals line the walls depicting scenes from town life, including the building of the *foguera*.

Leaving Canals, you can see a tower that once formed part of the palace in which Alfonso de Borja, later Pope Calixto III, was born on the last day of December, 1378. Follow the green-and-yellow signs for Oratorio and Torre that take you back to the main road you came in on. A few minutes after leaving the town centre, take a right turn towards Montesa (VV2085) and almost immediately turn left down a narrow street, still following the green-and-yellow signs. Moments later, you see the heavily restored 19-metre high tower on your right. Unfortunately the tower is closed to the public.

To continue, go to the top of this one-way street, turn left and left again, back on to the main road. Within moments you will see the Tanatorio, just after which is a set of traffic lights where you turn left. This takes you back to the road to Montesa.

As you crest a slight rise, you see over the orange groves the ruins of Montesa's castle rising from a great rock, all that is left of the physical and spiritual home of the religious-military order that took its name from the small town that sits below it. The castle is undergoing restoration. There is little else to detain you in Montesa.

When you reach the junction with the N430 autoroute, follow the signs for Albacete and Alicante. You are travelling through the narrow strip of land known as La Costera, with the Sierra Plana to your right and the Sierra Groso to your left. Fourteen kilometres further on, take the exit for Moixent (CV589). You will also see a large sign for La Bastida, an ancient Iberian town.

The road runs parallel to the N340 for about two kilometres. At a small roundabout in front of the empty Hotel Restaurant La Perla, turn left here towards the town centre, passing immediately under the autoroute. At a second roundabout, large letters leave you in no doubt that you have arrived at Moixent. Bear right, following signs for the centre.

You pass over a bridge reaching another roundabout with a statue of the Guerrero de Moixent, an Iberian warrior, in the centre. Turn right at this roundabout in the direction of Fontanares dels Alforins (VP2012). (NB: At the time of updating this book, just as you leave Moixent, a large sign says that the road to Fontanares is closed. This only applies to a stretch of about 100 metres, so take the track to the right of the road which runs along the river and rejoins the Fontanares road within a few moments.)

Enjoy a picturesque ride through almond groves, grape vines and pretty rolling hills. Soon you see the grand *masías*, beautiful houses built by the wealthy of Alicante and Valencia during the late 19th and early 20th centuries to escape the coastal heat in summer.

At the km10 marker, a sign directs you up a track to the left to the Poblat Iberic La Bastida de les Alcusses.

La Bastida is one of the oldest Iberian settlements in Valencia, dating back to the fourth century BC. The archeological finds when it was first discovered and excavated between 1928 and 1931 show it to have been a city of great importance, perfectly situated on a hilltop with a plentiful supply of water, large open tracts of land for cultivation below and forests to provide game and timber. Unfortunately, no-one has yet discovered its name or the reasons for its destruction and abandonment after less than a century of existence.

About half of the city has been excavated and shows a complete urban layout. Large houses are grouped in blocks around a central thoroughfare, with smaller streets running off it to meet in squares, one of which has a large cistern. The houses, terraced up the hillside, had a single storey and were 80 to 150 square metres in size, with the internal layout depending on the activities of its occupants. Central in most cases is the hearth, the hub of domestic life, around which are arranged livingrooms, storerooms, workshops and stables. There is ample evidence of remodelling where rooms have been added.

To experience life almost two-and-a-half millennia ago, a typical house of the time has been reconstructed, copied from the first house excavated in 1928 and using the same materials and construction techniques as those of the original builders. Inside, the ambience of Iberian life has been recreated with replicas of artefacts found on the site.

Return to the road to Fontanares and continue the ride through delightful countryside, now mainly vineyards, many of them organic. Where a sharp bend in the road is signposted to La Font de la Figuera, turn left for Fontanares. You have just entered the Vall d'Albaida, known to the Moors as al-Bàyda, the white land. To your right, set on a hill overlooking its own vineyard, is a beautiful salmon-coloured *masía* that has recently been restored. Five kilometres on, where you see the pretty blue-and-white cupola of the church at Fontanares to the right, turn left for Ontinyent.

Just after the km16 marker, the road curves downwards, leaving cultivation behind you as you travel through a land of beige-coloured earth and green scrub.

When you reach Ontinyent follow the signs for the centre. As you cross a bridge, you see to your right a church belonging to a convent of Carmelite nuns, founded in 1574 and the oldest in the city, opposite which is a large house painted yellow ochre.

This is the entry to the old town and you will be coming back here. At a sudden sharp right-hand turn, keep straight ahead to pass along the high side of the church and after a few metres you will see a piece of open ground to your right where you can park.

Ontinyent is the capital of the locality known as the Vall d'Albaida and, like most towns in the area, traces its origins back to Moorish times. From the 16th-century its fortunes have been tied to the textile industry, still the most important source of income for the town today. The *barrio de la Vila*, the original Moorish town, dates from the 11th and 12th centuries. After the conquest by Jaime I, the Moors were banished to the areas outside the town walls and the Christians moved in.

Return to the yellow-ochre house and pass through the archway to the left, the Portal de Sant Roc, the first entrance built by the

The church tower at Ontinyent

Village rooftops

Christians in 1256. The tiny square you enter betrays its past importance. On your immediate left is the Palacio de la Duqesa de Almodóvar, now in a sad state of repair but soon to be renovated, and the house in the corner at number 10 is the Casa de Pala, above whose door is the shield of the Borja family.

The street leading off to the left, Calle de Sant Pere, is a narrow confine of pastel-painted houses and *atzucas*, tiny dead-end alleyways. At the bottom of the short street you enter a small plaza with a statue of Sant Pere, looking remarkably unperturbed despite the huge knife lodged in his skull.

Continue downward on Calle de la Trinidad for a few metres before taking the steps to your right that wind upwards through the narrow streets to Santa María church in the Plaza de la Vila. The site was originally that of a Moorish mosque. The present church was built during the 14th and 15th centuries and enlarged in 1582. At 71 metres, the bell tower is the highest in the Valencia region, topped by a splendid cupola that looks like a mini-Victorian bandstand. Just behind the church is the tiny Placeta del Fossa, so called because it was used as a graveyard for the faithful who could not be interred in the church itself.

The old quarter continues below the steep walls of the church and, as you trip down the steps into the Plaça Mayor, you pass under the watchful gaze of three statuesque ladies representing justice.

Calle Maians, running off Plaça Mayor, is a mixture of the ancient and modern. A few metres along this street is the Círculo Industrial y Agrícola with a grand façade of columns in Doric and Ionic styles.

Leave Ontinyent by crossing back over the bridge you came in on and, turning right for Valencia at the first set of traffic lights. After some new cream-beige houses on your left you come to a roundabout.

To visit the Museo de Ciencias Naturales, take the third exit on this roundabout, on the left side of the bar El Comodi. You will see the beautiful twin Gothic towers of the San Franciscan monastery/college almost immediately on your left.

To exit Ontinyent, go back to the roundabout and follow the signs for Centro ciudad, crossing over a bridge. At the next roundabout take the left exit, down Avinguda Ramón y Cajal that takes you in the direction of Albaida. One kilometre further on you come to another roundabout where you take the CV40 to Albaida (10 kilometres) and Xàtiva. You will also see it signposted as the CV320.

Stay on this road until you begin to descend through olive groves into Albaida and follow the signs for the "Casc urba". These will lead you to Albaida's Plaça Major where you will be confronted by the majestic façade of the Palacio de los Milà i Aragó. There is parking in the plaza.

The Palacio, with its three fine towers, is undergoing massive restoration that will continue for some considerable time. Pass through its 15th-century arch to enter the Plaça de la Vila, a delightful square with slatted benches shaded by mandarin orange trees.

The most interesting places to see in Albaida are within a few seconds walk of here. To your right as you pass through the archway

The emblem of Moixent

and housed in the palace itself is the Museo Internacional de Titelles d'Albaida, a puppet museum unique in Spain. Ancient and modern examples of the puppeteer's art have been brought from around the world, with a separate floor devoted solely to Spanish and Valencia puppets. It is the home of the annual International Puppet Fair.

On the other side of the arch is the Museo de Belenes, a museum devoted to the Christmas cribs (*belenes*) that form part of Christmas celebrations throughout Spain and can range in size from a shoe-box display to a huge production filling a village square. It also houses a model of how Albaida looked in the 15th-century.

In front of the museum is Santa María church, built during the 16th and 17th centuries, behind whose double-arched doors and plain exterior are splendid altar paintings by Albaida's most famous son, José Segrelles. To learn more about the life of this distinguished artist, cross the square to the pretty Casa Museu José Segrelles, a charming modernist building where the artist lived from its completion in 1940 to his death in 1969 at the age of 84. It is said he died with a brush in his hand, having had that very day completed a huge religious painting.

The house was designed by Segrelles himself and has been kept much the same as when the artist lived in it, including the library with 11,000 volumes. On display throughout the house are his paintings, demonstrating the extraordinary range of his work, and many of the original illustrations he did for books by such famous authors as Blasco Ibáñez and Edgar Allen Poe and for magazines such as the *American Weekly* and *Illustrated London News* when he lived in New York and London.

To return to your base from Albaida, follow the signs for Xàtiva to the North and Alcoi and Alicante to the south.

The casino in Canals

WHAT TO SEE

CANALS:
Casino Gran, modernista club/café, Plaça de Mercat.
Open daily, 9am-9pm.
La Torre de los Borja, Calle Calixto III. Public viewing.
La Foguera, burning of the biggest bonfire in Valencia, on the
evening of 16 January.

MOIXENT:
Bastida de les Alcusses, Iberian settlement, Ctra. Moixent-Fontanares,
km10. Open Mon-Sat, Oct-Apr 10am-2pm & 4-6pm, May-Sep
10am-4pm & 6-8pm. Sun and holidays 10am-3pm. Free entry.
Guided tours in Spanish Wed-Sun 10.30am and 4pm.

FONTANARES:
The area around Fontanares is one of the major areas in Valencia
producing organic wines (as well as non-organic). The *bodegas*
listed below produce organic wine.
Bodega Los Pinos, Casa Los Pinos s/n. Tel. 96 222 20 90, 699 44
72 20 (English-speaking owner). A delightful one-man vineyard
still using antiquated equipment to produce excellent wines.
Has accommodation in a grand house with sun-drenched inner
courtyard. Visits to *bodega* by arrangement.
Bodegas Fernando Francés, Ctra Moixent-Fontanares, km11.
Tel. 96 323 93 00. Open Mon-Sat 10am-2pm or by arrangement.
Family-run bodega that has been producing wine since the early 1900s.

ONTINYENT:
Barrio de la Vila, original Moorish/Christian town.
Museo Arqueológico, Calle Regall, s/n (below church tower). Tel. 96

291 19 55. Open Wed-Sun 11.30am-1.30pm, 6-8.30pm. Free entry.
Museo Fester, Plaça de Baix, 26. Tel. 96228 0252. Open
Sat/Sun 11am-1pm. Newly opened museum with costumes,
arms, posters and anything to do with the Moors and Christians
fiesta in Ontinyent.
Museo de Ciencias Naturales, Colegio La Concepción, Avda San
Francisco, 5. Tel. 96 238 01 00. Open Mon-Fri 10am-1pm & 3.30-
6.30pm. Must telephone at least two days in advance to arrange
entry. Museum of natural sciences with exhibits from Spain, Africa
and the Americas. Also has a collection of Valencia ceramics.

ALBAIDA:
The following are all in the Plaça de la Vila:
Museo Internacional de Titelles, a unique international puppet
museum. Tel. 96 239 01 86. Open Mon-Fri 9am-2pm & 4-7pm,
Sat 11am-2pm and 5-8pm, Sun 11am-2pm. Entry €3.
Museo de Belenes, museum displaying belenes or Christmas
cribs. No fixed opening times. Check with puppet museum.
Casa Museo José Segrelles, home-museum of the town's famous
son, the painter José Segrelles. Tel. 96 239 01 88. Open Jan 1-
Jun 15 & Sep 16-Dec 31, Tues-Sat 10am-1pm & 4-6pm, Sun
10am-1pm. Jun 16-Sep 15, Tues-Sat 11am-1pm & 5-8pm.
Closed holidays.
Santa Maria, 16th-century church with splendid altar
paintings by famous local artist José Segrelles.

WHERE TO STAY

CANALS:
Pension Arnau Argent, Avda Vicente Ferri, 7. Tel. 96 244 53
71/54 59. Small family-run hostal in town centre. €

ALBAIDA:
Hostal Tarifa, Ctra Alcoi, s/n (just as you enter Albaida from
Ontinyent). Tel. 96 239 06 16. Basic family-run pension
accommodation. €
Fonda Comercio, Plaza Mayor, 3-1°. Tel. 96 290 14 15. Simple but
pleasant pension directly in front of the Palacio de los Milà i Aragó. €

WHERE TO EAT

CANALS:
Gavina, Avda Vicente Ferri, 6. Tel. 96 224 27 27. Open daily for
lunch and dinner, closed Sun. Modern, reasonably priced
restaurant serving local cuisine. €– €€

ONTINYENT:

El Tinell de Calabuig, Calle Gomis, 23. Tel. 96 291 50 48.
Open daily for lunch and dinner. Closed Sun all day, Mon
evening, Easter week, August 1-15 & second week in Oct.
Elegant modern restaurant with interesting menu created by
the chef/owner. Try the *jamón de pato con ensalada en
vinagreta de semillas tostada* (cured duck breast with salad
dressed in toasted seed oil) or lobster vol-au-vent with
seaweed salad. €€– €€€

ALBAIDA:

El Comodoro, Plaza Mayor, 1. Tel. 96 290 16 56. Open daily
for lunch. Dinner Thurs, Fri, Sat only. Closed last 2 weeks in
Aug. Large, cool restaurant, serves moderately expensive
cocina valenciana. A sign in *valenciano* above the door
boldly declares: "Here you eat the best *paella* in the world".
Ask for a copy of their leaflet that gives a few genuine local
recipes. €€– €€€
Tarifa, Ctra Alcoi, s/n (just as you enter Albaida from
Ontinyent). Tel. 96 239 06 16. Open for lunch and dinner
daily except Sunday. Simple restaurant, home cooking. €

MORE INFORMATION

CANALS:

Casa de Cultura, Calle Beato Factor, 17. Tel. 96 224 02 14.
Open Mon-Fri 10am-2pm & 5.30-8.30pm.
Ayuntamiento (Casa de la Vila*)*, Plaza de la Vila, 9. Tel. 96
224 01 26. Open Mon-Fri 8am-3pm.

MOIXENT:

Ayuntamiento, Plaça Major, 1. Tel. 96 229 50 10.
Open 8am-3pm.

ONTINYENT:

Tourist Information Office, Plaza de Santo Domingo, 13.
Tel. 96 291 60 90. Open Mon 4-730pm, Tues-Sat 10am-2pm,
Fri 4pm-730pm.

ALBAIDA:

Ayuntamiento, Plaza Mayor, 7. Tel. 96 290 09 60.
Open Mon-Fri 8.30am-3pm.

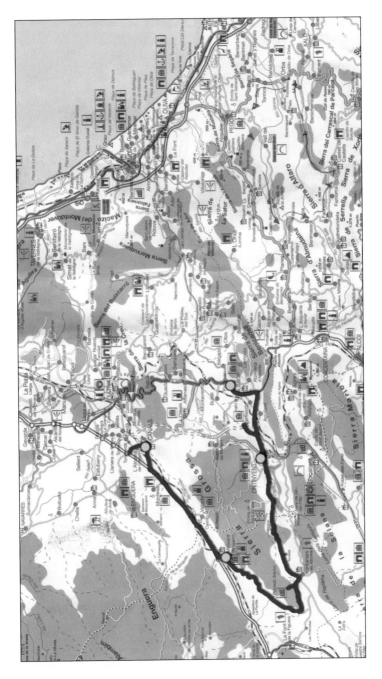

Xátiva Castle

THE WORTHY VALLEY

AREA: West of Gandia, northern Costa Blanca
ROUTE: Gandia – Simat de la Valldigna – Carcaixent –
Xàtiva – Quatretonda
DISTANCE: 73 kilometres

*See one of the splendours of the Valencian
region, be awed by an ancient bastion of defence
and be intrigued by Victorian pumps and pistons
in a village house.*

Following the N332 coastal road past Gandia, just to the
north of the city a slip road for the CV675 takes you in the direction
of Barx (13km). As you leave the roundabout that takes you under
the autoroute, directly ahead are the jagged peaks of the Sierra
Marxuquera to your left and the Macizo del Montdúver to your
right, crowned by a cluster of tall radio beacons.

You travel through dense orange groves and, as the pine-shaded road
begins to rise, you pass groups of attractive villas with the sierras
rising majestically above.

Pass through La Drova and Barx, following the signs for Simat de la
Valldigna (VV1083). To your left rises the Sierra del Buixcarró, where
marble quarries, according to Valencia's famous 18th-century botanist
and naturalist Cavanilles, are the same ones "from which the Romans
extracted huge slabs to make 30-foot columns without the least
imperfection". Marble from this region was used in the Vatican, New
York's St. Patrick's Cathedral and Valencia city's 15th-century Lonja
building (silk exchange) and the regional government palace, where
five centuries ago the Borgias allegedly hatched their political plots.

Just after Barx, as the road begins to wend downwards, you see a
picnic spot and photo opportunity to the left. Here you look down on
the vast fertile plain of Valldigna, a green quilt decorated with the

The Monastery at Valldígma

red roof tiles and white walls of Simat, Benifairró and Tavernes. The magnificent Santa María de la Valldigna monastery is the majestic centrepiece.

Entering Simat, follow the one-way sign to the right into the village and, as you reach the end of the street, you will see the grand twin towers of the monastery to your right.

Legend has it that Jaime II passed through the valley, then known as Alfandec, on his way from waging war against the Moors in Alicante and Murcia. He was impressed by the beauty and fertility of the area

and said to his chaplain, Friar Bononat de Vila-Seca, abbot of the Cistercian monastery of Santes Creus: "Vall digna per un monestir de la vostra religió (a valley worthy of a monastery of your religion)", to which the abbot replied "¡Vall digna! (a worthy valley indeed!")". In March 1298, the land was given to the abbot for the foundation of a new Cistercian order and the valley has been known ever since as Valldigna.

Three different stages of construction can be seen in the monastery: the original 14th-century Gothic renovations, undertaken after serious damage was caused by an earthquake in 1396, and a second major renovation in the baroque style after another earthquake in 1644.

In 1835, with the expropriation of church lands, the monks were expelled and the monastery sold into private hands. Many of the buildings were destroyed and the great stone blocks sold for construction. This splendid physical prayer to the glory of god fell into ruin.

In 1991, the Valencia government began a massive restoration project, spurred on by the 700th anniversary of its foundation. The monastery will never again be seen in its former glory but it is a delight to behold nonetheless. Restorers have done a splendid job on the entrance to the Santa María church, but even that doesn't prepare you for the magnificence of the interior which is, quite simply, stunning.

Sacked of altars and artworks, the bare walls at first seem pitiful in their nakedness, but look heavenward as you pass through the enormous brass-covered doors and you see a ceiling of such ornate plaster and paintwork that it makes you gasp. Once it must have been absolutely breathtaking, but even now, awaiting the restorer's caring hands, it is one of the gems of the Valencian Community's artistic heritage.

Village life in Simat itself seems to centre around Font Grand, a pond so shallow that you wonder how the fat fish in it don't scrape their stomachs on the bottom as they lazily drift around.

Leave Simat on the road that runs in front of the monastery, taking the CV322 to Tavernes and Alzira. Soon you come to a roundabout where you take the VV1082 to Tavernes and Alzira and, two kilometres later, take the CV50 left to Alzira (14 km) and Chiva.

After the 9km marker, note the beautiful entrance to a large orange grove, with its palm-lined drive leading to what looks like bits of a ruin sat on a mound of earth. Just behind, you get glimpses of a grand mansion.

Pass through Barraca d'Aigües Vives, Spanish suburbia with houses scattered through orange groves and pine woods. Four kms further on, take the CV570/VV1124 to your left for Carcaixent (4 km), where you pass alongside a dry riverbed full of bamboo, cactus and beautiful dusky pink oleander.

You enter Carcaixent on a dual carriageway that runs in front of a large shopping mall, the Ribera del Xúquer, and at the end turn left, following the signs for "Centro ciudad". When you reach the Carrer de Valencia, beside a blue building, go right and at the next junction right again (there is no left turn). At the next roundabout turn back and go up the road you have just come down. As you go through the first set of traffic lights, you see a building on the left with flags

The old pharmacy in Xátiva

where you pick up tourist info. Continue on this road until you see the town hall (another building with flags, opposite a fountain and church). Try to park in this area as you will be leaving by this road.

Carcaixent has some architectural gems that are unfortunately not open to the casual visitor, although given a couple of days' notice the tourist office will arrange a private guided tour. Even so, it is a pleasant little town with enough to see for a short and entertaining visit.

The 18th-century Palacio de la Marquesa (part of the town hall) was originally the home of gentry involved in the silk trade, and has the original gloriously tiled kitchen. The two main *modernista* buildings in the town, the Real Acequi and the Magatzem de Ribera, represent the wealth of the community.

The former, built in 1927, controlled the flow of water in the area, in both the literal and legal sense, while the latter, designed in 1910 by José Ríos Chiesta, is the most ornate orange warehouse you could imagine, although now no longer used for that purpose. What appear to be beautiful wooden beams in the Real Acequi are actually painted steel-reinforced concrete, the first of this kind to be used in the region. Anyone old enough to remember Dolly Blue, the deep blue cleaner that whitened clothes, will recognise the colour in the painted ceiling — a Spanish version was used to tint the paint.

La Asunción parish church (15 to 18th-century), with its sparkling blue, white and bronze tiled cupola, is stunning. You can even light a real candle, a rarity in these days of coin-fed electric fakes.

Wandering down Calle Julián Ribera, you come across an ochre-painted *cafetería* above which the town band practises, as well as on the aptly named Passatge del Musical. The barn-like interior, worth a glance to see how little changes in small-town Spain, has barely been touched since Edwardian times except to add a few battered Formica-topped tables.

You can stock up for a picnic at the Mercado Municipal at the bottom of Calle del Pare Marechena, a big, bright open market with all the stalls occupied (unusual these days) and as much a place for locals to meet and chat as a place to do the shopping.

Continue the excursion by taking the CV41 to Xàtiva (16 km), the road you entered Carcaixent on (passing in front of the Ayuntamiento). As you approach Xàtiva, its castle appears to be built on a ridge but, as you get closer, you will see that the walls actually rise up from the town itself.

Arriving at Xàtiva, follow the signs for the Casc Antic and Castell. As you wind up the hill through the narrow streets of the old town, you get tantalising glimpses of the castle high above. Soon you reach the lower walls scaling the hillside, but you continue on a twisting road upwards.

As you pass a pretty church on your left, you see the entrance to the Hotel Restaurant Mont Sant, one of the most delightful in the Communitat Valenciana, surrounded by orange groves and palm trees where once all was barren.

A fortress stood here in Iberian times and in his poem on the Second Punic War the poet Silius Italicus (101-25BC) refers to *Saetabis celsa arce*, Xàtiva with its tall castle, proof that a castle existed in Roman times. Its strategic value was due to its situation on the Via Augusta that began in Rome and crossed the Pyrenees and travelled down the Mediterranean coast before heading on to Cartagena and Cádiz. The grand structure you see these days is a mixture of Iberian, Roman and Moorish influences and later Christian fortifications.

The castle, with its 30 towers and four fortified gateways, must rate as one of the loveliest in the Valencian Community, not only because of its historical value but because a lot of thought and work has gone into its surroundings. Tinkling fountains, small orange groves and herb gardens that perfume the air give you a sense of what life must have been like in an important garrison town. (The fountains and gardens aren't just modern titivations but were an important part of the Moorish culture.) If you stand on the high tower at either end of the long, thin castle, you become aware of just how massive an undertaking it was to build such a structure in such an inaccessible place.

The town below the glowering castle walls is equally steeped in history. It was the birthplace of two popes of the Borgia clan (in those days it was spelled "Borja"). They were Calixtus III and Alexander XI, whose family held papal power for almost 200 years and sired the infamous Lucretia. It was the first town in Europe to manufacture paper, during the time of the Moorish occupation, and even today in Morocco paper is still known as *xativi*.

Not to be missed are the Royal Fountain of the Twenty Five Spouts, built in the late 18th-century, and the Museu de L'Almodi, where the portrait of Phillip V is hung upside down in retribution for his sacking the city in 1707. The streets themselves are like a splendid public gallery requiring no entrance fee. Mounted high on almost every wall of the old town, tiled plaques celebrate the lives of the saints.

In the Plaça de la Seu, the Basílica de Santa María stands opposite the 16th-century Hospital Real, whose gloriously ornate façade of cream stone is inscribed with centuries-old graffiti. A beautiful tiled plaque is dedicated to Sant Feliu Mártir, the patron saint of Xàtiva, and paid for by the Soler-Girenes family. Next to it is an even more elaborate confection, this one dedicated to Nuestra Señora de la Seu, female patron of Xàtiva, and financed by the Rus family.

To view the apotheosis of ceramic art, saunter around the corner to Calle Noguera. The Botica Central on Calle Noguera was once a pharmacy, and some wise person has retained the beautiful Victorian woodwork and glass cupboards full of ornately lettered dispensing bottles. Nowadays it serves as the office for OMIC, the Consumer Protection Office.

Alongside the shop front, a three-metre high, ornate tiled plaque with an inscription ends with the words *"Festa Ciudad, Gloria y esplendor del Mundo"*. Unfortunately, the craftsman doing the lettering ran out of space and improvised a little. Glorious still in its imperfection.

In your meanderings, seek out the Plaça del Mercat, a square hovering between semi-tumbledown and modern and suffused with a cock-eyed, cobbled charm. Set back in a corner in the shadow of the basilica is the Posada del Pescado, its name spelled out in intricate shell-like patterning with a fat fish dangling from a chain clenched in a lion's mouth. Its beautifully carved doors and shutters are weathered by years of neglect, but the building is now undergoing a complete restoration.

At the opposite end of the square, the restored pedestrian street, aptly named Carrer de las Botigues (Calle de Tiendas, Street of Shops, in its pre-*valenciano* days) reveals pockets of individuality. La Barraca displays rolls of the gorgeously rich fabrics used in the making of *Fallas* costumes (las Fallas is Valencia's fiesta marking the feast of San José). In the upper balconied floor, *señoras* toil over private commissions, hidden from public gaze. A few steps further on, Sombreros Matoses reveals that the trilby is alive and well.

The trip continues by leaving Xàtiva along the plane-tree-lined Alameda Jaume 1 (the street on which is the tourist office), in the direction of Gandia (CV610) and Tavernes (CV600). At the bottom of the Alameda, a right takes you up a rise where, moments later, you come to a sharp bend left. Almost immediately after this you will see a sign for Genovés (4 km) and Gandia to your left. (If you feel like a moment's respite, drop into the delightfully named Parque del Beso (Park of the Kiss), just after you turn right, which has gurgling fountains, a beautiful cupola and lions' heads shimmering in the sun.)

You quickly leave Xàtiva behind, passing olive groves and rugged, pine-covered hillsides, with roadside stands of bamboo. As you approach Genovés, it appears to consist of only an enormous, twin-spired church, perched on a hilltop and surrounded by a few houses. The village is actually long, narrow and mainly modern, and the recently built church is devoid of architectural delight. On a roundabout at the end of the village you see the Monumento al Pilotari, a statue celebrating the villagers' skills in this ball game.

Follow the CV610 for Gandia and Quatretonda (10 km). The road climbs upward through hills of pine and scrub. Just after the km7 marker, the road peaks and you begin to descend through an attractive landscape with pockets of cultivation in the valley below. Orange, olive and almond trees blend pleasantly with a few small vineyards and the occasional apple orchards as you enter the Vall d'Albaida. Just after the km10 marker, you will come across a sign for a rest area, where you can stop to relax and picnic.

Moments later you rise a hill and see the pretty five-sided bell tower of the parish church of Quatretonda, the late Gothic Sant Joans. With its plateresque and Renaissance embellishments it is very attractive and the focal point of historic interest in the town.

19th century oil press pumps

A family olive mill

In 1875, the Domingo Alberolo family made their home at 22 Carrer Sant Josep in Quatretonda and, in a large room at the back of the house, installed an olive mill to produce oil for the villagers.

The mill is still in operation today, using the original great Victorian press to crush the olives. The only difference these days is that the millstones are no longer turned by animal power and the oil is collected in plastic Coca-Cola bottles or five-litre water containers.

This little family-run *almasera* (olive mill) that bears no name is one of only a handful remaining in the Communitat Valenciana, and probably in Spain. Though the product does not bear such fancy names as "virgin" or "first green pressing", it is as pure an olive oil as you can get. When the workers sat down to lunch they would simply scoop up a glassful of the oil straight from the barrel and pour it over their salad.

Return to the CV610 Gandia road once more, going in the direction of Llutxent. Stay on this road until it joins the CV60, turning left for Gandia (16 kms). As you enter Gandia, you pass under the *autovía* and shortly after come to a roundabout directing you to the N332 to Alicante and Valencia.

WHAT TO SEE

SIMAT DE LA VALLDIGNA:

Santa María de la Valldigna, a magnificent monastery originally built in the 14th-century for the Cistercian order of monks. Tel. 96 281 16 36. Open Tues-Sun 10am-2pm. Free entry. English guide by appointment. Has a series of exhibitions and concerts.

CARCAIXENT:

Real Acequi, Calle Julián Ribera. An important *modernista* building from where the flow of water in the area was controlled. Tel. 96 246 70 66. Open weekdays 9.30am-1pm (or as part of the guided tour — see below).

Magatzem de Ribera*, Calle Marquese Campo. The other main *modernista* building in the town. Designed in 1910 by José Ríos Chiesta, it was originally used as a warehouse for oranges.

Palacio de la Marquesa*, Calle Marquessa de Montortal. Once the home of gentry involved in the silk trade, it still has the original gloriously tiled kitchen.

La Asunción, a beautiful 15 to 18th-century parish church with blue, white and bronze cupola.

*The interiors of these buildings can only be visited by prior arrangement with the Centro de Promoción Económica. A two to three-hour guided tour (Spanish only) can be arranged through the Centro and covers all the main sites in the town, including interiors. Fees are modest but depend on size of

Tomatoes drying in the sun

group. Small groups can borrow an audio guide on MP3. Contact Centro de Promóción for details.

XÀTIVA:

Castell, the castle. With 30 towers and four fortifield gateways and beautiful gardens, rates as one of the region's loveliest castles. Tel: 96 227 42 74. Open Tues-Sun, Summer 10am-7pm, Winter 10am-6pm. (Hours change when the clocks change.) Entry €2 adults, €1 children 10-18 years.

Museo de l'Almodi, Calle Corretgeria. Municipal museum housed in Renaissance building. Exhibits include archeological remains, Roman and Iberian relics, baroque paintings and the famous upside-down painting of Phillip V. Tel. 96 227 65 97. Open Tue-Sun 15 Jun-15 Sep 10am-2.30pm, 4-6pm, 16 Sep –14 Jun, 10am-2pm, 4-6pm (closed Sat/Sun afternoons Sep-Jun). Entry €2 adults, €1 children 10-18 and retired persons.

Colegiata Basílica de Santa María, Plaça Calixto III s/n. 16th-century basilica. Open daily 10.30am-1pm.

QUOTRETONDA:

Almasera, Carrer Sant Josep, 22. Olive mill in private house. Open every day except Sunday, no fixed hours but a member of the family is usually there — knock on the door. Otherwise, there is a list of telephone numbers, call and someone will come to attend to you.

WHERE TO STAY

CARCAIXENT:

L'Horta de la Iaia, Partida del Barranquet. Tel. 635 795 156. Charming, recently restored *casa del huerto* (small country house), set in orange groves 1 km from town centre. Opened in Spring 2003. €€

XÀTIVA:

Hotel Mont Sant, Carretera del Castillo, s/n. Tel. 96 227 50 81. Privately owned hotel set in orange groves and a palm garden. One of the most delightful hotels in the Communitat Valenciana. Swimming pool, sauna, gym, jacuzzi and little sitting areas for quiet contemplation in the enormous garden. Wooden cabins for rent have own balconies overlooking the gardens and town. Highly recommended. €€€€

Hotel Huerto de la Virgen de las Nieves, Avda de la Ribera 6. Tel. 96 228 70 58. info@huertodelavirgendelasnieves.com.

www.huertodelavirgendelasnieves.com. Originally built in the 14th-century by one of King Alfonso XIII's doctors, though adapted by succeeding generations the building still retains much of its original form. €€€- €€€€

WHERE TO EAT

CARCAIXENT:
Salon Royal 1915, Calle La Misa, 22 Tel. 96 243 40 50 or 651 143 990. An original *modernista* façade on the oldest street in Carcaixent, though the entrance/bar is as camp as a row of tents, with carved multicoloured bunches of flowers, bowls of fruit and fat little cherubs. Elegant restaurant serving regional cuisine.

XÀTIVA:
Mont Sant, Carretera del Castillo, s/n. Tel. 96 227 50 81. Open for lunch and dinner daily. Splendidly elegant restaurant. Small rooms with nooks and crannies in variety of styles and a large terrace. Surrounded by orange groves. Awarded three forks by the Michelin guide. Be sure to try the delicious homemade ice creams, such as mango, apple or carob. Highly recommended. €€€
El Mirador del Castell, inside the castle walls. Tel. 96 228 38 24. Elegant restaurant with a large terrace. Superb views over the town and surrounding countryside. Specialising in country food of the region. Open daily for lunch except Monday. €€
Casa de la Abuela, Calle Regna, 17. Tel. 96 227 05 25. Open daily except Sunday for lunch and dinner, serving carefully preserved local recipes. €€– €€€
Hotel Huerto de la Virgen de las Nieves, Avda de la Ribera 6. Tel. 96 228 70 58. Stylish restaurant in library of restored 15th-century house. Open daily for lunch and dinner. €€€

MORE INFORMATION

CARCAIXENT:
Centro de Promoción Económica, Calle Marquesa de Montortal, 56. Tel. 96 245 76 58, Email turisme@ayto-caircaixent.es

XÀTIVA:
Oficina de Turismo, Alameda Jaume I, 50. Tel. 962 27 33 46. Open Tue-Fri 10am-1.30pm, 4-6pm, Sat/Sun and holidays 10am-1.30pm.

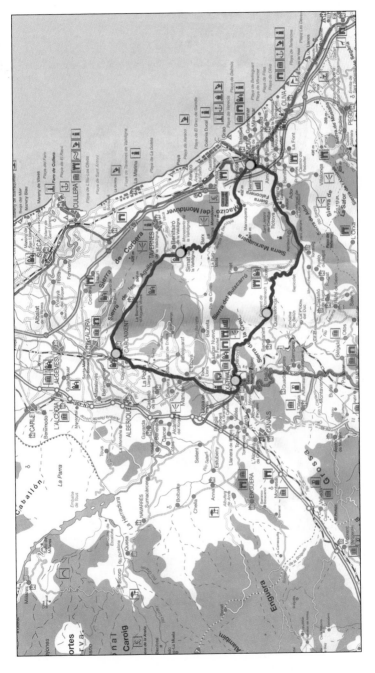

A mountain pool near Margarida

FOLLOWING OLD BLUE EYES

AREA: Mountains west of Denia in northern Alicante province
ROUTE: Pego – Vall de Ebo – Vall d'Alcalà – Castell de Castells – Pego
DISTANCE: 97 kilometres

Take to aromatic hills in search of The Blue-Eyed One, a legendary Moorish leader, delve into enchanting chasms and marvel at Neolithic man's artistic endeavours.

Leave the A7 motorway at junction 61 (just south of Gandia) and take the road for Oliva and Pego. When you arrive at Oliva follow the CV715 (also signposted C3318) for Pego (this also applies if you are on the N332 coastal road). Keep following the signs for Sagra and Callosa d'en Sarrià until you leave Pego. Two kilometres after leaving the town, immediately after the sign on your right for the Das-Ding factory, a sharp right heads you uphill in the direction of Vall de Ebo (12km on CV712).

This steep zigzag climb quickly takes you away from the modest urban sprawl of Pego. As you rise above a band of pine trees, the views get steadily more splendid, until the whole patchwork quilt of olive, orange and lemon groves, and few remaining rice fields, spreads all the way to the sparkling blue of the Mediterranean. At the summit, marked by a white-and-blue windmill to your right, the road begins a languid descent into Vall de Ebo. A right-hand turn immediately after a blue-railed bridge (signposted Vall d'Alcalà) runs along the bottom of the village to another bridge that takes you back over the river. Park before crossing this second bridge if you wish to have a look at Vall de Ebo. (These names can be a little confusing as Vall d'Alcalà refers to the valley of Alcalà, whereas Vall de Ebo is the name of a village.)

Margarida village

Like many small villages, Vall de Ebo has suffered badly due to depopulation as the young people move to the coast in search of work. Those who have stayed work mainly in agriculture, but the beauty of the surrounding countryside is attracting an increasing number of visitors to sample the peace and tranquillity and excellent mountain cuisine. Lamb — roasted, grilled or in rich stews — is popular on local restaurant menus, as are *minjos,* small pancakes stuffed with meat or wild mountain vegetables, *blat picat,* a pork stew with vegetables and barley, and of course, being so near the ricefields of Pego, a wide range of rice dishes.

A couple of minutes´ drive up the hill from Vall de Ebo, following the signs for Vall d'Alcalà, is the Cova de Rull. Discovered in 1919 by one José Vicente Mengal when trying to rescue his dog after it had disappeared down a rabbit hole, the Cova de Rull (Curly Cave) is estimated to be between five and seven million years old. Visitors take a 20-minute wander through caves with splendid formations of stalactites and stalagmites with such endearing names as Catedral de Diamantes, where the rock sparkles in the light of the guide's lamp, and La Flor, an opening in the cavern roof which has petal-like stone layers overlaying each other resembling a beautiful flower in full bloom.

Back in daylight, continue to Vall d'Alcalà, a small valley with only two villages, Alcalà de la Jovada and Beniaya. The land appears uncultivated apart from the occasional olive and almond groves, with spiky gorse and palmetto interspersed with the odd copse of pine trees. But don't be deceived. Since medieval times this area has been known as the medicine chest of Europe, and herbalists would travel hundreds of kilometres to pick the provender of these apparently sparse lands. The intense heat of this high, rolling terrain produces some of the finest-quality rosemary, thyme, camomile and lavender, and even today local people can be seen roaming the hills gathering medicinal and culinary herbs. A number of restaurants in the area offer wild vegetables picked from the mountains as well as using the herbs found on their doorstep.

Just before Alcalà de la Jovada, at the K7 marker, beside a car park and picnic area on your left-hand side, is a *nevera*. This is a snow well, one of the man-made shafts that proliferate in this region. They were used to store the mountaintop snow, brought down from high ground in panniers carried by mules, that would later chill the summer-time drinks of the coastal elite, as well as preserve the abundant fruits for which the local valleys are still renowned.

Park and walk up the rough track to the right for a few moments. To your left you will see a gray dome, reached by another small path. This *nevera* is one of the best preserved in the area. Two short footpaths, one to the top of the *nevera* and another, which allowed access half way down, give a good idea of the structure of these pre-industrial freezers.

As you look into the deep, dark reaches below through openings at the top, you can imagine the pulley suspended through the metal ring at the pitch of the dome, via which chilled workers would be lowered to stamp down the snow. When the compacted snow reached the level of the arched openings a layer of rice would be spread over it to conserve the temperature. When the snow became ice, it would be packed into straw-lined wooden boxes to be carried by mule down mountain tracks to the clients on the coast.

Return to the road and continue to the yellow-and-white km6 marker. Take the concrete road to the right and you will almost immediately see the ruin of Adzubieta. Far from the opulent centres of art and science that were Córdoba and Granada, Adzubierta is Valencia's most perfectly preserved Moorish village, albeit a ruin. As you step gingerly over the stones that now clutter what were formerly the alleyways of the village, it is easy to imagine yourself back in the *aljame*, the Moorish *barrio*, listening to the call to prayer from the minaret of the *mezquita* (mosque) in nearby Alcalà de la Jovada.

An easy walk to fabulous views

This walk is a moderately easy ramble of about an hour and a half. Park your car at the small parking area beside Adzubieta, the Moorish village outside Alcalà de la Jovada. Follow the track from the village for about 20 metres to a track on your right (the first you come across, on a bend).

After about three minutes' walk, the footpath splits. Take the left fork, going uphill. The path dips and rises, and after 10 to 15 minutes you see a ruined Moorish farmhouse on your left. Just beyond, the path bends sharply to your right, and tucked in the bend a couple of metres from the track is a *pozo*, the original well for the farm. Be careful, because it is uncovered and still contains water.

Fifty metres or so after the well is another fork. Again, take the left fork (waymarked with yellow and white stripes on the path and also on a rock a couple of metres up the hill). As you climb, you walk through the terracing created by the Moors, now mostly in ruin, and see scattered houses, long abandoned. There are occasional well-tended olive groves that seem all but inaccessible, indicating that there are still a few hardy folk around.

Wheatears (known until prudish Victorian times as "whitearses" because of their distinctive markings) skitter low over the scrubland, and if it is your lucky day you could see a Bonelli's eagle scouring its hunting territory. Most of the walk is gentle, except for the last 30 metres that might have you catching your breath as you scramble over the rock and scree, but it's worth it for the breathtaking view down the Vall de Gallinera to the coast.

For those who really feel adventurous and have a head for heights, a steep rough path leads you into the rock hole of La Fordada, from where it's said that on a clear day you can see all the way to Ibiza. Retrace your steps to the car park at Adzubieta to complete the walk.

Return to the main road, turn right and within a couple of minutes you will arrive at Alcalà de la Jovada, which overlooks Adzubieta. From this village, Alsahir Ibn Al-Azraq (known as the blue-eyed one long before Frank Sinatra's time) ruled his domain. Born in the village around 1218, he was a thorn in the side of Jaime I in his

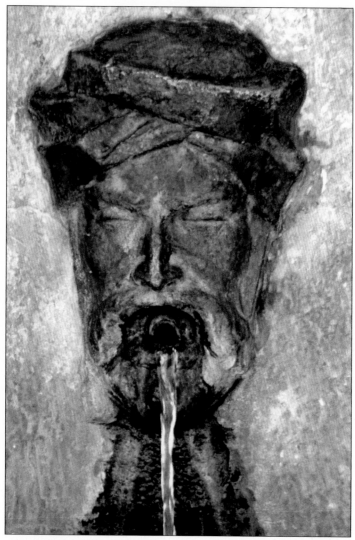

Al-Azraq, the "Blue Eyed One"

conquest of the Kingdom of Valencia, until in 1254 he was defeated by the Christian king and banished to North Africa.

Longing for his home, the Moorish leader returned 22 years later to lead an uprising to reclaim his lands. He failed in the attempt and was killed in 1276 while laying siege to the walls of Alcoi.

In the village square, remnants of the mosque that Al-Azraq built as part of his palace now form part of the parish church, La Purísima Concepción. A bust of Old Blue Eyes in the street behind the Town Hall commemorates his rule, and another, in the shape of a brass fountain in the main square, pours forth fresh mountain water.

Two kilometres after leaving the village, heading in the direction of Planes, a turn left leads to a twisting road that mounts the hill to Beniaya. With Alcalà de la Jovada, this village makes up the Vall d'Alcalà. Follow the sign through the village towards Tollos, a winding country road with stunning views as you pass over the top of the tail end of the Sierra d'Almudaina.

As you begin the descent just before the km5 mark, the valley to your left is the Barranco Malafi, the route by which, in 1609, thousands of Moriscos (Moors who had converted to the Christian faith when the country finally came under Christian rule), who had been given only three days' notice of their forced departure, were herded down the twisting track through high cliffs to the port of Denia. Rumours of hidden treasure are still bandied about.

Turn left as you enter Tollos and left again at the T-junction and follow the road for Castell de Castells (13 kilometres). As the road descends into Castell, it crosses a small bridge and immediately begins to rise again. Fifty metres further on an ornate lamp standard stands at a junction that points right to the village or left for Benichembla. Take the left fork. Just after the marker km28, a sign indicates the Pla de Petracos to your left, 1.5km.

The narrow road takes you to some of the most important rock paintings in the Communitat Valenciana. Park in the small area beside the next sign and take the steep footpath that begins with a set of steps right beside the sign. This takes you up to a viewing platform where large panels explain the history and significance of the paintings. The footpath is quite a scramble so not advisable unless you are wearing flat shoes.

Thought to be about 8,000 years old, and discovered in 1980, five of the eight drawings are visible. At first they are a bit difficult to see, but your eyes soon focus on them in the brown concave depressions of the rock face.

Return to the road and turn left. When you reach the junction at Parcent you can return to the coast via the Jalón valley (picking up some of the wine for which the valley is renowned, particularly the full-bodied red) and taking the road to Pedreguer. To return to Pego turn left and follow the road to Orba and Pego.

Cova del Rull

WHAT TO SEE

VALL DE EBO:
Cova de Rull, underground caves with spectacular stalactite and stalagmite formations. Open daily, Apr-Sep 10.30am-8.30pm, Nov-Feb 11am-5pm, Mar-Oct 11am-6.30pm. Entry €3.80 (includes entrance to ethnic museum in Vall de Ebo). Last ticket sold 40 minutes before closing time. Guided tour in Spanish only but the guide speaks slowly and clearly for those with a modest understanding of the language. In any case, worth a visit for the visuals alone.

ALCALÀ DE LA JOVADA:
Nevera, historic snow well at Km7 on the CV712. Accessible to public, no charge.

ADZUBIETA:
Remains of Moorish village at Km6 on the CV712. Accessible to public, no charge.

PLA DE PETRACOS:
Neolithic rock paintings at Km28 on the Castell de
Castells–Benichembla road. Accessible to public, no charge.
(There is a small museum at C/San Roque, 1, next to the
Ayuntamiento of Castell de Castells that explains the paintings,
but opening hours tend to be haphazard.)
During February and March the whole of this area and the
valleys surrounding it are awash with various fruit trees in
blossom. A major visitor event.

WHERE TO STAY

PEGO:
Casa Rural Louise, Ptda Michanes. Tel. 96 557 17 56. English-
owned *casa rural.* €€
Beniaya, El Chato Chico, Plaza de la Iglesia, 6. Tel. 96 551 44
51. Cosy, English-owned *casa rural.* €€- €€€
Parcent, Casa Carrascal, Carrer D'Alt, 14. Tel. 679 043 130.
www.casacarrascal.com Delightful British-run small hotel in
tastefully restored 17th-century village house. €€€

WHERE TO EAT

Vall de Ebo:
Bar Capri, Carrer les Eres, 47. Tel. 96 557 14 23. Said to
make the best *paella* in the area. Good-value *menú del
dia.* €

ALCALÀ DE LA JOVADA:
Campament de Turisme La Valle, Camí d'Andón. Local dishes,
including game and wild boar when in season. Tel. 96 551 43
33. €– €€

TOLLOS:
L'Antiga Escola, Calle Salamanca 9. British-owned restaurant
with eclectic menu devised by owner, and adaptations of
regional/Spanish food. Highly recommended. Tel. 96 551 83
28. Open lunchtimes only, Wed-Sun. Evening meals by
arrangement. €€

PARCENT:
Casa Carrascal, Carrer D'Alt, 14. Tel. 679 043 130. Inventive
menu created by Savoy Hotel-trained chef. Very good fixed-
price menu including wine. Dinner only. €€

MORE INFORMATION

None of the towns on this excursion have tourist offices,
although most of the venues, hotels and restaurants mentioned
will have some leaflets about the area.

VALL DE EBO:
Ayuntamiento, Plaza Mayor, 2. Tel 96 557 14 13. Open
9.30am-2pm.

ALCALÀ DE LA JOVADA
Ayuntamiento, Plaza Bis Villaplana. Tel. 96 551 41 07.
Open 9.30am-3pm.

CASTELL DE CASTELLS:
Ayuntamiento, C/San Roque, 1. Tel 96 551 80 67.
Open 9.30am-2pm.

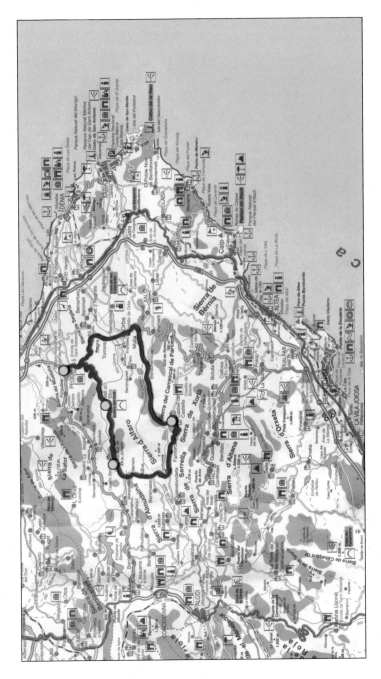

A níspero orchand in Bolulla

TRIP 14
SUCCULENT FRUIT AND PRIZE-WINNING WINES

AREA: Vall de Pop, west of Benidorm.
ROUTE: Benidorm – Bolulla –Tàrbena – Alcalalí –
Xaló (Jalón) – Fontilles – Pedreguer
DISTANCE: 70 kilometres

*Taste Valencia's succulent fruit, the prize-
winning wines of the Jalón valley, spicy sausages
made to an historic Mallorcan recipe — and
enjoy the tranquillity of Spain's last sanctuary
from a terrible scourge.*

From Benidorm take the C3318 to Callosa d'en Sarrià, passing
beneath the N332 coastal road, or from the A7 motorway exit at
junction 65 to join the N332, travelling in the direction of Alicante, and then take the next exit, following the signs for Callosa, 15
kilometres further on.

When you arrive in the center of Callosa, take the second exit on your
right from the roundabout with the new fountain, heading towards
Bolulla (5 km away) and Tàrbena on the C3318/CV715.

Passing the Font d'Algar Water Park, the meandering road carries you
through orange and *níspero* groves with the foothills of the Sierra de
Xorta to your left and the Sierra de Bernia to your right. As the road
straightens out, you see the village of Bolulla, a small huddle of
houses tucked into the hillside.

Apart from a rumour that Hannibal and his elephants stopped off at
Bolulla castle (of which nothing remains) on his ill-fated journey to
besiege Rome, Bolulla is of little note historically. Nonetheless it is a
pleasant stroll through the narrow streets with nooks and crannies
filled with pots of flowers (though, be warned, the streets are so steep

they should be fitted with escalators). The alleyway of Canto de Coca overflows with greenery and during summer months is a riot of floribunda.

The affluence of Bolulla comes in part from the groves of *níspero* that surround the village. Known as the loquat in English, the *níspero* is a yellowy-orange fruit about the size of an egg that, when eaten at its prime, is deliciously juicy and sweet. Unfortunately its prime doesn't last very long, but shops throughout the area sell the fruit preserved in a number of ways.

During the picking season from mid-April to early June, as you wander the streets you will see garage and basement doors open to reveal ladies trimming the stalks from the fruit before grading and packing them in boxes, using scissors to snip the stalks being as near to automation as they get.

On the opposite side of the main road is a picnic site with rows of barbecues. Should you have forgotten the salt or need something to nibble at while you wait for the *paella* to cook, in the center of the village is Comestibles Montiel, a choc-a-bloc tiny supermarket that seems to be open at all hours and is run by a delightfully chatty lady who can help you out in fluent French if your Spanish isn't up to scratch.

Return to the main road and continue onward to Tàrbena, the road zig-zagging furiously as you climb. Glance backwards and you see Bolulla sitting like a white pearl set in the deep green of the orange and *níspero* groves. As you get higher these begin to give way to almond trees that surround a scattering of white, beige and pink houses. One km after you pass a viewing point on your left (four kilometres after Bolulla), you enter Tàrbena. The narrow streets make parking difficult, so it's best to leave your car on the edge of the village.

After the banishment of the Moors in the 17th-century, Tàrbena was repopulated with 17 families from the island of Mallorca. They brought with them recipes for Mallorcan sausages that later brought fame to Tàrbena. The village still has a reputation for its sausages.

You can buy them at Embutidos Petito on Parada Font del Botó, where a diminutive grandma sells long chains and fat balls of *sobrasada*, a slightly spicy sausage with a creamy texture, *butifarras,* rich black puddings, a mixture of pork, onions and spices, and the rough-textured *blanquet.* Whenever she plonks a sausage on the scales, she will tell you it is *"muy bueno"* — and indeed it is.

In the village square, Casa Pinet styles itself as a Bar-Restaurant-

Restaurateur Jerónimo Pinet making his herb liqueur

Museo, and justifiably so, as it is packed with an eclectic mix of *objets d'art*, bric-a-brac and memorabilia, much of it related to the Civil War. The restaurant, serving local dishes, is the domain of Jerónimo Pinet, without doubt one of the most colourful characters in the village.

For decades the one-handed Jerónimo (the stories as to how he lost his right hand are many and varied) always dressed from head to foot in black, his head topped off with a beret, and his tongue-in-cheek socialist rantings brought in the crowds. They came not only for the museum and his showmanship but also for the country food, which was excellent. And it still is.

The once-infamous Señor Pinet has mellowed greatly and is now a charming host (minus beret) who still puts specially selected herbs into bottles to make the fiery *hierba* that he offers at the end of the meal, all the while keeping a watchful eye on his museum.

The colourful restaurant Casa Pinet

From the Plaça Santa Anna, the small square just above the road that leads to the village cemetery, you get a wonderful view through a cleft in the hillside over the *níspero* groves to Benidorm and the Mediterranean beyond.

From Tàrbena, you drive uphill in the direction of Pego. You pass through a rugged, rocky mountainscape where tiny roads disappear in all directions. On your left the abandoned and disintegrating terraces look like a giant stairway traversing the side of the sierra, while on your right sinuous terraces of almond and olive groves snake around the lower hills.

The views are picture perfect — at least they would be if you could find a place to stop and take a picture along the narrow road that twists and turns relentlessly. Great swathes of vivid yellow gorse and pale, blushing rock roses line the road and the aroma of rosemary and wild mountain thyme perfumes the air.

As you cross over the Coll de Rates at 780 metres above sea level (eight kilometres after Tàrbena), you see the village of Parcent and the scattered urbanisations of the Jalón valley laid out before you, with orange groves separating the developed areas as they spread down to the sea. As the road descends towards Parcent, it takes you into the Val de Pop.

It was from the rough landscape surrounding the Coll de Rates that, during the last quarter of the 19th-century, the bandits El Tona, El Durá, El Mixana and El Sabateret rode out to terrorise the surrounding areas.

The story goes that the last outlaw in the nearby Sierra Bernia was caught in the 1950s. He was not your typical bandit of old who robbed stagecoaches. He would stop a car and force one of the male occupants to exchange clothes with him, and would not be seen again until his "new" outfit had worn out. He was eventually caught but, unfortunately, nothing is recorded of his name or what happened to him after his capture.

The writer Gabril Miró lived in Parcent and his home is soon to be turned into a museum celebrating his work, but for the moment there isn't a great deal to see in the village, so when the road levels just before Parcent take the first right to Pedreguer and Alcalalí. Shortly after this it joins another road where again you go right. After two kilometres you reach Alcalalí where, just as you enter the village, you will see a small sign for the centre of town to your right (opposite the larger sign to Orba on your left). Just as you turn off the main road you will see parking spaces.

As Alcalalí is a rural wining and dining centre for coastal dwellers, there is no shortage of good restaurants in the area. Even though the development of rural tourism has brought a building boom to the region, Alcalalí itself still feels like a small Spanish town.

The central square, the Plaça de l'Ajuntament, is entered by a low arch that gives it a nice historic feel, even though it wasn't built until 1984. A large tiled plaque to the side of the 18th-century Natividad parish church in the Plaça de l'Ajuntament tells the history of Alcalalí in a dozen lines. The church itself houses the Museo Parroquial San Juan de Ribera.

The restoration of the 15th-century tower opposite the church, all that is left of a baronial palace, aroused mixed feelings amongst the locals. Some thought putting a modern, dark-glazed cupola on top of a medieval stone tower was cultural vandalism while others considered it a tasteful mix of the old and the new.

The leper colony of Fontilles

The last leper hospital in Spain

These days leprosy is easily treated and is usually attended to in a general hospital, but in December, 1901, when a Jesuit priest, Father Carlos Ferris, visited his friend Joaquín Ballester at Tormos, the disease was a scourge that respected neither class nor creed.

Shocked by the living conditions of a leper living nearby, the two friends raised the money to buy the land to create a sanctuary, later to be known as the Sanatorio de San Francisco de Borja-Fontilles. But it wasn't until January, 1909, that the first six patients entered Fontilles, to be attended by the sisters of the Franciscanas de la Inmaculada and by Jesuits of the Compañía de Jesús, the two religious orders that tend to the needs of the patients to this day.

As lepers would usually be simply forgotten by their families (there was no medication available until the 1940s), the priests and sisters tried to create as far as possible a family atmosphere in the sanatorium.

Within the stone wall that encircled the santorium, the patients learned crafts, and Fontilles became a village in its own right, with a bakery, carpenter's shop, smithy, printing office, bindery, shoemaker, hairdresser, and gardeners. It even had its own theatre, still in use until the late 1990s. Fontilles is still home to 60 people, some of whom have spent most of their lives there.

The tower now houses the municipal archives on the second floor, while the third and fourth floors are home to the Museo de la Pasa (Raisin Museum). This may sound like the ultimate joke museum, but the economic value of the dried grape to the Marina Alta, the region in which the Vall del Pop sits, was massive from Moorish times up to the mid-1900s. In the latter years, ships laden with Valencia raisins would sail from the port of Denia to London and Liverpool and the good old British Co-op had an enormous warehouse in Denia that, while no longer storing raisins, still exists.

The fifth floor of the tower, protected from the elements by its new roof, is poetically called the "Mirador de la Vall del Pop" (Lookout Point of the Vall del Pop), recreating its original role as a watchtower. On this floor is displayed a model of a *riu-rau*, one of the ancient barns typical to this area that comprised a small room where the farmer would sleep during harvest time and a series of open-arched storerooms where grain would be left to dry.

Returning to the main road (CV720), turn right for Pedreguer and 200 metres later you take another right to Xaló (usually referred to as Jalón). After a short narrow bridge you bear left and enter Xaló/Jalón (some two kilometres from Alcalalí) and see on your left the tourist office that serves the Vall del Pop. There's parking space here.

Xaló, a sleepy little *pueblo* a couple of decades ago, was the first village in the area to be encroached upon when residents, both foreign and Spanish, began the drift away from the coastline. It has become so popular with the British that most newsagents in the village now stock English newspapers.

Nevertheless, there are still a number of good reasons to visit Xaló. Historically speaking, there's little to see except the attractive hexagonal church tower in the village square, but most visitors don't come for history. They come to find a bargain at the Saturday antiques market or to stock up on the local wines that can be bought at excellent prices from one of the numerous *bodegas* along the road in front of the tourist office.

The *Denominación de Origen Vall de Xaló* is famous for its muscatel white wine, *mistela* (sweet muscatel), rosé and full-bodied reds. If you wish, you can sample the wines the Spanish way by drinking from a *porrón*, the glass vessel with a long spout that you hold high in the air to aim an arc of wine into your mouth — or down the front of your shirt if you lack expertise.

Reverse the directions to return to Alcalalí. Once more in Alcalalí, turn left on the CV720, following the sign for Fontilles, and after 200 metres, beside a garage opposite the parking place where you parked earlier, turn right for Orba (5km).

The Jalón valley has the reputation of being overbuilt but, as soon as the road begins to rise, you can see that there's still plenty of greenery, with the Sierra del Carrascal de Parcent creating a backdrop to the white houses.

Two kilometres further on, turn right onto the CV715 for Orba and La Val de Laguar (also known as Vall de Laguart). Bypass the entrance to Orba and shortly after, as you descend a low hill, take the left for Fontilles and Val de Laguar. Two kms later, you arrive at a junction on a bend in a mountain road where you take a left, going uphill.

The road takes you through dramatic cliffs with occasional views of cultivated groves spreading down to the Mediterranean. Look up to your left a few minutes later and you will see a stone wall tracing the contours of the hillside as it surrounds Fontilles, the last remaining leper hospital in Spain.

The architecture of Fontilles demonstrates the architectural styles of Spain, from the grand edifices of the *modernista* period through Art Deco to the ultra-modern design of the Residencia Borja, a recently opened residence for retired people that is bringing new life to Fontilles.

But the essence of the Sanatorio is its peacefulness. As you walk the grounds, you can imagine how comforted those afflicted by this terrible disease must have felt when they arrived somewhere where they would no longer be rejected.

Leave Fontilles and continue uphill. As you rise, you pass through the villages of Campell, Fleix and Benimaurell, none with a population of more than 400 souls. Benimaurell appears to be tucked into the side of the sierra, but as you get closer you realise that it is stuck on the top of a hill of its own.

Keep on through the village, following the signs for the Hotel Alahaur. When you reach the hotel you are as high as the road will take you and, from its car park, your steep drive is rewarded by wonderful views over the hills, crags and almond groves down to the glittering Mediterranean 30 kilometres away.

Another reversal of route and you eventually end up back on the outskirts of Orba (7km). Turn left in the direction of Pego and Ondara, turning right moments later when you see a sign for the Cueva de Benidoleig. At the next set of traffic lights turn right for Benidoleig and Ondara.

Continue through Benidoleig (3km), across the small roundabout in the centre of the village, going in the direction of Pedreguer and the Cuevas de las Calavaras. Just after the km5 mark you see the entrance to the caves on a U-bend (badly signposted, but there is a large sculpture in the car park and a cafeteria to the right of the entrance). The caves lack much of the extravagance found in some others in the Valencia region, but nonetheless still have a charm of their own.

The succulent níspero fruit

Your footsteps echo off the wooden boardwalk and through the vaulted chasms distorted with rock forms that flow like something designed by Gaudí after a harrowing nightmare. A monstrous stalactite in the Sala de la Campana, that has taken millions of years to form, is now barely 30 centimetres away (i.e. some 2000 years) from the stalagmite growing beneath it. All around, the mottled deep purple and green colouration of the rock gives the impression that prehistoric cavemen have decorated their domain with great pots of paint.

Turn right leaving the Cuevas and 10 minutes later you enter Pedreguer. Follow the signs for Valencia and Alicante (A7/N332) and when you reach the junction with the N332 turn right for Alicante via the coast road and left for Valencia. If you wish to join the motorway, turn left at this junction and a few minutes later you will see signs for the E15/A7 Autovía to Alicante and Valencia.

WHAT TO SEE

TÀRBENA:
Restaurante/Museo Casa Pinet, Plaça Mayor. Tel. 96 588 42 29. Open daily from 9am-5pm. Closed Wed. Unusual cafeteria/restaurant packed with objets d'art, bric-a-brac and memorabilia of the Civil War. You are not obliged to eat a meal to view the displays covering the restaurant walls, but you would be well advised to do so.

ALCALALÍ:
Torre Museo, Calle Mayor, 1. Collect key from Ayuntamiento during office hours. Entry €1.
Museo Parroquial, housed in the parish church in Plaça de l'Ajuntament. Open during mass times.

XALÓ (Jalón)
Saturday market. Open market held every Saturday morning (approx 9am-2pm) near tourist office on edge of the village. A mixture of antiques and bric-a-brac.
Bodegas. There are a number of *bodegas* in Xaló, most of them on the edge of the village on the Xaló-Alcalalí road (opposite tourist office). Most keep normal shop hours for tasting. The Cooperativa Valenciana Virgen Pobre de Xaló is the main one. Open summer Mon-Fri 9.30am-1.30pm, 4-8pm, Sat 9.30am-2pm, 4-7.30pm, Sun 9.30am-1.30pm; winter Mon-Fri 9.30am-1.30pm, 3-7pm, Sat 9.30am-2pm, 3-6.30pm, Sun 9.30am-1.30pm.

FONTILLES:
Sanatorio de San Francisco de Borja-Fontilles. Open daily. Visitors are welcome to visit the sanatorium grounds. No entrance fee but the sanatorium is grateful for any donations.

BENIDOLEIG:
Cueva de las Calaveras, Ctra. Benidoleig-Pedreguer. Tel. 96 640 42 35. The caves have complex opening hours depending on time of year, weather etc. but are usually: summer 10am-8.30pm and winter 10am-6pm. Entry €3.

WHERE TO STAY

TÀRBENA:
Hotel de Tàrbena, Calle Santísima Trinidad, 1. Tel. 96 588 40 06. htarbena@paralelo40.org. Attractive, newly opened small hotel in village centre. Has singles, doubles and suites. €€

PARCENT:
Casa Carrascal, Carrer D'Alt, 14. Tel. 679 043 130. *Casa rural* with excellent restaurant. English-owned. €€€

ALCALALÍ:
Casa Almar, Calle Mayor, 16. Tel. 96 648 20 15. Elegant new *casa rural* in village centre with that rarity in hotels in Spain, tea-making facilities in the bedroom. €€€

XALÓ:
Caserío del Mirador, Camino les Murtes, 13. Tel. 607 433 349 or 607 811 197. Splendid new accommodation of apartments and rooms with beautiful views over the mountains. €€€€

BENIMAURELL:
Hotel Alahuar. Tel 96 558 33 97. Newly built rustic-style hilltop hotel with stunning views. Also has small cottages to rent as suites. €€€

WHERE TO EAT

BOLULLA:
Bar Era, Calle Era, 16. Tel. 96 588 15 28. Open daily for lunch and dinner, closed Thurs. Small family-run cafeteria/restaurant serving well-priced country food and Mediterranean cuisine. Good selection of *tapas.* €
Venta Figural, Ctra Bolulla-Tàrbena km42. Tel. 96 588 19 56. Open daily lunch only. An 18th-century goat farm where locals gathered for a glass of wine is now a delightful rustic restaurant with beamed ceilings and flagged floors, a big open fire where they burn wood from the surrounding orange, lemon and *níspero* groves, and a large, vine-shaded terrace for summers with splendid views down to the sea. Choice of well-priced *platos combinados.* €€

TÀRBENA:
Casa Pinet Plaça Mayor. Tel 96 588 42 29. Open daily for lunch, closed Wed. Fixed daily menu that includes local sausages, *paella, fiduea* (similar to *paella* but made with pasta) lamb and pork chops, and rabbit. Good country food. If you want to try the roast suckling pig or special roast lamb you need to order in advance. Highly recommended. €– €€
Sa Cantrella, Partida Foya Ganach, s/n. Tel. 96 588 41 54. Open 10am-10pm daily June, July, Aug, Sep, other months same hours but closed Sat. Specialising in wild boar, venison,

duck, rabbit, quail, pheasant, turkey and partridge. You can sample their home-made sausages and fruit and veg from their own organic kitchen garden. You can dine on the large terrace with panoramic views of the mountains (free use of swimming pool if you are dining, €3 otherwise). The large, open restaurant interior is decked out with baskets, dried gourds, pots and grinning boars' heads to remind you of what's on the menu. €– €€

PARCENT:
Casa Carrascal, Carrer D'Alt, 14. Tel. 679 043 130. Excellent, recently opened restaurant. The inventive chef has a wealth of experience, including a stint at London's Savoy, which shows in the highly polished menu. The fixed price menu is top value for both quality and choice. Highly recommended. Open dinner only. €€

ALCALALÍ:
Pepe Casa Jaume, Partida la Solana, Ctra. Alcalalí-Pedreguer. Tel. 96 648 24 56. Open daily for lunch and dinner, closed Sun night and all day Mon. Excellent value rustic-type restaurant serving man-sized portions. Try *filloas rellenas*, stuffed pancakes crammed with seafood and oven baked, or the *pierna de cordero*, leg of lamb baked in a faintly curryish sauce. As you get *two* legs per serving, you can either share or ask for a doggy bag. Highly recommended, but get there early as it fills. €– €€

BENIMAURELL:
Hotel Restaurant Alahuar, in town. Tel. 96 558 33 97. Attractive modern restaurant with superb views over the surrounding countryside. Excellent rustic food and local cuisine. Recommended. €€– €€€

OTHER INFORMATION

TÀRBENA:
Ayuntamiento, Calle San Miguel, 1. Tel 96 588 42 34. Open Mon-Fri 9am-3pm.

ALCALALÍ:
Ayuntamiento, Plaça de l'Ajuntament, 1. Tel. 96 648 20 24. Open Mon-Fri 9am-2pm.

XALÓ:
Tourist Information Office. Paseo de la Alameda, s/n. Tel. 96 648 10 17. Open summer (15 Jun-15 September) Mon-Fri 10am-2pm, 4-8pm, Sat 10am-2pm. Other months Mon-Sat 10am-1.30pm, 4.30-7pm, Sun 11.30am-2pm

Bocairent´s monument
to a local industry,
blanket making

TRIP 15
THE ICE MAN COMETH

> **AREA:** Inland towns of the Sierra Mariola, Alicante province.
> **ROUTE:** Cocentaina – Agres – Bocairent – Alcoi – Cocentaina
> **DISTANCE:** 66 kilometres

Drive through glorious countryside and discover two medieval gems on a trip that's short on kilometres but long on history.

Cocentaina, where this excursion begins, is a small town five kilometres north of Alcoi (Alcoy on some maps). To get to it coming from the south on the A7 motorway, take exit 67 (just after San Juan) on to the N340 and follow the signs for Xixona and Alcoi. From the north take the N340 at Xàtiva.

At first glance Cocentaina looks like little more than an industrial estate and rarely gets a mention in a tourist guide but, like many other small mountain towns in these parts, an historic heart beats behind all those factories producing textiles and furniture.

Towards the end of the 11th-century, Cocentaina was the capital of a large Islamic region that covered the entire northern part of present-day Alicante province. Around the mid-12th-century the Christians began their conquest of the town, and in 1258 Jaime I raised his standard as its saviour. Less than 50 years later, in 1304, the Moors of Granada attacked and burned the town, earning the locals the soubriquet of *socarrats*, the scorched ones.

The historic part of Cocentaina is divided into two zones: El Raval, the ancient Moorish neighbourhood whose streets rise in terraces up the hill towards the Ermita Santa Bárbara, and La Vila, the Christian part that contains most of the town's architectural and historical points of interest.

The tumbling village of Bocairent

The epicentre of Cocentaina was the Palau Comtal, historic home of the Corella family, whose crest features a woman's head atop the body of a serpent. When the Countess Corella took over the building in the 15th-century, she wasn't happy with the 13th-century Gothic appearance and turned it into a Renaissance palace with lots of painted and carved ceilings, ornate tiled floors and columned arches. And she did a good job.

The Sala de los Embajadores, now a museum of Gothic art, has stunning ceramic tiles and carved panelled ceiling, and the Sala Dorada has an impressive painted ceiling. Panels depicting the kings of Navarra (the Countess's family) are surrounded by scenes of the battles between Moors and Christians, notably that of Jaime I sitting on a hilltop prior to his successful invasion of Valencia city.

Adjoining the Palau, the church of Virgen del Milagro convent and monastery is a haven of ornate intimacy, where the locals pop in and out

all the time. The decoration and artistic embellishment is worthy of a cathedral, in a structure that, when packed, could hardly accommodate more than a couple of hundred souls. Elaborate paintwork covers large areas of the walls and huge sections are painted to imitate irregular stone blocks, the overall effect being of a slightly kitsch rustic church with a nod in the direction of decadence.

While Cocentaina has a number of splendid edifices, it also has tiny, twisting streets with magnificent charm. Sneaky little alleyways lead to dead ends and worn narrow flights of steps lure you on Alice-in-Wonderland style.

The streets are decorated with beautifully painted plaques depicting the lives of saints and religious goings-on. Just around the corner from the Santa María church, stone steps lead up to the street Mare de Déu del Miracle. If you turn left here you will come across the oldest ceramic panels in Cocentaina. They date from the mid-18th-century and represent the suffering of the Virgin, giving their name to the street in which they are located.

Keeping a watchful eye over the town is the recently restored castle. More tower than castle, this emblem of Cocentaina was built in Gothic military style during the 13th and 14th-centuries. You can reach it by car, but it's a steep climb and the view is marred somewhat by the industrial buildings spread out below. Alternatively, enjoy the vista from the picnic area around the chapel of San Cristóbal, where you can sit on stone blocks (it's advisable to take a cushion) with a huge stone slab as a table and with the aroma of rosemary in the air. Continue your trip by returning to the N340 and taking the direction to Valencia on a dual carriageway. After three kilometres take the exit for the C3311 to Muro de Alcoi and Agres (it's the second exit for Muro). At the roundabout at the end of the slip road turn left onto the CV700 signposted Agres where it goes over the N340.

Ignore the first sign for Agres. After the km8 marker turn left by a sign bearing the Costa Blanca logo with tourism symbols and "Agres" in large letters. Follow the road straight up the hill (it bears left after 200 metres or so but keep straight ahead) and as you top the rise alongside a pillared handrail (just after a row of green rubbish bins) turn hard left. This brings you into a small square beside the Restaurant Pensión Mariola.

Agres is one of those delightful mountain villages of narrow twisting streets, bougainvillea-covered cottages and fountains gushing sparkling mountain water. To get to the Santuario at the top of the village by car, take the first right after the Restaurant Mariola on to Calle Mayor, a very narrow road despite its grand name. When you reach the first square, the Plaza de España, turn right again and immediately turn left after the church (there's a sign saying Quiosc on the wall in front of you). This leads you directly to the Santuario.

The Santuario is dedicated to the Mare de Déu de Agres (Mother of God of Agres) and commemorates a 15th-century miracle. On the night of August 31, 1484, the church of Santa María in Alicante was destroyed by fire. The statue of the Mare de Déu was seen to disappear into the sky. The following day she was discovered near Agres castle by a disabled shepherd, who instantly and miraculously was cured. The Mare de Déu de Agres, now kept in the Franciscan monastery, became the destination for a major pilgrimage, and on September 1 each year her discovery is re-enacted by villagers, the texts handed down from father to son. At other times it is a delightfully peaceful place to sit and ponder awhile.

The Sierra Mariola is rich in flora. Thyme, rosemary, lavender, sage, all make walking in these mountains an aromatic delight to complement the visual pleasures of rockroses and orchids. There are numerous walks around Agres.

The snow cave of Cava de Agres

A drive to a snow cave

If you prefer to drive, you can scale the dizzy heights that rise over the Santuario without getting out of your car, although the route is not for the faint-hearted nor anyone suffering from vertigo. The road leads to a rough track, often no more than the width of a car, that twists and turns erratically. Once you begin there's nowhere to turn around until you get to the top.

When you leave the car park in front of the monastery, instead of taking the right fork back down through the village, take the left and follow the sign that says "*Pujada al refugi i caves*", quickly turning left again and up a steep slope. When you reach the top, you are rewarded with stunning views, some of the best in the whole area.

You will also find one of the most beautiful *neveras* in the Valencia region, the Cava de Agres (also known as the Cava Arqueda). These snow caves were used to store compacted snow that would later be taken, when it had turned to ice, to the major cities throughout the area.

This beautiful 16th-century construction, which still has the six arched spines that formed the original roof, was last used in 1926. If you are one of the faint-hearted, you can see a model of the *nevera* in the Restaurant Mariola.

From the Santuario, retrace your route to the CV700 and, turning left at the bottom of the village, head in the direction of Alfafara and Ontinyent. When you get to the T-junction of the Ontinyent-Villena road (CV 81), turn left and a couple of minutes later you see the tiered houses of Bocairent on your right, clinging to the side of the hill for dear life.

Bocairent is a weird and wonderful mixture of architectural styles. In the centre of the roundabout at the entrance to the town is a monument with apparently no official title but referred to locally as "the monument to the blanket". It depicts an angular figure of a man with a heavy plaid blanket draped over his shoulders, a reference to the town's leading handicraft, although now sadly in decline.

Cross the Pont Nou, the bridge that connects the town with the main road, and you soon pass a number of good examples of the wrought ironwork and curved stylism of the *modernista* (Art Nouveau) period. Unfortunately you also pass a number of 1960s excrescences. Eventually, passing under an arch called the Portal de l'Arc de L'Aigua, that looks convincingly Moorish but was built recently, you arrive in the Plaça del Mercat, also known as the Plaça de l'Ajuntament.

Around the square are old houses towering up to eight storeys, like medieval high-rises. It used to be said that in Bocairent the donkeys leaned out of the windows — meander up the steep, narrow cobbled streets from the square and you will see why. What appear from the square to be eight-storey houses are four two-storey houses, one on top of the other. The animals would be kept on the ground floor. Thus a donkey on the ground floor of the top house could poke its head out of what seemed below to be a seventh-storey window. It seems a pity there are no more donkeys left in this part of town to resurrect this bizarre vision.

In lieu of gardens in this rather unusual *pueblo* there are countless balconies, steps and low walls festooned with pots of geraniums, cacti, ferns and all manner of greenery. The further you walk down the steeply raked streets, the more tumbledown the buildings become. Nothing moves except scuttling cats shocked from a siesta by the ring of your feet on the cobblestones.

In 1843 the town council decided it wanted a bullring but was short of money and there was no level land on which to build it, so the citizens hacked one out of solid rock — from the tiered seating to the underground bullpens — using only pickaxes and chisels. Big enough for 1000 spectators, this Roman-style amphitheatre is now used for musical and cultural events throughout the year.

At a nearby cliff overlooking the Barranc de Fos, 53 inter-connecting caves have been carved out of the rock. No-one knows when they

An unusual corner window in Bocairent

were built or what they were used for, or even why they are called the Moorish Caves because the Moors had nothing to do with them. Just another Bocairent oddity.

Without doubt, Bocairent's outstanding monument is the Verge de L'Assumpció (Virgin of the Assumption) parish church. Begun in the 16th-century on the site of an Arab castle, the Gothic-style temple was heavily revamped in the 17th-century and is today considered one of Valencia's finest examples of classic baroque.

Return over the Pont Nou to the main road and turn right at the roundabout. At the third roundabout, after two kilometres, reach the Alcoi road by taking the slip road to your right and crossing over the main road. Take the first right and follow it uphill. This route takes you through the picturesque Font Roja, the natural park in the heart of the Sierra Mariola. Rolling pastures, wheat fields and acres of yellow sunflowers make this a delightful ride home in the fading hours of the day.

Keep following the signs for Alcoi. From Alcoi follow the sign for Valencia to go north or Alicante to go south. Both directions are via the N340.

WHAT TO SEE

COCENTAINA:
Palau Comtal, Plaça el Pla. 15th-century palace of the Corella family. Includes the Sala de los Embajadores, Sala Dorada, private chapel, now deconsecrated, and town library in the beautifully restored Gothic Room. Same opening hours as the tourist office. Free entry.

Convento y Monasterio de la Virgen del Milagro, Plaça el Pla (next to Palau Comtal). Beautiful 17th-century church built to commemorate a "miracle" in 1520 when an image of the Virgin is said to have cried tears of blood. (The original image is now in the monastery, but a copy can be seen in the chapel of the Palau.) No access to the convent or monastery, but the church is open daily.

Dolores de la Verge, Calle Mare de Déu del Miracle. The oldest street ceramic plaques in Cocentaina, part of the *circuito urbano de taullels,* the route of tile paintings.

Walks: the tourist office provides a reasonably detailed map and guide to some of the walks in the surrounding hills of Montcabrer.

AGRES:
Santuario Mare de Déu de Agres. Small church housing statue of the Virgin next to the monastery (now used only for groups on religious retreats) on the hill above the village. Opening times vary, especially during the annual fiesta celebrating the arrival of the statue, the focal point being September1. There are some pleasant walks and a picnic area around the Santuario.

Cava de Agres (also known as the Cava Arqueda). One of the most beautiful *neveras* (snow caves) in the region, with fabulous views over the Sierra Mariola and beyond.

BOCAIRENT:
Verge de l'Assumpció, off Plaça de l'Ajuntament. Stunning baroque church. Houses museum, containing examples of sacred art, including the Sant Blai altar piece by one of Valencia's most famous artists, Joaquín Sorolla, and a chalice by the Florentine sculptor and goldsmith, Benvenuto Cellini. Open briefly on Sundays and fiestas at 12.30pm, after mass.

Plaza de Toros, a 1000-seat bullring carved out of rock. Ask at the tourist office for programme of cultural and musical events. Open daily, noon-2pm and 6pm-7.30pm Entry €1.20.

Covetes dels Moros, just outside village opposite the medieval part. 53 inter-connecting caves. Open daily, 11am-2pm and 5.30-8.30pm. Entry €1.20 euros

SIERRA MARIOLA:
If you would like to see the Sierra Mariola from the sky, Totglobo offers balloon rides as part of their programme of rural adventures. Tel. 629 611 889. Web page www.totglobo.com

WHERE TO STAY

COCENTAINA:
Nou Hostalet, Avgda Xátiva, 4. Tel. 96 559 10 95. Email: nouhostalet@moibatec.com Newly opened basic hotel on edge of the old town. €€
Hotel Odón, Avgda País Valencia, 145. Tel. 96 559 12 12. Email: odon@hotelodon.com Charmless businessman's hotel near town centre (parking €3). €€€

AGRES:
Pensión Mariola, Calle San Antonio, 4. Tel 96 551 00 17. Web Page www.restaurant-mariola.es Thirteen ensuite rooms above the restaurant on the edge of the village with superb views over the valley. € (They also have a number of cottages for rent sleeping 2-6. Check for rates.)

BOCAIRENT:
Hotel L'Estació, Parc de L'Estacio s/n. Tel. 96 235 00 00. Elegant hotel and restaurant, refurbished in 2006.
Hotel L'Agora, Calle Sor Piedad de la Cruz. Tel. 96 235 50 39. New hotel with rooms themed on China, Pakistan, Thailand and Kenya.

WHERE TO EAT

COCENTAINA:
L'Escaleta, Subida Estación del Norte, 205. Tel. 96 559 21 00. Part of a group of restaurants called Parlant Menjant (Associació Gastronómica Muntanya d'Alacant) with a reputation for good regional cuisine. €€– €€€
El Laurel, Juan M Carbonell, 3. Tel. 96 559 21 00. Part of the same group as above. €€– €€€

AGRES:
Pensión Mariola, Calle San Antonio, 4. Tel 96 551 00 17. Owned by the same family for three generations, highly recommended for excellent country fare at low prices. Big grills, rich stews and home-made desserts. Try the *nueces y*

miel, walnuts dipped in local honey, and sip the restaurant's own *hierba*, a liqueur made from fresh herbs from the surrounding hillsides. Reasonably priced with excellent-value lunchtime menu. €– €€

BOCAIRENT:

El Riberet, Avinguda Sant Blai, 16. Tel. 96 290 52 11. Creative cuisine. Considered by some to be the best restaurant in the area. €€€

El Cancell, Sor Piedad de la Cruz, 3 (Bajo). Tel. 96 235 50 38. Same owners as El Riberet but here they specialise in local dishes. €€

Hotel L'Estació, Parc de L'Estacio s/n. Tel. 96 235 00 00. Elegant hotel restaurant, specialising in *carne de piedra*, meat cooked on a hot stone at the table.

MORE INFORMATION

COCENTAINA:

Tourist office, in entrance to Palau Comtal, Plaça de Pla. Open daily 10am-2pm (from 15 Jun to15 Sep, 11am-2pm and 5-8pm). Tel. 96 559 01 59. If closed you can get information from the town library in the courtyard of the Palau.

MURO DE ALCOI:

Tourist office, Plaza Ramón González, 1. Tel. 96 553 20 71. Open 9.30am-2pm and 5-7.30pm Mon-Fri and 11am-1.30pm Sat.

BOCAIRENT:

Tourist office, Plaça de l'Ajuntament, 2. Tel 96 290 50 62. Open 10am-2pm and 4pm-6pm Mon-Fri, and 10am-2pm Sat and Sun.

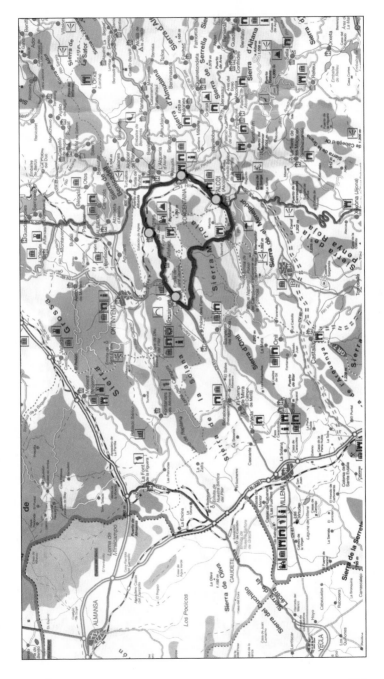

The bell tower of Guadalest

HITTING THE HIGH SPOTS

AREA: Mountains west of Benidorm, northern Costa Blanca
ROUTE: Benidorm – Callosa d'en Sarrià – Fonts d'Algar – Guadalest – Penáguila – Quatretondeta – Benidorm
DISTANCE: 122 kilometres

Take a dip in a cool mountain stream before anointing yourself with aromatic oils, delve into a latter-day Moorish bazaar, and get lost in a 200-year old maze.

From Benidorm take the CV70 in the direction of Callosa d'en Sarrià, passing beneath the N332 coastal road. From the A7 motorway, exit at junction 65 to join the N332 in the direction of Alicante and take the next exit, following the signs for Callosa.

When you arrive at Callosa town centre after 15 kilometres, take the second exit on your right from the roundabout with the new fountain on it, heading towards Bolulla and Tàrbena on the C3318. After two kilometres along this winding road, you will see a large sign indicating the Fonts d' Algar. Take the right hand turn beside it. Soon, after a series of parking signs, the road begins to climb and you will see a small wooden booth on your left. This is the entrance to the Fonts, opposite which is a free car park (many of the car parks you pass either belong to bars and restaurants or have to be paid for).

The Fonts d'Algar is a natural park of waterfalls and pools, with tumbling cascades that vary from tiny, tinkling streams at the upper level to the rumbling Cascada del Toll de la Caldera, the waterfall that fills the main pool at the bottom.

From the entrance, visitors pass along wooden walkways and across slatted bridges to reach a set of steps set into the rocks alongside the

The gateway to Guadalest village

waterfalls, lined with bamboo, oleander and reeds. As you climb higher, level areas offer natural swimming pools. The higher they get the chillier they become.

If a dip in a cooling mountain stream doesn't tempt you, follow the path alongside the narrow canal on the opposite side of the river until you come to some steps and the Arboretum, a garden full of most of the typical Mediterranean spice plants. Next to this is the Museo del Medio Ambiente (Museum of the Environment) which houses a small collection of aromatic and medicinal herbs and the essences of oils and perfumes made from them, all of which are on sale.

When you leave the Fonts d'Algar, take the road back to Callosa d'en Sarrià, passing through hillsides covered in the lush green foliage of *níspero* (loquat) trees and plastic sheeting. Callosa is one of Spain's main areas for *nísperos*, and the plastic sheeting is there to protect and force fruit growth. You can buy cans and bottles of *nísperos*, as well as fresh fruit in season, at a small stall at the Fonts d'Algar and in local supermarkets.

When you get to the roundabout in the centre of Callosa, take the road almost directly in front of you (C3313) heading toward Alcoi and Guadalest.

This weaving road carries you through the rugged mountains of the Sierra d'Aitana, the highest in the province of Alicante. You are entering the Guadalest Valley, whose 18-kilometre length is covered in Mediterranean pine, holm oak, maple, ash and yew, as well as *nísperos*, apples, cherries, pears, olives, oranges, lemons and figs. It is a hunter's paradise, with an abundance of rabbit (a major part of the local cuisine), and wild boar. A wide variety of wild herbs go into the making of *hierbas*, a herbal liqueur for which every home and restaurant has its own recipe.

An animal sanctuary with a royal seal

Continuing on the C3313 in the direction of Alcoi, a mere 300 metres after you leave the car park at Guadalest, a sign on your right directs you down a rough track to El Arca de los Animales. A lion's roar, the holler of a gorilla, or the howl of a dingo could welcome you as you pass through the gateway to one of the most unusual sights in the Comunitat Valenciana.

El Arca is an animal sanctuary in the true sense of the word, home to more than 60 species peacefully living out their lives instead of ending up as mounted heads on some hunter's wall or as fancy fireside rugs.

The protected inhabitants include a tiger whose feet were terribly burned when circus trainers tried to teach it to dance by putting it on heated metal plates, a vulture with its tongue cut out, an albino fawn that would never survive in the wild and a pair of lynx terribly weak with advanced rickets, the debilitating bone disease.

Far more than just a zoo, it is also used as a study centre and received the royal seal of approval when Queen Sofía visited the park in May, 2002.

Shortly after leaving Callosa, on your left is a recently opened motor-cycle museum, where more than 100 *motos* and motorbike/sidecar combinations are on display, the result of 25 years of collecting.

Stay on this road and it will bring you to the hilltop village of Guadalest, which, in 2002, stole the crown from the Prado Museum in Madrid for being the most visited tourist destination in Spain. And it shows. There is not a single business in this tiny village of only 200 permanent residents that is not involved in removing the euro from the pockets of its visitors. But what redeems this eagle's nest of a *pueblo* is that it really is extremely pretty, and most of the souvenirs on sale here are of good quality.

Guadalest is split into two parts by the Puerta de San José, an imposing wooden door and narrow passageway hewn through solid rock. The upper part of the village is what used to be the fortress where the Christian population lived. As you exit the tunnel going into the fortified village, directly in front of you is the Casa Orduña. Originally the palace of the Orduña family, it is now the Municipal Museum and entrance to the Castillo de San José.

The Orduñas were the most influential family in the town from the mid-18th until the early 20th-century, and the building is a delightful example of a wealthy 19th-century home.

As you climb the metal stairway to the heights of the castle and Spain's highest cemetery, you are watched by a permanent collection of life-size bronze sculptures, one of which is a mop-capped, bespectacled granny armed, for some unknown reason, with a machine gun. The views from this eyrie are spectacular, with forested and terraced mountains and valleys sloping down to the sea and the reservoir that feeds the towns on the coastal plain far below.

Below the Puerta de San José are the narrow streets of the *Arrabal*, the Moorish quarter. This resembles the bazaar of old for most of the commercial activity of modern-day Guadalest is conducted in these crowded streets. You can buy fine-quality leather handbags and tasteful knick-knacks for the home or choose from 12 different varieties of the local honey and a wide range of honey-based products (look for the shop with no name at 20 Calle Virgen).

Return to the main road and head once more in the direction of Alcoi. The scenery on this winding mountain road is dramatic: glowering mountains, olive groves, high crags and pine forests, pockmarked with tiny mountain villages and scattered houses seemingly dropped into inaccessible places.

Most of these villages will have restaurants serving wholesome regional cuisine with such favourites as *conejo al alioli* (rabbit in

Keeping cool at the Fonts d'Algar

garlic mayonnaise), *verdura al horno* (oven-baked vegetables), *arrós amb fesols i penques* (rice with broad beans and artichoke stems), or *pilotes de farina de dacsa* (meatballs in corn flour). Just as mouth-watering are the local sweetmeats, *patissets d'ámetalla, almendrado,* or *caruinyoles,* almond-based pastry soft or hard.

Continuing on the C3313, at Confrides, three kilometres further, on a tight left-hand bend you see a shop which was once the excellent restaurant El Rincón Olvidado (The Forgotten Corner). So famous did the restaurant's home-made jams and sauces become that the owners closed the eating place and took up sauce production full-time. The shop also stocks regionally made products.

Several kilometres further on a sign to the left directs you to Alcoleja and Vila Joiosa (exactly opposite the sign at the entrance to the village of Benasau.) Beside this sign is a smaller one for Jardín de Santos, a recently restored 19th-century formal garden. Take this turn, and after two kilometres of twisting road turn right at a junction with the CV781. Within a few kilometres a large sign on the right directs you down a rough track to the garden.

The Jardín de Santos was laid out as a summer retreat by one Joaquín Rico, an apt name for a 19th-century aristocrat who had amassed a fortune in South America. Neglected for many years, it was eventually handed over to the local community and has been restored to its delightful former glory. On your left as you pass through the arched cast-iron entrance gate is a summer house painted glowing bright blue, and just beyond a fountain plays in a large rectangular pond.

When in private hands, the local hoi-polloi were only allowed to visit the gardens on one day a year, but now visitors can promenade under the shady arbour bordering the pond, admiring the *jardineras* (large pots for plants) of geraniums and ferns that top stone columns and the palms, chestnut, yew and magnolia trees. A grotto provides a romantic touch and an antique maze with a central Lebanon spruce has been replanted to the original design.

Beside the gardens is a recreation area with barbecues, and if you want to stretch your legs you can follow the *ruta fitoclimática,* a 45-minute walk offering information on the different species of flora in the area and the results of climatic change on natural environment. After a rather busy start to this excursion, the second half is more relaxing, with a drive that reveals the incredible variety of scenery in this part of the Alicante mountains.

Pick up the road to Alcoi once more. You are now driving through the high valleys of the Sierra de Serrella and the rugged mountains you passed through half and hour ago are replaced by beautiful rolling acres of cultivated farmland, interrupted by the occasional *masía*, a large farmhouse with walled courtyard. Some are in ruins but others have been restored to become beautiful *casas rurales*, such as one called Mas de Pau on your right shortly after you leave Penáguila. Ancient watchtowers dot the skyline above the pine-covered slopes that rise up from the wide valley floor.

You drive through Benifallim and when you reach the T-junction with the N340 you turn right in the direction of Alcoi. Just over one kilometre further, turn right on the C70/A160 towards Benilloba, 11 kilometres away, and Callosa d'en Sarrià.

As you begin to climb, Alcoi is spread out to your left. Not exactly a thing of beauty, but its claim to fame is that it celebrates the most important Moors and Christians fiesta in Spain, and is one of the main cities manufacturing the gorgeously ornate costumes used in this fiesta throughout the country.

As you drop down into Penella, five kilometres from the N340, a ruined tower (all that is left of Penella castle) stands guard over the village, while in the distance the restored castle of Cocentaina stands like a nipple on the fulsome bosom of the hill overlooking that town. Passing through Benilloba, just after the km9 marker, a left-hand turn puts you on the C710, the road to Millena and Gorga. When you reach the main junction in Gorga (a sign indicates "Millena 2 km" straight ahead), turn right and immediately right again, almost doubling back on yourself to go in the direction of Quatretondeta. You know you are on the right road when about 200 metres after the turn the road narrows briefly to one-car width and passes between two buildings, one of them a pharmacy.

You now leave the softness of the rolling uplands and enter a dramatic moonscape of tumbling gorges, where olive trees hang on for dear life to the narrow terraces running to the edges of sheer drops. Grey and haggard as the terrain sometimes looks, it has a rugged beauty all its own.

When you get to the T-junction in Fachega, turn right and drive the 10 kilometres to Castell de Castells. Turn right just before the bridge as you enter Castells (you will see a playground on the right). Drive 12 kilometres through pleasant and varied scenery to a T-junction, where you turn right for Tàrbena and Callosa d'en Sarriá to return to Benidorm.

WHAT TO SEE

CALLOSA D'EN SARRIÀ:

Fonts d'Algar. Natural waterfalls and swimming pools. Open daily, Apr-Sep 9am-5pm, Jul-Aug 9am-8pm, Oct-Mar10am-5.30pm. Entry Apr-Sep adults €3, children (under 12) €1.17, Oct-Mar adults €2, children €1.50. Price of admission includes entry to Arboretum, a garden full of typical Mediterranean spice plants, and Museo del Medio Ambiente, which houses collection of aromatic and medicinal herbs, and oil and perfume essences made from them. Open times as Fonts.

Motorcycle museum. Ctra Callosa-Guadalest, km7. Tel. 96 588 21 97.
Winter 10.30am-6pm, summer 10.30am-8pm, closed Sat. €3. Sometimes closes earlier if weather is poor.

GUADALEST:

Guadalest has about 10 museums of one sort or another, displaying everything from antique toys and miniature dolls' houses and *belenes* (nativity scenes) to microscopic sculptures of such things as a flea riding a bike. Surprisingly enough, most are quite interesting.

Casa Orduña, Municipal Museum, Calle Iglesia, 2. Open daily Apr-Sep10.15am-9pm, Oct-Mar 10.30am-5.30pm. Entry adults €3.50, children €1.50. A reproduction of 19th-century family life using furnishings supplied by the Orduña family. The top floor has a small gallery with exhibitions changing every two months. Access to the castle is through the Casa Orduña and included in the price.

Museo Etnológico, Calle Iglesia, 1. A small, interesting museum housed in an original cottage, displaying scenes of everyday rural life. Information cards in a variety of languages. Open daily (except Sat in winter) Apr-Sep10am-8pm, Oct-Mar 10am-6pm. Entry free, although it is polite to make a small donation to running costs, a €2 donation is requested to visit the exhibition of antique firearms.

Museo de Tortura Medieval, Calle Honda, 2. Open daily Apr-Sep 10.30am-9pm Oct-Mar 10.30 am-6pm. Entry adults €3, children €2. Mixture of original and reproduction torture instruments. Information plaques in Spanish and English.

El Arca. Animal sanctuary with compounds set in indigenous Valencia flora. (300m from Guadalest car park on C3313, direction Alcoi). Open daily from 10am until dusk. Entry adults €5, children €3.

PENÁGUILA:
Jardín de Santos. 19th-century garden with pool, maze and grotto, on the C3313 just before village. Open Sat/Sun/holidays 11am-2pm, 4-6pm. Entry €1. Short opening hours, but a delight to visit and a surprise for garden-lovers.

WHERE TO STAY

CALLOSA D'EN SARRIÀ:
El Repos del Viatger, Calle Mayor, 4. Tel. 96 588 23 22/639 902 930. Very pleasant pension in what was the residence of the village pharmacist. The chatty English-speaking owner will proudly show you the largest private library of historical books in the region. €€

GUADALEST:
Cases Noves, Calle Achova, 2. Tel. 676 010 171. Opened in 2005, *casa rural* in restored village house that maintains original features while incorporating a hydro-massage, flat-screen TV and Internet connection in every room. €€€

CONFRIDES:
El Pirineo, Calle San Antonio, 52. Tel. 96 588 58 58. Small, family *hostal* and restaurant with 10 double rooms. Ask for one with views down the valley. €

PENÁGUILA:
Mas de Pau, Ctra Alcoi, km 9. Tel. 96 551 31 11. Beautifully restored farmhouse with tennis court and indoor swimming pool. Also has wood cabins. Restaurant with local cuisine open for residents only. €€€

QUATRETONDETA:
Els Frares, Avda País Valencia, 20. Tel. 96 551 1234. Email elsfrares@terra.es, website: www.inn-spain.com. Highly recommended English-owned rural hotel specialising in walking tours of the area. Totally refurbished in 2006. €€€

WHERE TO EAT

GUADALEST:
Nou Salat, Ctra Callosa-Guadalest, Km 11. Tel. 96 588 50 19. Closed all day Wed. Medium-price restaurant with typical food of the region, especially fish dishes. Try the

hojaldre relleno de merluza, puff pastry stuffed with hake, or *favas con almejas,* broad beans with clams. €€

BENIMANTELL (village after Guadalest):
Venta La Monaña, Ctra Alcoi, 9. Tel. 96 588 13 41. Highly regarded restaurant in what used to be the courtyard of a coaching house. Serves value-for-money *comida del pueblo,* robust meats and stews. Excellent *pierna de cabrito lechal al horno,* roast kid's leg, and *butifarras,* locally made sausages. Recommended. €€

QUATRETONDETA:
Els Frares, Avda País Valencia, 20. Tel. 96 551 12 34.
Email elsfrares@terra.es, web: www.inn-spain. The English owner/chef is highly skilled and inventive, using and adapting recipes found on family holidays throughout Spain, often with produce shipped directly from each region's local producers. Excellent menus, including gourmet for that special occasion. Highly recommended. Open daily except Monday. Advisable to reserve a table. €€

MORE INFORMATION

CALLOSA D'EN SARRIÀ:
Tourist Information office, Calle Sant Antoni, 2.
Tel. 96 588 01 53. Open Mon-Fri 9am-2pm.

GUADALEST:
Information Office (in main car park). Tel. 96 588 52 98.
Open daily Apr-Sep 11am-2pm and 3-7pm,
Oct-Mar 10am-2pm and 3-6pm, daily except Sat.

PENÁGUILA:
Ayuntamiento, Plaça l'Esglesia,1. Tel. 96 551 30 01.
Mon, Wed and Thu 9am-2pm and 5-8pm.

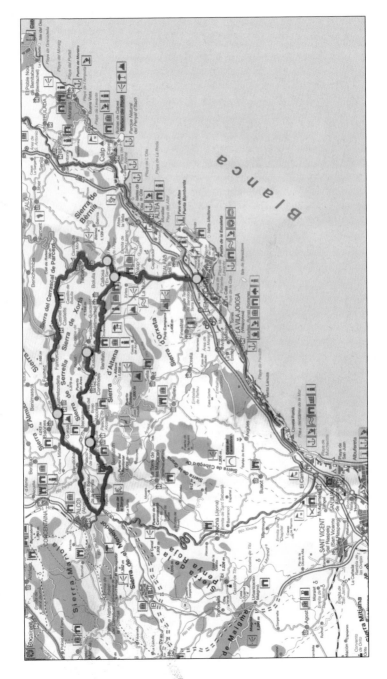

237

The unique Bread
Fiesta of Torremanzanas

TRIP 17
SWEET-TOOTH COUNTRY

AREA: Inland North of Alicante
ROUTE: Aigües – Torremanzanas – Xixona - Busot
DISTANCE: 85 kilometres

Bless the bread in a pagan ritual with the villagers of Torremanzanas and indulge your sweet tooth in Xixona, the home of Spain's favourite Christmas treat.

As you leave the N332 coastal road just north of El Campello, taking the CV775 to Aigües, you enter pleasant rolling country-side largely undisturbed by cultivation, although the terraced slopes that date back to Moorish times speak of a different agricultural history. Shortly after you leave the coastal road you will see on your left what looks like a scrapyard but is in fact a vintage vehicle restorer's workshop from where the rusted old wrecks eventually leave in pristine, show-room condition.

After nine kilometres you enter the pleasant little village of Aigües, or Aguas de Busot as it is also known, at the foot of the Sierra de Cabecó d'Or, so called because of rumours of pockets of gold waiting to be discovered.

The few streets of the tiny village were once on the banks of a great river (which gave the town its name) and formed the southern border of the kingdom of Valencia. At various times belonging to Murcia, Castilla and Aragon, Aigües has had a chequered history and very little is known about the origin of the spa that brought the village fame.

As you enter, take the small road that goes off to your left in front of a row of painted terraced houses (it looks as if you are going straight ahead as the main road curves to the right). As you reach the junction you will see a sign for the Banys de Busot and a few moments later the beautiful buildings of the *balneario* (spa), now in a very dilapidated condition.

In the early 19th-century, during the building of the luxurious Hotel Miramar that dominated the *balneario*, equestrian paddocks, Arab arches and coins bearing the bust of Julius Caesar crowned with laurel were discovered, demonstrating that visitors bathed in these waters centuries ago.

The Marchioness of Bosch, Countess of Torrellano, acquired the baths in 1816 and set about creating a spa which, when the government categorised establishments offering waters of medicinal value, was recorded as one of the top five in the whole of Spain.

The last word in architecture and hygiene, the magnificent Hotel Miramar, grandly described as "that salutiferous establishment offering the most attractive perspective", catered for the cream of society where "250 people could lodge decently or in great luxury". Elegance and simplicity, comfort and hygiene were the sovereign rules.

The spa gradually acquired a casino, parks, dairy and woods, swimming pools and a solarium and, in 1844, its then proprietor, the Count of Casas Rojas, added further baths and 33 small houses in which to lodge families.

"Taking the waters" fell out of fashion and the state took over operations at the end of the Civil War, converted the spa into a sanatorium for people afflicted with tuberculosis. By the mid 1960s, the waters had run dry and the aged building was abandoned and left to fall into ruin.

Nonetheless, the Baños de Busot are an impressive sight and worth visiting. But be careful. There are signs around warning you not to enter as the building is in a dangerous condition. It is easy to see the layout of the grounds and wonder at its past magnificence from *outside* the protective fence.

Follow the rough track around the *balneario* and it will bring you into the village. Apart from the parish church, a Moorish tower and the antique and craft fair held in the main street on the first Sunday of every month, there is not much to see or do. But there is a delightful café and tiny cave restaurant, called La Taverna, on Calle Canalejos that is highly recommended — if for nothing else than the owner (a comedian Tommy Trinder look-alike — remember him?) and his excellent home-made liqueurs.

Continuing the trip, return to the junction where the track from the

"Masia Mas Blanca" near Aigües

spa meets the main road and take the sharp left on the A180 in the direction of Relleu, 16 kilometres away.

This is a lovely ride as the road snakes its way up the pleasantly rough hills of the Cabezón de Oro. As you climb the slope around the km17 marker, look to your right for Mas Blanch, a wonderfully restored *masía* whose turrets stand out proudly against the ragged edges of the Sierra Aitana. Sadly, although restored, it seems to have been abandoned and is inhabited only by pigeons.

When you arrive at Relleu there are parking spaces on your right as you enter the village. Relleu, like most of these mountain villages, has a grand church, a hermitage and a ruined castle, but that is not

241

all. If you take the street opposite the door of the San Jaime Apóstel church and follow it all the way to the bottom, you will come across a tiny *palacio* on the side of a small gorge where once a river flowed. Though of no great cultural or historical significance, it's a pretty sight looking like a doll's house and guaranteed to raise a smile as you wander the shady streets.

To leave Relleu, follow the road through the village for two minutes or so. Immediately after a sharp left-hand bend on the edge of the village take a road to the left with a sign indicating Torremanzanas 14 kilometres away. This road takes you around the back of Relleu, where you will see the ruins of the Arab fortress sticking up like a row of ill-kept teeth, just after which another road to the left also directs you to Torremanzanas.

The landscape changes as you drive over the Sierra de la Grana. The slopes are still terraced but more rugged and with occasional almond groves and a number of ruined houses built up against the rock face. Signs along the road warn drivers of falling rocks. Major rock slides are rare, but you will often see a scattering of small rocks on the road, especially after rain.

The hearty food— *pericana,* a dish of cod and peppers, *cocido de pelotas*, stew with dumplings and *pelotas de maíz,* corn dumplings, to name just a few local dishes — reflects the colder temperatures in this mountainous zone. Famous for its *turrón,* the area is also known for its honey and *yemas,* a sweet made from egg yolk.

As you approach the km7 marker, the scenic views delight you on both sides of the road. There are small houses hidden in the pine-covered mountainside to your left and tiers of olive and almond groves to your right. The road straightens out and the drive is much smoother through the upland valley for a kilometre or so until you begin the slow curving descent to Torremanzanas.

The small town takes its name from an ancient fortified Almohad tower. Just as you enter the village, you can see on your right a rather strange and more modern fortication, the Villa Edelmira, a fortified *masía* or farm house. Immediately after this you will see parking spaces to your right.

The Blessing of the Bread festival called *Pa Beneit,* celebrated as part of the town's Fiesta de San Gregorio, is one of the oldest and most original in Spain. Its roots are thought to date back to the pagan rites of Egyptian times, when cakes of the god Isis and water from the river Nile were blessed and distributed among the people. Brought to Spain by the Romans, the tradition was maintained during the Moorish occupation and, in the case of Torremanzanas, embraced by the villagers when they adopted Saint Gregory as their patron saint.

Cardinal Gregorio Ostiense was despatched to Spain during the 11th-century by Pope Benedict IX to rid the country of a plague of locusts that had caused devastation in the regions of Navarra and La Rioja. Legend has it that he accomplished this by preaching to the locusts and sprinkling the affected areas with water. Two centuries later he was declared a saint. In the 17th-century, a further plague came to the land and it is said that the locusts were driven from Torremanzanas in 1658 by using water blessed in the saint's name. From that day, Saint Gregory became the patron saint of the town. The townspeople blended paganism and Christianity by incorporating the blessing of the bread as part of their religious devotions during the fiesta.

For five days in early May the villagers pay homage to Saint Gregory. Before the fiesta begins, several youths called *llumeners (valenciano* for the one who carries the candle) are chosen. They each select a young girl called a *clavariesa*. During the fiesta the youths wear the traditional farmers' black trousers and waistcoats with white shirts, while the girls wear long white skirts and beautifully embroidered shawls.

A parade takes place on the morning of the third day when the *llumeners*, escorted by the town band, visit the homes of their chosen girls and escort them to the town square. Each of the *clavariesas* balances a large round loaf of sweet bread on her head. The loaves, weighing between six and eight kilos, rest on a *llibrell*, a padded support draped with hand-embroidered organdie and topped off with a bouquet of flowers.

The procession assembles in front of the town hall, from where the priest leads them through the narrow streets to San Gregorio church. When the bread has received the blessing by being anointed with holy water it is distributed among the parishioners.

Follow the one-way signs through the *pueblo* and at the end of the main street follow the road over a bridge on the left that will take you up a hill to a T-junction. Turn left here for Xixona, 16 kilometres away. As the road begins to drop down to Xixona after the km10 marker, look out for the ostrich farm to your right where the ungainly creatures strut around flicking their stunted wings.

When you reach the N340, cross over and follow the signs for Xixona. This will lead you on to the N340 but you exit almost immediately.

Known as *La Cuna de Turrón* (The Cradle of Turrón), Xixona is a town with a sweet heart whose fortunes are built on the twin delights of nougat and ice-cream. From the beginning of September the surrounding area is filled with the sound of trees being whacked with long poles as the almonds that go to make the traditional Christmas treat are knocked from the trees. The production season lasts only until December but around 8 per cent of the town's population are employed in the turrón industry.

At first view the town has a rather untidy, uncared for look and the elegance of the wide Avenida Constitución comes as something of a surprise. At its lower end there are some delightful *modernista* (Art Nouveau) buildings and the town hall, with its ornate blue-and-gold tiles and painted griffons, catches the eye.

You can visit the Museo del Turrón just outside the town or wander around a few narrow streets displaying tiled images of the saints they are named after, but the real reason for visiting Xixona is to sample its mainstay, which you can do at any number of shops and factories.

From Xixona, take the road to Alicante and when you see a sign for Busot, turn left (this is the road you will be on if you have visited the turrón museum), following the country road until you see a sign for the Coves del Canelobre (Caves of the Candelabra).

Turrón, Xixona's famous Christmas treat

To describe *turrón* as simply nougat is rather inadequate as a number of different types are produced in a wide variety of flavours. Textures can be brittle and crunchy, smooth and creamy and the flavours would remind people from Arab countries of *halva*. In fact, it was 15th-century Moors and Jews who began producing the famous Christmas treat adored by Spaniards.

In its traditional form, *turrón* is a blend of sugar, almonds, orange blossom, egg white and honey from bees that have dined solely on rosemary. The two main varieties are Alicante, the nougat you are most likely to recognise, and Jijona, a softer, sweeter variety. Different types require different almonds. Marzipan and egg yolk are added to make the softer *turrón* but it is claimed that colouring or preservatives are never used.

Even though it is now a major industry and has been for more than 200 years, the best *turrón* is still blended by hand, after which it is fed through a rolling mill to achieve the standard thickness and blocked shape. El Lobo's 1880 brand is said to be one of the most luxurious. These days, large quantities of *turrón* from Xixona are exported worldwide.

A local bandsman practicing in a field near Torremanzanas

You'll see why the caves get their name as soon as you enter for the millennia of dripping water have created strange, often whimsical forms. The fine acoustics of the interior, one of the highest cave vaults in Spain, has led to the caves hosting musical concerts, especially in the summer months.

Go back to the Busot road, turning right to return to the coast.

WHAT TO SEE

AIGÜES:
Baños de Busot, semi-derelict 19th-century spa.
Iglesia Paroquial, dedicated to St Francis of Assisi, with a
17th-century altar-piece painted by Antonio Vallanueva.
Torre Morisco,14th-century Moorish tower.

TORREMANZANAS:
La Casa Alta, Calle del Castell. 13th-century Almohad tower.
El Pou de la Neu del Rontonar, ice cave and *El Brull*,
waterfalls and natural pools.
Two points of interest to be visited on walks from the village.
Inaccessible by car.
Parque Municipal. Attractive park with picnic facilities,
barbecues and children's playground.
Pa Beneit, the festival of the blessing of the bread. The parade
of loaves is especially worth seeing. Takes place around May
9. Confirm dates with the town hall.
Sunday Market, in the main street.

XIXONA:
Museo del Turrón, Polígono Industrial Ciudad del Turrón,
Carretera Xixona-Busot, km1 (4km from town centre off the
Alicante road). Tel. 96 561 02 25. Displays of *turrón*-making
through history. Open daily 10am-7pm (1pm on
Sat/Sun/holidays). Guided tours every hour, including visit to
modern production plant. Entry €1. Leaflets in English.
Most of the *turrón* factories are open to visits and tastings.

WHERE TO STAY

AIGÜES:
Finca El Otero, Calle Atalaya, 60. Tel. 96 569 01 16. Email:
elotero2001@yahoo.es Web page: www.elotero.es.vg. Small,
pleasant hotel with sea view. In warm weather breakfast can
be taken on terraces overlooking the 6,000-square-metre
gardens.The five rooms are named after local fruits.
Swimming pool for clients' use. €€€

RELLEU:
Almassera Vella, Carrer Mare de Déu del Miracle, 56.
Tel. 96 685 60 03. Email christopher@oldolivepress.com.
Stunningly restored olive mill on edge of village owned by

English/Spanish couple who also run residential and weekend courses in literature, painting and cooking. Dinner for residents if required. €€€

El Almendral, Ptda Rural El Terme. Tel. 659 165 085, email info@almendral.com, web page www.almendral.com. Elegant newly built hotel with rooms named after the seven deadly sins. €€€- €€€€

Las Puertas del Indiano, Calle Alicante, 23. Tel. 96 685 63 26 or 605 253 188. Email correo@puertasindiano.com, web page www.puertasindiano.com. Delightful village house converted into small hotel that is also a spa. Massage, beauty and remedial treatments available as well as use of spa. Treatment, relaxation packages available. €€€

TORREMANZANAS:

El Sester, Calle Finestrat, 2. Tel. 96 561 90 17. Email: elseber@arrakis.es, web page: www.hostelsester.com. Attractive small hotel in a restored farmhouse. Disabled access. €€€

WHERE TO EAT

AIGÜES:
La Taverna, Calle Canalejas, 10. Tel. 96 569 27 36. Delightful café and tiny four-table cave restaurant specialising in local recipes. The spoken menu (nothing is written down) changes daily. Try the rich stews such as *borreta*, made with meat and vegetables, or *bollitori*, another stew but this time using *bacalao* (cod). Good value, with main course 10 to 12 euros. Good range of *tapas* including *chorizo* cooked in rum. Choice of 40 homemade liqueurs. Bar/café open Tue-Sun from 10am, restaurant open daily for lunch and Fri/Sat for dinner. €– €€

RELLEU:
El Almendral, Ptda Rural El Terme. Tel. 659 165 085, email info@almendral.com, web page www.almendral.com. Elegant restaurant in newly built hotel. Inventive adaptations of regional cuisine and chef's own recipes. €€- €€€

TORREMANZANAS:
El Sester, Calle Finestrat 2. Tel. 96 561 90 17. Restaurant attached to hotel serving excellent menu of local dishes including *jabalí* (wild boar) and *rabo de buey estofado* (oxtail

stew). Open daily for lunch and dinner Jun-Sep and weekends only during winter, when it is advisable to make a reservation. €€

A number of bars in the village serve *tapas* and good-value *menús del día*.

XIXONA:
Bar-Restaurant Pichoc, La Vila, 74. Tel 96 561 05 75. Basic family-run cafeteria serving good portions of local food at sensible prices. Lunch only, *tapas* at other times. €
Numerous bars around the town centre serve *tapas*.

MORE INFORMATION

AIGÜES:
Ayuntamiento, Calle Pintor José Vila, 1.
Tel. 96 569 00 61. Open 11am-3pm.

TORREMANZANAS:
Ayuntamiento, Avenida de Espanya. Tel.
96 561 90 51. Open 8.30am-3pm.

XIXONA:
Ayuntamiento, Avenida de la Constitución, 6.
Tel. 96 561 00 80. Open 8am-3pm.

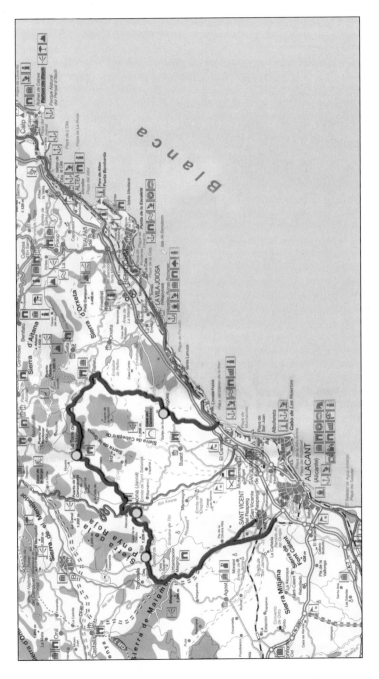

A rugged mountain landscape

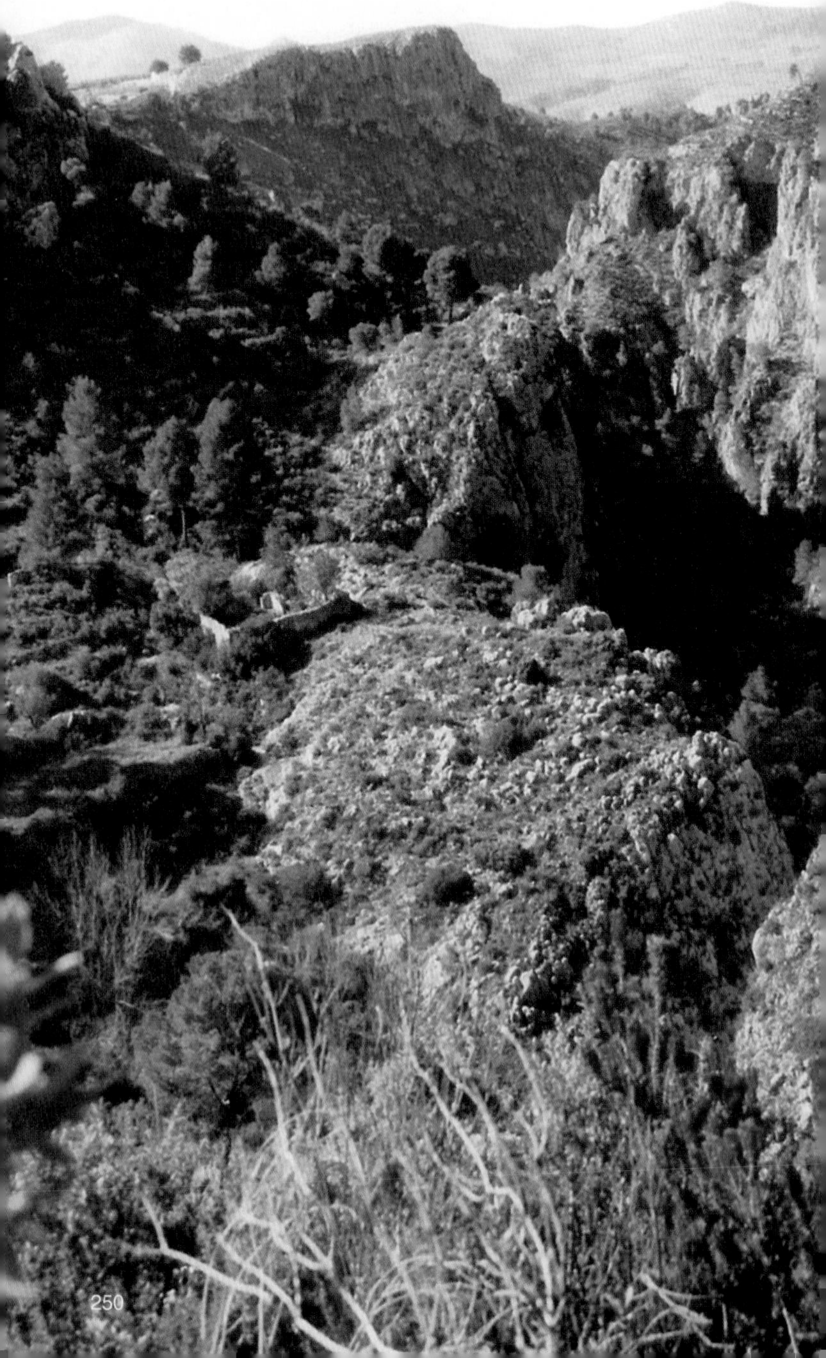

TIN TOYS AND KEYS OF THE KINGDOMS

AREA: High Vinalopó, Alicante province
ROUTE: Ibi – Banyeres de Mariola – Biar
DISTANCE: 128 kilometres

Mountain beauty combined with mouth-watering cuisine and the splendid Alicante wines make this an excursion to savour as you travel highlands once the scene of ferocious disputes between Castilla and Aragon.

From the coastal motorway (the A70 as it bypasses Alicante) take the A36 towards Alcoi, Castalla and Ibi, passing Sant Vicent del Raspeig. When you exit from the A36, follow the signs for Alcoi and Banyeres until you join a dual carriageway in the middle of Ibi. Stay on this road (following the signs for the Ajuntament and Museu de Joguet) until you get to the top of a gentle rise and you see a Repsol garage on your left beside a set of traffic lights.

To take this left you first have to take the short slip road on the right just before the traffic lights and cross over the main road and go down the other side of the garage. This leads you to the Ajuntament (town hall), beyond which you see the blue-tiled dome of a church. The Museu de Joguet (toy museum) is just behind the church, but it is advisable to park near the town hall as it is difficult near the museum. Also the road by which you will be leaving Ibi is directly opposite the Ajuntament.

Ibi's wealth rests on plastics these days, but at the turn of the 19th century the town owed its existence to agriculture and ice cream, the latter made from snow gathered from the surrounding mountaintops and sold throughout the region.

The tinsmiths of Rafael Paya kept the town supplied with cans and ladles, lamps and candlesticks. Then, in 1905, his three sons, Vicente, Pascual and Ismael, founded La Sin Rival – Paya Herma-nos factory (Paya Brothers, Without Rival) that eventually came to supply more than half the toys in Spain.

With the factory's closure in the early 1980s, the Fundació Paya was formed and the company's collection of tin toys — including clockwork railways, whizzing jugglers, big-wheeled prams and mechanised motorbikes — was donated to the town. It is now on display in the Museu del Joguet, housed in the beautiful 18th-century villa of the Pérez family, where you can also buy hand-made replicas made from original Paya patterns.

Leave Ibi by the road opposite the Ajuntament. Soon you will enter the Parque Natural del Carrascar de la Font Roja. Gentle pine-covered hills give way to cornfields and sunflowers, disappearing into the distance among regimented olive groves and the occasional small field of low blue/grey lavender bushes.

The park has one of the best-preserved Mediterranean forests in Valencia, with oak, yew, flowering ash and kermes oak. Wild boar, genets, wild cats and badgers roam free while Bonelli's eagles and golden eagles, vultures and eagle owls prowl the sky.

At the new road junction 10 kilometres from Ibi, bear left on the C795 to Banyeres (the town's full name is Banyeres de Mariola and you will see references to both names). Dusty roads lead off into the park at regular intervals, many of them leading to picnic areas.

You are entering the High Vinalopó, a beautiful mountainous region, ideal for walkers and nature lovers. The area's cuisine — featuring such hearty dishes as *arroz con conejo* (rice with rabbit) and *gazpacho de coca con liebre,* a thick, almost pasta-like dish made with noodles and hare, a world away from the chilled *gazpacho* of Andalusia — provides sturdy sustenance for the local farm workers.

Aromatic herbs are found in abundance on the mountainsides and feature heavily in the local cooking. In most of the villages in these parts you can treat yourself to sweet potato pie and almond cakes and sweets made with wine and liqueurs. There is no shortage of excellent restaurants on this excursion.

Locally produced *turrón* (a type of nougat), *peladillas* (sugared almonds) and *miel de romero* (rosemary honey) carry the special label specifying *denominación de origen* that guarantees a high standard of quality. A separate D.O. also verifies the quality of the table grapes grown in the High Vinalopó, some of the best in Spain and almost always those used to pop into the mouth at the 12 strokes of midnight that bring in the New Year.

The High Vinalopó is one of the major wine-producing regions of Mediterranean Europe. When Ferdinand Magellan set off on his circumnavigation of the globe he took Alicante wine with him, making it the first wine to make it around the world. Rumour has it that the Sun King, Louis XIV of France, spurned his own country's *vin rouge* and drank Alicante wine on his deathbed.

After a sudden right-hand twist in the road 20 kilometres from Ibi, you see Banyeres castle, keeping watch over the steep streets of the town. The castle was part of a chain of fortifications (Los Castillos de Vinalopó) that played their part in skirmishes between the Castilians and the Aragonese, when they laid claim to these lands during the 12th and 13th centuries.

The first paper mill in Alicante province was opened in Banyeres in 1779, although records show that paper had been produced in the town since the end of the 14th-century. A charming museum, the Museu Molí Paperer, is housed in the Villa Rosario, a small palace set in a park of the same name on the edge of town. The museum, unique in the Valencia Community, charts the history of paper-making since its origins in China in 105 BC and its introduction to Europe via Xàtiva, the city now in Valencia province. It has a whole section devoted entirely to cigarette papers.

Nearby, the Museo Arqueológico occupies the 17th-century Torre Font Bona, a defensive tower dating from the 15th to 16^{tth}-centuries that contains local artefacts from the Iberian, Roman, Islamic and Christian periods. A short drive from the town centre is a leisure area beside the Vinalopó river called the Molí l'Ombria, an ideal spot for a stroll or picnic.

Leave Banyeres and head for Villena and Ontinyent, joining the CV81 a kilometre out of Banyeres heading towards Villena. As you travel the arrow-straight road, in front of you the towering blue cupola of Beneixama's San Juan Bautista church rises from the plain, accompanied by its twin towers and large clock. In Beneixama you can also visit the 12th-century Torre de Negret and the 18th-century Ermita de la Divana Aurora (the chapel of the Holy Dawn), which was built by Valencian sculptor Josep Esteve and is thought to have pagan origins.

A warming and sometimes fiery digestive

Almost every mountain restaurant in these parts will offer you a glass of *herbero* (also called *hierbas*), a warming and sometimes fiery digestive. Each has its own recipe handed down from generation to generation, which usually consists of a mixture of medicinal herbs such as thyme and camomile macerated in sweet anisette.

Most of these concoctions are delicately referred to as *clandestino* (unlicensed). The sole producer of legal *herbero* in the area is Fabricación Artesanal de Licores de Hierbas Rufo, and their premises can be found in what is little more than a garage at Calle Penya Roja, 10.

Three generations of the Rufo family have been making *herbero*, using between 15 and 20 different herbs to create the range of four flavours the small shop has on offer. The shop is open to the public mornings only from Monday to Friday (Tel. 96 556 63 33/606 61 29 57).

Earthenware pots can be bought in many Valencian villages

Biar´s elegant Town Hall

At a roundabout take the CV81 to Villena. A few minutes later you come to another roundabout that directs you to Cañada, a village that lives mainly from fruit-farming and a small industry of textiles and leather. Here you can buy a fresh white cheese called *queso tierno*, made from a mixture of goat and cow's milk, and Terreta Rosé wine, made exclusively in the village from the *monastrell* grape.

Cañada is best known for the mystery play enacted every January 6 and 7 since 1764 and grandly titled *La venida y adoración de los Santos Reyes Magos al Niño Jesús* (the coming and adoration of the Child Jesus by the Three Kings). There are only 18 main roles, but almost the whole of the village joins in as shepherds and villagers. On the first day, Epiphany, historically the day when children were given their presents long before Christmas Day was celebrated nationally, the Three Kings come from different parts of the village to meet at the *belén* (crib) to present their gifts. On the following day they re-enact the flight to Egypt and Herod's massacre of the innocents.

In the parish church, in the heart of the village, hangs a painting entitled "*El rey San Luis de Francia*" by the famous 19th-century Valencian painter Joaquín Sorolla.

Leave Cañada by Calle Mayor that passes in front of the church. Cross a road with a Stop sign and, when you reach a junction at the edge of the village, turn right (a sign for Beneixama points to the left but there is none for Biar to the right).

A seven-kilometre rural drive from Cañada on the CV807 brings you to Biar, said to have one of the best-preserved 16th to 18th-century building heritages in the Valencia region. The name of the town originates from Roman times when it was called Apiarium (beehive), as it was one of the most important areas for honey in eastern Spain due to the abundance of flavoursome mountain herbs.

If you have the energy to climb up to the castle through steep winding streets from the Plaza de la Constitución (the town square), you will be rewarded with glorious views of the Vall de Vinalopó. The Torre de Homenaje (the castle keep) is one of the most important in the region and one of only three in Spain with ribbed vaulting on its arches (on the second storey) that intertwine to form a rosette in the middle of the vault, a feature that dates it to the second half of the 12th-century.

The lower two floors are of Islamic design, while the third is a 15th-century addition, built at the same time as the double bailey that protects its southern face. A plaque inside the keep, placed there when it was conquered for Aragon by Jaime I in 1245, declares in Latin "Only the king has two keys", signalling his dominion over both warring factions.

Biar's 15th-century parish church, La Asunción de la Virgen, has a Levantine-Plateresque façade, much weathered by the centuries but still highly impressive. Inside, the Shrine of the Communion is one of the leading examples of Churrigueresque baroque. Just off the square on Calle Mayor is the little Museo Municipal.

Modern-day Biar thrives on the production of dolls, blankets, and hand-forged metalwork, including gates, verandas, bed heads and balconies, which are still made in the traditional way. Small-scale ceramics factories, which have been a major part of Biar's economy since the 18th-century, produce everything from vases, dishes and bowls to flower pots, draining boards and large earthenware jugs.

Leaving Biar by the A210 to Castalla, after seven kilometres you join the A36, which bypasses Castalla. The road splits shortly after, one route going to Alicante and the south and the other to Alcoi and the north.

A tin car from Ibi´s Paya Brothers factory

WHAT TO SEE

IBI:
Museu del Joguet, Calle Aurora Pérez Caballero, 4.
Tel. 96 655 02 26. Tues-Sat, 10am-1pm and 4-7pm.
Fiesta days 11am –2pm. Entry €1.50.

BANYERES DE MARIOLA:
Castillo, one of a chain of castles involved in skirmishes
between Castilla and Aragon in the 12th and 13th centuries.
Open Sun, 11am-dusk. The **Moors and Christians Museum**
within the castle is open by appointment with the town hall.
Museu Molí Paperer, Parque Villa Rosario. Tel 96 556 77 70.
Paper mill museum. Open Tue-Sun, 11am-1pm, 5-7pm.
Free entry.
Museo Arqueológico, Torre Font Bona. Tel 96 656 78 96.
Open Tue-Sun, 1-2pm, 7-9pm. Free entry.

BIAR:
Castillo, 12th-century castle with one of the most important

keeps in the region. Open Tues-Fri 11am-1pm, Sat 10am-2pm, 4-6pm, Sun 10am-2pm. Entry €1. (Please note: as the ground within the castle walls is very uneven, it is advisable to wear sensible shoes.)

Museo Municipal (Museo Etnográfico), a small museum displaying local artefacts. Calle Mayor, s/n. Open Tues-Sat noon-2pm, 6-8pm, Sun noon-2pm. Free entry.

Iglesia Parroquial, 15th-century parish church in the Plaza de la Constitución.

Acueducto Ojival. 17th-century aqueduct on the edge of town in the direction of Banyeres.

Cerámica Maestre, Camino de la Virgen s/n. Tel. 96 581 00 62. Pottery with public viewing, Mon-Fri 9.30am-1pm, 3-8pm, Sat 9.30am-1.30pm, Sun 11am-1.30pm.

WHERE TO STAY

IBI:
Hostal el Laurel, Calle L'Escoleta, 4. Tel 96 555 29 45. Comfortable modern hostal. €€

BANYERES:
Venta el Borrego, Ctra. Villena-Ontinyent, Km 18. Tel 96 656 74 57. Converted coaching-house that celebrated its centenary in 2001. With gardens and swimming pool. Horse-riding can be arranged. €

BIAR:
Hotel Rural Mas Fontanelles, Ctra Biar-Banyeres, km 4. Tel. 686 426 126 or 639 707 924. Email info@masfontanelles.com, web page www.masfontanelles.com. Splendid restoration of old family farmhouse. €€- €€€

Finca Fanecaes, Ctra de Banyeres s/n. Tel 902 220 052. Email finca@fanecaes.com, web page www.fanecaes.com. Elegantly restored rural house. €€€

Los Dos Tilos, Calle Barrera, 54. Tel. 676 988 836, Email cataliv@hotmail.com, web page www.losdostilos.com. Family home in the middle of the town, with large garden. A testament to the *modernista* period. €€- €€€

WHERE TO EAT

IBI:
Casino Primitivo, Calle San José. Tel 96 555 35 10. Serving good-value local food. Open daily, 9.30am-midnight (breakfast,

lunch and dinner). €
Restaurante Niagra, Paca Guillem, 5. Tel 96 555 05 08.
Elegant modern restaurant serving reasonably priced traditional
Mediterranean dishes. Open 12.30-4pm and 8-11pm. Closed
Monday. €€

BANYERES:
Restaurante Piramide, Pintor Segrelles, 8. Tel 96 556 64 71.
Open for lunch Mon-Fri 1.30-4pm, and for dinner Fri/Sat
8.30pm-midnight. Comfortable modern restaurant elegantly
furnished. Speciality of the house is lobster soup. Part of the
Parlant i Menjant association. €€– €€€
Venta el Borrego, Ctra. Villena-Ontinyent, km 18. Tel: 96 656 74
57. Open for lunch and dinner Mon-Sat, lunch only Sun. Also part
of Parlant i Menjant. Specialises in mountain cuisine and well
known for its charcoal-grilled lamb and roast leg of kid. €€

BIAR:
El Solet, Maisonnave, 6. Tel 96 581 00 22. Housed in an
18th-century *bodega*, the menu is traditional Mediterranean
and regional cuisine. Try the *dulce tomate*, a village pudding
recipe that is basically a cheesecake blended with honey and
topped by a sweet tomato sauce. Open for lunch and dinner
Tues-Sat, lunch only Sun. Closed Mon. €€–€€€
Finca Fanecaes, Ctra. De Banyeres s/n. Tel: 902 220 052.
Highly inventive menu. Try the marinated salmon with
rosemary honey or steak with prune sauce and pastry filled
with mushrooms. A choice of menus. Open daily for lunch
and dinner. €€–€€€

MORE INFORMATION

IBI:
Ayuntamiento, Calle Les Eres, 48. Tel. 96 555 24 55. Web
page www.ibirural.com Open Mon-Fri 8am-3pm.

BANYERES:
Ajuntament, Plaça del Ajuntament, s/n. Tel. 96 656 73 15.
Open Mon-Fri, 8am-2pm.

BIAR:
Tourist Information Office, Avda de Villena, 2. Tel 96 581 11
77. Web page www.biar.es or www.biarrual.es. Open Tue-Fri,
8.30am-2.30pm, Sat 10am-2pm.

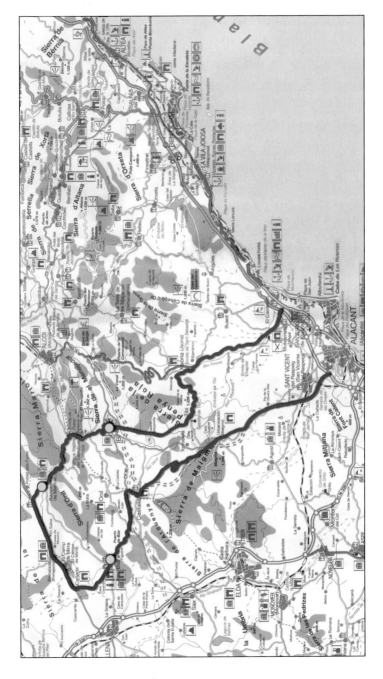

Alicante´s lunar landscape

TRIP 19
ALICANTE'S LUNAR LANDSCAPE

AREA: Inland southwest Alicante
ROUTE: Alicante – Santa Eulalia – Pinoso – Baños de Fortuna – Abanilla
DISTANCE: 135 kilometres

Visit a semi-deserted village with a murderous past and wallow in the warm waters of a natural spring on an excursion that passes through Alicante's wine-producing hinterland.

From the A7 motorway that circumnavigates Alicante, take the N330, the main road to Madrid that begins just south of the city. Stay on this dual carriageway for 46 kilometres passing Novelda and Elda until, a couple of kilometres after you see Sax castle perched on top of a sheer precipice, you come to the exit for Santa Eulalia. You exit with a large Cepsa filling station on your right. Follow the signs for Santa Eulalia as you cross over the motorway and come to a T-junction. Turn right.

As you drive down the narrow road, a rooftop rises over the pine trees before you. A few moments later you enter the Colonia de Santa Eulalia, a peaceful, picturesque village surrounded by cornfields but with a semi-derelict air and a past shrouded in mystery.

Sit in the centre of the square of baked earth and neglected plants in front of the church — its clock pointing permanently to one minute past two as if signalling the time when the old town died — and try to imagine it as it was in its heyday. Once the square was adorned with statues, pools, fountains and gardens and the Condesa de Santa Eulalia entertained her guests in the Teatro Cervantes behind La Unión, the towering *fábrica de alcohols* at one side of the square. In its day, the most important performers in Spain trod the boards of the tiny theatre.

The story goes that at the end of the 19th-century, with funds supplied by the Conde de Alcudia, an agricultural engineer built here a village of 20 houses, a farm, a flour factory, a distillery, café and shop, and a small *palacio* surrounded by beautiful gardens. Some time later the count was murdered by someone, it was rumoured, in the pay of his wife, who then inflamed local gossip by setting up home with the engineer.

Little by little the lady's wealth was frittered away by her lover, who later abandoned her. What was left she spent defending herself against an accusation of murdering her husband, until she was reduced to penury and the deepest misery. This is just one story of many that haunt the slowly disintegrating *colonia*. Others involve a miracle and a giant serpent.

Although the flour factory finally closed its doors in the 1970s, Santa Eulalia isn't as deserted as it appears at first glance. The permanent population of a dozen or so families is increased at weekends and on fiesta days by visitors, some of whom have holiday homes in the village.

There are moves afoot to restore some of the buildings, including the palace, which has a stunningly painted interior. But things are slowed down by the fact that Santa Eulalia is located in two municipalities (the border runs right through the palace), and it's feared this odd but rather engaging little village could tumble into ruin before anything is done to save it.

Leave Santa Eulalia by Calle de Salinas, the narrow road that runs up the side of the Teatro Cervantes in the direction of Cabreras and the El Plano picnic area. At the first T-junction turn right. Take care on this road. Most of it is in quite good condition but there are sections, mainly where old water courses have been filled in, that are a bit rough.

You are now travelling through flatlands of corn, vines and olive groves, passing rows of tiny, ancient terraced houses typical of this area, some of which have been joined together and converted into weekend retreats for city folk.

In the fields you will see dozens of one-room *casitas* (huts used by farmers to store their tools or cook meals) and what look like tall chimneys but are in fact towers housing pumps to draw water for irrigation. Turn left at the next T-junction.

The countryside is a cornucopia of jagged rocks, pointed hillocks, undulating mountains and rolling fields, a multi-hued valley of different crops each displaying its own colour and shade of green.

The ancient liquor factory at Santa Eulalia

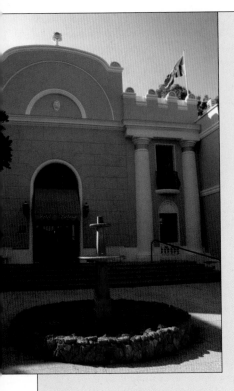

One of Spain's top spas

A marble plaque just above the main entrance to the subterranean thermae informs you that Don Juan Cascales Font and his wife Doña Carlota Bocio Boucha opened the spa to the public in 1863. Two decades later the elegant Gran Hotel, now known as the Hotel Balneario, was opened, together with two rows of cottages, each with its own heated bath, which could be rented on a daily or weekly basis.

Don Juan was a fierce advocate of the reigning *modernista* (or Art Nouveau) style of that time and the hotel reflects this elegant architectural form. Many of the public rooms, including the splendid sweeping staircase and the beautiful dining room with its central row of ornate, cast-iron pillars based on the dining room of the ill-fated Titanic, are still in their original condition.

As the decades rolled by, the elegant Hotel Victoria replaced the cottages, the Casino with its spacious ballroom was built, gardens were laid, swimming pools and a golf hall with an indoor pitch-and-putt course were installed.

These days the casino, ballroom and *salón de golf* have been converted into small treatment centres specialising in various thermal remedies, but many of the facilities used in the water treatment rooms beneath the two hotels are original, including the huge marble baths with lion's-head spouts carved from a single block of marble.

A short drive brings you to Salinas. When you get to a large new roundabout beside some industrial units on the edge of town, take the second right, leading you into the village. Follow the road as it curves around taking you on to the main road. Just after you turn you will see an ochre-coloured building on the left with a sign for the Asociación Amas de Casa. Stay on this road (CV830) as it leaves the village.

You pass through a fertile valley with barely a millimetre of the land uncultivated. On your left you catch glimpses of the Laguna de Salinas, a small lake that irrigates the patchwork quilt of vineyards, olive groves and almond trees. Seen from a distance, the vines look like rows of well-regulated stubble in the brick red earth, interspersed with the occasional cornfield that adds a golden haze. By summer they will be heavy with the grapes that make this one of the most bountiful wine-making areas in Valencia.

Ten kilometres after Salinas you come to a junction where you turn right on the CV83 and drive to Pinoso, 13 kilometres away. The sleepy nature of Pinoso belies the fact that, per capita, it is one of the richest towns in Spain. Its fortune is based on the three "Ss": salt, shoes and sausages. Most people who see giant mounds of salt on the coast at La Mata think it comes from the salt lake of Salinas de Mata; in fact it is deposited there after having travelled 60 kilometres propelled by gravity through an underground pipeline from the purple salt mountains above Pinoso.

Despite being an ancient crossroads, Pinoso isn't exactly packed with historical content (apart from the pretty clock tower that also served as the town jail), but it is a pleasant town with a good indoor market. It also has some good walks in the vicinity and is part of a wine route dotted with "Venta de vino" signs inviting you to stop to sample locally produced wines.

Leaving Pinoso, take the CV836/C3223 to Fortuna 26 kilometres away. The road descends into another valley full of vineyards and fields edged with grey stone walls. The landscape is strangely impressive, far removed from the mountains only an hour's drive north.

In the distance you can see what looks like a metropolis of white, high-rise buildings but are actually the sides of mountains cut away to extract marble. This sight is especially spectacular by night when the searing arc lights of the quarries light up the sky.

Just after the Bodega Sanbert, a new building six kilometres from Pinoso that looks rather out of place in this beautiful countryside, you crest a small hill and a stunning vista of orange groves and vineyards laid out along the valley floor comes into view. The landscape changes rapidly as you twist through barren hills, the earth taking on a peculiar colouring of striated red and pale green, where hilltops have been lopped off to provide more space for cultivation.

You pass plenty of ruined *masías* (old farmhouses) just waiting to be restored, and what look like man-made stumps sticking out of the ground are actually the chimneys of troglodyte houses. Historically, these cave homes were inhabited by poor people but are now becoming much sought-after, partly because they maintain a year-round temperature of 18 degrees C and can be easily and cheaply enlarged. If you need an extra room, you just hack it out of the sandstone.

As you drive on, the terrain becomes more lunar-like and takes on a peculiarly rugged and barren beauty. When you cross the long narrow bridge at Compules, keep an eye open for cacti growing on the roof of a semi-derelict house.

The village of Baños de Fortuna, three kilometres after the cactus house, looks dusty and careworn, but as you pass the first few houses you see a large tiled sign to the left indicating the entrance to the Balnearios Fortuna-Leana, one of the foremost spas in Spain.

Drive under the shady pines that welcome you to the Balneario and you enter a world of Victorian elegance whose health-giving waters have attracted a constant stream of elderly and not-so-elderly Spaniards for almost a century and a half.

If you don't feel the need for lumber sprays, mud massages or being bombarded by high-pressure hoses, all of them wonderfully stimulating, you can relax in a pair of naturally heated swimming pools.

From the spa, continue on the road you came in by, following the sharp bend left just after the blue painted building and the entrance to the *piscina*. It isn't signposted, but 10 minutes later you will enter the village of Mahoya. Turn right at the T-junction (signposted Abanilla) and very quickly you will come to a roundabout indicating Abanilla is two kilometres further on. When you get there, follow the signs through the twisting streets for the church, behind which is a small car park.

San José, with its gilded and marbled retablo, is one of the most beautiful churches you will ever see. The side chapels alone would grace any cathedral. But this is only one of the jewels in Abanilla's crown.

Impressive stairway at Balnearios Fortuna-Leana

In front of the church is the beautifully restored façade of a mansion, once home to the commander of the local forces of the Knights of Calatrava, Spain's oldest military order. Founded in 1158 by a group of Cistercians monks from Navarra, who formed themselves into a military confraternity as a defence against the Moors, the order was very powerful, holding large tracts of land until the 13th-century, when it fell into decline.

The house is now a private home, but you can sometimes get a brief glance through the heavy, studded doorway into its tree-shaded central courtyard.

Walk a few metres up Calle Mayor, a narrow street that runs off the Plaza de la Constitución, the square in front of the Ayuntamiento, and you come to a beautiful fountain, decorated with ceramic imagery telling the folkloric history of the area.

Elderly women of the village spurn the bottled water available from shops and bring large plastic buckets to fill up here, proselytising on its excellent quality. "*Es muy dulce; en verano es fresca y en invierno es caliente,*" they will tell you. "It is very sweet; in summer it's cold and in winter it's warm."

Climb up the 177 steps from the Plaza de la Constitución to a pleasant garden of cactus and palm and you find yourself beneath a 10-metre-high statue of Christ of the Sacred Heart. It is completely white except for the vivid red heart emanating golden rays and the stigmata in the hands.

Walking back down the steps, you can enter one of the narrow side streets that meander through the old town and stop off at the Plaza de la Lonja to relax in the shade of a bougainvillea-covered arbour where the locals gather to chat and enjoy the cool of the evening.

Leave Abanilla in the direction of Orihuela and Benferri. At Benferri you can pick up the E15/A7 for Alicante or Murcia. If you wish to return to Costa Blanca south, continue on the C4140/CV870 to Orihuela until it reaches the junction of the N340. (Ignore the road to the right signposted Orihuela just before you reach the N340.)

Turn right and a few hundred metres on you will see a road passing over the N340, just before which is a right-hand turn almost opposite a Repsol garage. This turning is badly signposted as the direction sign for Orihuela is almost obscured by a large blue-and-white traffic bollard. Take the turn, going over the N340, and follow the signs for Bigastro and Torrevieja.

The decorative font of Abanilla

WHAT TO SEE

COLONIA DE SANTA EULALIA:
A picturesque, semi-abandoned village with a colourful past set amid cornfields.

PINOSO:
Torre del Reloj, clock tower that also served as the village jail.

BAÑOS DE FORTUNA:
Balnearios Fortuna-Leana. Thermal spa with residential accommodation. Thermal pools open to non-residents who can also arrange treatments on the day of their visit. For information about treatment and reservations call 902 444 410.

ABANILLA:
San José, beautiful church with a gilded and marbled retablo.
La Fuente, Calle Mayor. A fountain decorated with 12 metres of ceramic imagery telling the history of the area.
Sagrado Corazón, 10-metre-high statue of Christ overlooking the Plaza de la Constitución.

WHERE TO STAY

PINOSO:
Hartendale, Paraje Purgateros, 5, Encebras (a small village 10-min drive from Pinoso). Tel. 96 597 80 12. Pleasant, newly opened B & B run by an English couple. €

ABANILLA:
Restaurante La Posada, Carretera Salzillo, 22. Tel. 96 868 00 06. Basic rooms with shared bathroom. €

WHERE TO EAT

PINOSO:
El Timón, Carretera Jumilla, 9. Tel. 96 697 01 03. Open daily for lunch. Good-value set menu, and reasonably priced local dishes. €– €€

FORTUNA:
Balneario Fortuna-Leana. Hotel restaurant open to public for lunch and dinner. €– €€

ABANILLA:
Restaurante La Posada, Carretera Salzillo, 22. Tel. 96 868 00 06. Old coaching house serving regional dishes with large sit-in fireplace. Good-value hearty meals. €– €€

MORE INFORMATION

PINOSO:
Ayuntamiento, Plaza de España, 1. Tel. 96 697 02 50. You can pick up a small booklet here giving information about the town and locality.
There are no other information offices on this route.

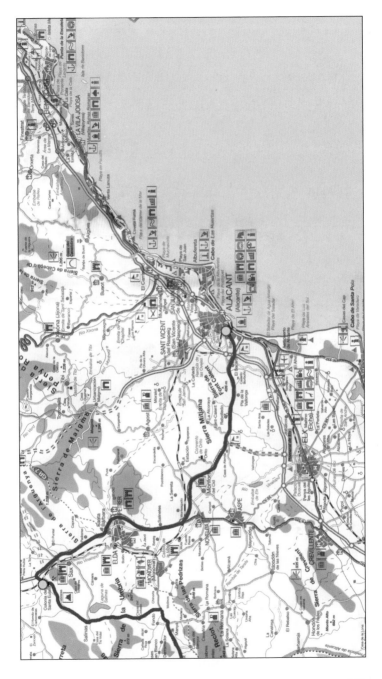

Santuario de Santa María Magdalena, Novelda

ROUTE OF THE CASTLES

> **AREA:** Valley of the Vinalopó, west of Alicante
> **ROUTE:** Alicante – Novelda – Monòver – Elda - Petrer –
> Sax – Villena – Castalla
> **DISTANCE:** 142 kilometres

Trace the necklace of castles that kept warring Aragonese and Castilians apart, raise your eyebrows at a bizarre shrine and admire a copy of the world's most expensive shoes.

This excursion takes you to some of the main castles in an area that was one of the most heavily fortified in the region, much fought-over by the kingdoms of Aragon and Castilla. For non-castle lovers there's still plenty to see.

From the centre of Alicante or the A7 that bypasses the city take the N330 Autovía del Mediterráneo towards Madrid, leaving this road at the junction for Novelda, 24 kilometres from Alicante. Cross over a new roundabout and at the next set of traffic lights turn right, following the signs for Elda and Castillo (next to a Citroen garage). At the T-junction a couple of hundred metres later turn left, passing along a dry riverbed. At the next traffic lights, beside the Kia service station, turn left and right at the next lights. At the following junction turn right (you join the Paseig de Molins) and follow the signs for the Castillo.

La Mola castle is unique in Europe in that it is the only one with a triangular tower called, not surprisingly, the Torre Triangular. The tower is thought to have been built in the early 14th-century to fortify the crumbling ruins of a 12th-century Moorish castle, although references are made to there being fortifications on the site since Roman times. It is therefore one of the first examples of a Gothic civic-military building in Catalan style in the land of Valencia, and its peculiar shape conjures up tales of alchemists and the search for magical formulae in secret rooms.

A sanctuary with Gaudiesque charm

Beside the Castillo La Mola is the Santuario de Santa María Magdalena, one of the strangest-looking shrines in the area. It looks like something Gaudí cut his teeth on before getting stuck into the Sagrada Familia in Barcelona, but in fact was the brainchild of one José Sala Sala, an engineer who studied in Cataluña and built the church in the Catalan *modernista* style.

The sanctuary was begun in 1918 but, because of a series of delays, was not completed until 1946. This bizarre edifice has a knobbly charm, being made of rough-hewn stone and pink-tinted marble and rubble lifted from the Vinalopó river.

With its arched façade and twin towers rising heavenward, you can imagine it in some Gothic horror movie, backlit with forked lighting against a stormy Transylvanian sky. In bright sunlight though, you can see that it is decorated with delightful polychrome tiles with motifs of medieval and baroque origin and the naturalised floral forms of the *modernista* period. Some of the designs carved into the blocks that form the triple arch of the entrance are decidedly pagan in origin.

In complete contrast to the outrageous exterior, the interior is surprisingly simple. Light filters through arches of alternating red-and-colourless glass panels, illuminating a minimum of architectural details. Around the walls, religious scenes are depicted in a series of three-metre-high paintings, many of which include Santa María Magdalena, patron saint of Novelda. Despite their appearance of antiquity, they were painted during the 1960s.

Return to Novelda and when you reach the T-junction at the end of Paseig de Molins turn right, heading for Monòver and Aspe. At the next junction (almost a T, with a dead end ahead of you) turn left and then right with the one-way system at the end. You come to a square with a church in front of you, to the right of which is a sign directing you to Monòver. At the next major junction, just across the road to your left is the ornate entrance to the Parque del Oeste, an intriguing little park and pleasant picnic stop. Stay with the signs for Monòver (CV835), but be aware that this junction is a bit complicated and the exit slip road is very short before you are brought into the rush of traffic on the main road.

Musician at medieval market

You pass through a barren, rubble-strewn landscape of no great appeal. When you arrive at Monòver, after nine kilometres, you will see the Casa Cuartel (Guardia Civil Barracks) on your right, partially hidden by some trees on a grassed area. On the corner after the barracks is a sign pointing to Pinoso, 19 kilometres. Turn right in front of this sign and follow the signs for Elda, eight kilometres.

Birthplace of the novelist José Martínez Ruiz Azorín, one of Spain's most renowned 20th-century literary figures, Monòver is a busy little town that forms part of a "wine route" and you will have ample opportunities to sample the local vintage. It is potent stuff, with often

277

as high as 14 degrees alcohol, and very light on the pocket. It also has a museum dedicated to its most famous son and a good art and craft museum with a fully equipped 19th-century pharmacy and shop and examples of local industry from times gone by. The latter can only be visited by appointment.

Keep following the signs for Elda. Miss the first exit for Elda (also signposted for the Polígono Industrial) and take the second one. As you enter the town look out for the large Porcelanosa sign on your left. Elda is as near a gridlocked town as you can find, so it is advisable to park in this area and go on by foot. It's only a short walk to the next venue. Just after the Porcelanosa sign a large green bollard with white arrows directs you either side of a narrow strip of garden. Stay on the left side. After the junction at the end of the garden you join Avenida de Chapi where, at number 32, you will find a museum that celebrates the product on which the city's fortunes are built, the Museo del Calzado (Footwear Museum).

The first records of shoemaking in Elda go as far back as the mid-18th-century but within a century the industry became the mainstay of the city's economy and these days Elda and its near neighbour Elche vie for the title of shoe-making capital of Spain. The museum is a collection of the weird and wonderful tools and equipment used in the early years of shoe production and some of the equally weird and wonderful shoes they made, showing what agonies people would go through, all in the name of fashion. Donations from the rich and famous are on display, including some from King Juan Carlos and Queen Sofía, and a copy of what are said to be the most expensive shoes in the world, worn to the Oscars by Mexican actress Laura Elena Harring.

To leave Elda follow the white arrow in the green bollard to the *right* of the garden and at the traffic lights turn right. A couple of hundred metres later look out for the small sign directing you left in the direction of Madrid and Petrer. Cross over a roundabout with a tall wrought-iron lamp standard in the centre, and at the next junction turn right. Follow this all the way to the roundabout at the top where you will see the two-storey, red-brick building of the Cervecería Cruz Blanca, which forms part of the bus station, where you will find the information office of the Conçorcio la Isla del Interior. This represents five of the surrounding towns and is a central pick-up point for tourist information, including a neat little pack of walks in the area endearingly called the Rutas del Caracol (Routes of the Snail).

Turn left at the roundabout on Calle Madrid which forms the border line between Petrer and Elda, although you would think you are in the same town except that Petrer has retained much of its old-town whereas Elda has only a few tumbledown streets surrounding what's left of the castle.

Vineyards near Monover

Continue along Calle Madrid to the traffic lights and turn right. Stay on this road as it narrows beside a blue-and-white painted building and at the next junction, a slightly awkward crossroads, go straight across to the narrow road that almost looks like a left turn. (To visit Petrer's castle and the meandering streets of the old town, you go straight ahead instead of turning left at this junction, but it's tricky to get back here so you would be advised to park and walk.) At the next traffic lights turn right at a slightly angled crossroads and stay with the signs for Madrid until they take you once more on to the N330, heading in the direction of Sax.

(Please note, at the time of revising this book, Elda was undergoing extensive road works, which were expected to be finished in mid-2006. If the directions mentioned above are blocked, look for signs to Madrid which will take you to the motorway.)

Four kilometres after joining the N330 Sax castle rises in front of you, snaking along the ridge of the hill overlooking the town. It's only when you get close or pass it on the autoroute that you realise just how precipitous the rock face is. While the imposing castle has been well-restored the rock on which it stands has been disintegrating due to frost erosion. Millions of euros are needed to support the castle before it collapses on to the medieval streets below. This might account for some of the houses bearing such names as Las Penas (The Sorrows), El Peligro (Danger) and El Milagro (The Miracle).

Continue on the autoroute to Villena to find one of the best-preserved castles in the province. In the soft rays of the evening sun the pinkish-cream stone of the castle glows. Rigorously restored, it still has a fairytale charm. La Atalaya (meaning watchtower) is one of the most imposing constructions once used to defend the extensive marquisate of Villena. Perched on a hill, surrounded by the meandering streets of the old town, the castle is composed of a double ring of solid walls protecting two inner baileys (main defensive walls) with circular turrets at its corners. To enter the inner bailey you pass through a Moorish arch in a crenellated gatehouse with slits for archers.

The great square Torre del Homenaje (keep) stands 25 metres high, its four storeys marked by two building styles, the lower section being mud walling and the upper having a rubblework finish. The keep has ribbed vaulting indicating its Islamic origin and was constructed during the late 12th-century and the early 13th-century, a date confirmed by Arab sources that mention the castle in 1172. The plastering of the keep's lower section is characteristic of the style of Al-Andalús (as the Moorish states were called at that time) during the late 12th-century. This lower section of the tower is the only part of the castle remaining from that period. Having passed through the hands of numerous invaders, the structure you see today was built during the mid-15th-century under the governorship of Don Juan Pacheco, Marqués de Villena, whose armorial bearings adorn the building.

While La Atalaya can be seen as one of the jewels in the necklace of castles that gird the Vinalopó, Villena's greatest treasure is tucked away in the town's vaulted Museo Arqueológico, in the 16th-century Palacio Municipal. Such is the value — monetary, historical and emotional — that one of the most important finds of gold jewellery and artefacts in the western world is kept in an ornate, metal-studded cabinet, specially constructed and only opened in the presence of a curator.

In 1963 José María Soler, director of the Municipal Archeological Museum, discovered 35 pieces of ancient gold jewellery, including rings, necklaces and a belt, on Cabezo Redondo, a nearby mountain that was being mined for gypsum. Understandably pleased with that find, in December of that year he, the town and the international archeological community were stunned when a beautifully made gold bracelet was discovered while workmen were clearing a piece of land in what used to be known as the Rambla del Panadero.

Then, on closer inspection, Soler and his team came across a ceramic pot measuring 50 centimetres across containing the biggest single find of Bronze Age golden artefacts ever recorded (later dating estimated them to be from 1000 BC): 11 bowls, 28 bracelets, three bottles and an assortment of other priceless items, richly decorated with geometric and circular relief patterns. Weighing almost 10 kilos, the find became known as El Tesoro de Villena (The Treasure of Villena).

Just around the corner from the Museo Arqueológico, in the Plaza de Santiago, the 14th-century Santiago church with its helicoidal (twisted) columns and baptismal font attributed to Jacobo Florentino, an associate of Michelangelo, has been splendidly restored and is said to be one of the region's finest Gothic-Renaissance buildings. (It is usually only open during mass but ask at the tourist office, just opposite, as there are plans for the staff to provide access to the church.)

Villena has some fine examples of Art Nouveau architecture, in particular the Teatro Chapí. Named after Ruperto Chapí, the illustrious composer born in the city, the theatre was inaugurated in 1925 after 11 years in construction. Following years of neglect, the theatre was returned to its former grandeur at the turn of the millennium and now hosts performances of dance, opera, theatre and the *zarzuela* (Spanish light opera), for which the composer was famous.

Leave Villena by following the signs for Alicante that take you past the front of the Teatro Chapí. At a T-junction for Madrid, Alcoi and Alicante, turn left, and left again just before the road passes under the motorway, then follow the signs for Biar to the right (seven kilometres).

As you approach Biar along a straight road through pleasant countryside, you see its castle looming over the town. The castle keep is one of the most important in the region of Valencia and one of only three in Spain with ribbed vaulting on the arches on the second storey that intertwine to form a rosette in the middle of the vault, a feature that dates it in the second half of the 12th-century.

The lower two floors are of Islamic design, while the third is a 15th-century addition, built at the same time as the double bailey that protects its southern face. A plaque inside the keep, placed there when it was conquered for Aragon by Jaime I in 1245, declares in Latin *"Claudo et aperio regnum"*, only the king has two keys, signalling his dominium over both warring factions.

The views of the Vall de Vinalopó from the castle are stunning, and you will be further rewarded if you have a smattering of Spanish as the guide is very friendly and knowledgeable.

Leave Biar by the A210 to Castalla. A few kilometres further on you see the ragged outline of Castalla castle, with Onil to your left, where more dolls are manufactured than in any other town in the Valencia Community.

From the top of the limestone rock, 785 metres above sea level, on which Castalla castle stands, you have a commanding view of the Verde river. Archeological remains show that the castle was most likely of Moorish origin, probably from the 11th-century, although no remains from this period are to be seen.

The parts still standing date from the second half of the 15th-century. When Pedro IV of Aragon granted the castle to Ramón de Vilanova in 1362, he said it should be razed to the ground and built anew because of its decaying fortifications, a small job that lasted a mere 217 years. The keep was finally finished in 1579.

The remains belong to the ancient manor house that had two circular towers on each end. Stretches of wall around the main bailey are still much in evidence and enclose the remains of a number of medieval storerooms. The *pièce de résistance,* however, is the huge circular Torre Grossa.

The locals fought their own battle a few years ago when the local council tried to asphalt their Cami de la Bola, a rough piece of ground on the outskirts of town where the local game of *joc de la bola* has been played at weekends and fiestas for 300 years, with steel balls weighing three kilos handed down from father to son. Vociferous protests and hundreds of signatures saved the day.

From Castalla take the road for Alicante until you join the A36, where you can go to Alcoi and the north or continue on to Alicante 24 kilometres to the south.

WHAT TO SEE

NOVELDA:
Castillo La Mola, the only castle in Europe with a triangular tower.
Santuario de Santa María Magdalena, a bizarre-looking sanctuary beside the castle.

ELDA:
Museo del Calzado, Avenida de Chapí, 32. Tel. 96 538 30 21. Open Tues-Sat 10am-1pm and 4-8pm, Sunday 10am-2pm. During August Tues-Sat only, 10am-2pm.

VILLENA:
Castillo de La Atalaya. Open Mon-Fri 10.30am-1pm, Sat/Sun & holidays 10.30am-1.30pm. Guided tours every half hour. Free entry.
Museo Arqueológico, Plaza de Santiago, 1. Tel. 96 580 11 50 ext 66. Priceless gold treasure. Open Tues-Fri 10am-2pm, 5-8pm, Sat/Sun 11am-2pm. Free entry.
Teatro Chapí, Calle Lucián López Ferrer, 17. Tel. 96 581 47 50. Restored early 20th-century theatre with neo-Moorish external decoration. Open at performance times.
Museo del Botijo. Calle Párroco Azorín, 7. Tel. 96 580 05 71. Private collection of over 1500 examples of wine and water-cooling jars from around the world. View by arrangement with the tourist office
Museo del Festero, Plaza de Santiago (in the Casa de Cultura). Tel. 96 534 30 50. Museum of the Moors and Christians' Fiesta. View by arrangement with the tourist office.

CASTALLA:
Castle & 15th-century parish church.

Villena Castle

BIAR:
For more information on Biar see Excursion 18: Tin Toys and
the Keys to the Kingdom.

WHERE TO STAY

PETRER:
AC Hotel, Avenida de Madrid, 10. Tel. 96 695 60 80. Info and
reservations 902 292 293. Modern hotel, part of national AC
hotel group. €€€€

VILLENA:
Hotel Restaurante Salvadora, Avenida de la Constitución,102.
Tel. 96 580 09 50. Web page: www.hotelsalvadora.com
Villena's only hotel, but comfortable and well-priced. €

WHERE TO EAT

NOVELDA:
L'Alarich, Calle San Roque, 22. Tel. 96 560 75 82. Highly inventive chef who changes the menu regularly. €€€
Azafrán, Av. Alfonso X El Sabio, 24. Tel. 96 560 62 98. Mediterranean cuisine and chef's own recipes. €€– €€€

PETRER:
La Sirena, Avenida de Madrid, 14. Tel. 96 537 17 18. Email: info@lasirena.net. Web page: www.lasirena.net. Open daily 1-3pm and 9-11.30pm. Best to reserve. The simplicity of the exterior belies the beauty of the interior of this splendid restaurant. Muted tones of glowing wood with panelled walls. Prices reflect the fact that La Sirena is part of the superb restaurant association Cuina i Tertulia Alicante. *Menú degustación* €42 or *menú viajero* €18. You can sample a wide range of original *tapas* at the bar. The web page is a work of art too. €€€
Cerveceriá Cruz Blanca, Estación de Autobuses, Avenida de Madrid. Good range of *tapas* and *raciones* from €7-13.

VILLENA:
Hotel Restaurant Salvadora, Avenida de la Constitución, 102. Tel. 96 580 09 50. Typical food from the region with a good range of *tapas* at the bar. The *menú degustación* (a sample of different dishes from the main menu) changes monthly. €€– €€€
El Rincón de la Espuela, Calle José Zapater, 4. Tel. 96 581 48 28. Good range of local dishes and own recipes. Large choice of rice dishes including *paella de ajos tiernos, pulpo y verdura* (paella with garlic stalks, octopus and vegetables). Meat dishes include ostrich, or you can choose from a wide range of *tapas*. €€

MORE INFORMATION

NOVELDA:
Tourist Information Office, Calle Mayor, 6. Tel. 96 560 92 28. Opening hours Mon-Fri 10am-7pm (8pm in Summer), Sat 10am-2pm.

PETRER:
Conçorcio de la Isla del Interior, Estación de Autobuses, Avenida de Madrid, 10. Tel . 96 695 25 86. Open Mon-Fri 10am-2pm and 4-8pm.

VILLENA:
Tourist Information Office, Plaza de Santiago, 5.
Tel. 96 580 38 04. Open 8am-3pm Mon-Fri, Sat/Sun
10.30am-1.30pm.

CASTALLA:
Ayuntamiento, Plaza Mayor, 1. Tel. 96 658 08 01.
Open Mon-Fri, 8am-2pm.

Tourist Information Office, Plaza Mayor, 3.
Tel. 96 556 10 18. Open Tue-Fri 9.30am-2.30pm,
4.30-6.30pm, Sat 10am-2pm.

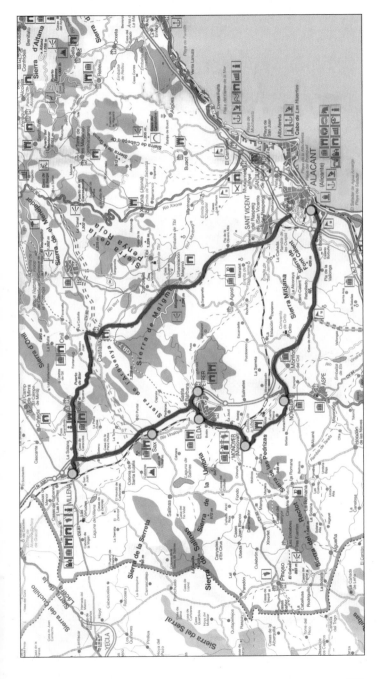

Elche's
Imperial
Palm

SEA OF PALMS

> **AREA:** Southwest of Alicante city
> **ROUTE:** Elche – Aspe - Novelda
> **DISTANCE:** 42 kilometres

Stroll through Europe's largest palm forest which provides the white fronds used in Easter celebrations all over the world, and marvel at how the other half lived at the turn of the 20th century.

Palms are the one thing you can't miss in Elche. It has the most extensive palm forest in Europe, covering more than 445 hectares (1,100 acres). With more than 200,000 trees, there is said to be one for each of the city's inhabitants.

The older part of Elche (Elx in *valenciano*) is set in the middle of this palm forest like an urban oasis, which is exactly what the Moors who planted the palms intended it to be — an oasis on the trade route between Africa and the interior of the Iberian peninsula. Their original irrigation system is still in use today in some places and has ensured the continued existence of Europe's most northerly palm forest.

There are 67 *huertos* (gardens or orchards) of palm trees in total, but the most historic is the 13,000-square-metre Huerto del Cura, famous for its 200-year-old Imperial Palm, a single tree with eight branches.

It is also renowned for its baptised trees, which bear a plaque in honour of the person in whose name it was baptised. One palm carries the name of Queen Sofía. The patron attends a ceremony during which their palm is baptised with wine and each year they receive a bunch of dates from their own tree.

The influence of the palm extends far beyond that of providing a

Elche, the city of palms

few dignitaries with dessert or visitors with a bit of exotic shade. The fronds of the white palm cultivated in Elche are sent throughout Europe for Palm Sunday processions. Black plastic hoods are placed over the tops of male palms to keep the light out and stop the young branches from turning green. When they are harvested they are kept moist in special refrigerators before being woven into ornate confections of stars, crowns, donkeys and castles, which can be anything up to 2.4 metres (8 feet) high.

Almost as numerous as the palm trees are replicas, from finger-sized to monumental, of the bust of the Dama de Elche to be seen throughout the city. Thought to be the earliest example of Iberian sculpture (dating from 500 BC), the Dama was discovered in 1897, then sold to the Louvre in Paris for the equivalent of about 35 euros. It returned to Spain in 1941. The beautifully carved head of a woman with ornate headgear went on show in Elche for six months in 2006 but its permanent home is in the Museo Arqueológico Nacional in Madrid.

But the Dama is just one example of the art and architecture brought to Elche, or Illici as the original Iberian residents knew it, by conquering hordes.

Phoenicians, Carthaginians, Romans and Moors all adapted the city to suit their needs and left their mark. The original 12th-century Arab baths are hidden inside the 14th-century convent of Our Lady of Mercé, while the town hall looming over the Plaza de Baixa was built in the 13th-century to a Moorish design but acquired a new façade during the Renaissance period. Most overwhelming is the Basílica de Santa María, the 15th-century baroque church that dominates the city centre, built on the site of a mosque.

Apart from its historical significance, Elche produces 42 per cent of the shoes made in Spain and has some splendid shoe shops to prove it, as well as shops selling virtually anything you can think of to do with palms and dates.

Elche's medieval mystery play

Vying with the Palm Sunday procession as one of the city's most important fiestas, the Misteri d'Elx is the only medieval choral religious mystery play allowed to be performed inside a church after the Council of Trent's ban in the 17th century. In true medieval liturgical style, no women are allowed to participate and all the angels, and Mary herself, are played by young boys.

Performed and sung by amateurs, the re-enactment of Mary's death and ascension to Heaven takes place over five days in mid-August, in the Santa María basilica. A three-day dress rehearsal (open to the public) is followed by the full two-day performance.

In the early part of the performance the Mangrana, an enormous gilded pomegranate, descends through an opening in a painted canvas representing heaven, slowly opening to form a palm tree of brilliantly coloured leaves. It shelters an angel carrying a golden palm, which he delivers to Mary, la Virgen de la Asunción, 22 terrifying metres below. The audience goes wild when Mary rises triumphantly heavenward, accompanied by a guitar-strumming angelic choir.

An ancient, complex contraption of beams, pulleys and stout ropes is used to send the actors flying upwards and downwards during the performance. The operating instructions were passed verbally from father to son and only were finally written down in the year 2000.

To continue the excursion, leave Elche by the road that passes in front of the tourist information office and crosses over the Pont d'Altamira in the direction of Crevillente and Aspe 12 kilometres away. A couple of hundred metres after the bridge, a small sign to the right directs you to Aspe and the Polígono Industrial Carrús. (The sign is not easy to see, so look for St Andrew's School of English on a corner and turn there.)

Follow the signs for Aspe, Murcia and Alicante, with the Polisportiu Municipal de Camps on your right, taking the right at the first roundabout. Take a left at the next roundabout, signposted for the Hotel AC and the Hotel Campanillo (there is no motorway sign here but you will soon see one). You pass through an industrial estate, where you turn right at a large roundabout directing you to the motorway and a few moments later join it heading toward Aspe and Alicante. When you see an overhead sign for Aspe-Asp, cross over to the left lane as you come to a left-hand bend, immediately after which is the turn-off for Aspe (CV84). If you aren't in the left lane, you could miss it.

Stay on this dual carriageway (ignoring the small sign to your right that indicates Aspe and Zona Industrial) until you come to the exit for Aspe and Crevillente (N325). Follow the signs into Aspe town centre. Aspe has been an independent wine-producing area since the 16th-century, but these days the town forms part of an association with neighbouring Novelda, Hondón de las Nieves and Monforte del Cid and shares with them the Denominación de Origen Uva Embolsada del Vinalopó, which guarantees the high quality of the table grapes from this area.

The mature grapes are covered with paper bags while ripening to protect them from insects and to ensure their sweetness — an unusual sight during the months of September and October. These grapes are the sweetest available and much favoured during the New Year's Eve celebrations, when Spaniards traditionally gulp down one grape on each of the twelve chimes of the clock at midnight to bring them luck for the coming year.

The original Moorish town of Aspis was founded in the 12th-century on a site about four kilometres from the present town. A few ruins are still visible there. Modern Aspe was built on the banks of the Tarafa River, a tributary of the Vinalopó, which later dried up and earned the town the nickname of *uvas mil y agua poca*, a thousand grapes and little water.

At its heart Aspe is a pretty little town with a liking for pastel-shaded paintwork. Even some of the modern buildings are decked out in coats of ochre, pale blue, brick red and other pleasantly muted tones. In the Plaza Mayor, the 17th-century *palacio* of the Duque de Maqueda, until recently used as the town hall, is undergoing extensive restoration. The new town hall next door has been designed by someone with obvious good taste and the modern frontage blends in beautifully with the stone of its 300-year-old neighbour. It's worth nipping inside to admire its arched glass ceiling.

Facing the palace in the Plaza Mayor is the attractive Casino Primitivo, one of a number of *modernista* (Art Nouveau) buildings in the town, but the square is dominated by the grand baroque façade of the Iglesia de Nuestra Señora del Socorro. The church celebrated its 400th anniversary in 2002. Unfortunately it is often closed, but there is a pretty little side chapel on the narrow lane to the right of the building.

The attractive streets radiating from the Plaza Mayor are a mixture of *modernista* and medieval. It's worth walking up Calle Don Francisco Candela (to the left of the Casino Primitivo) to see the wonderfully archaic Droguería Andújer. The stock may have changed since the shop opened 70 years ago, but the style hasn't. The shelves are packed with every conceivable product for cleaning, painting, polishing, staining and a hundred-and-one other household chores. Brushes, paint-rollers, buckets, watering cans and fly swats hang on bits of twisted metal coat hangers from aging shelving. In its own fascinating way, it's a museum.

Two minutes or so walk from the town hall is the splendid 1930s Mercado de Abastos with its glorious Moorish-style horseshoe arch for an entrance and its cream-and-rust-red stonework. You can shop here for a picnic and take it to the nice little park beside the market. To find out more of the history of Aspe visit the Museo Municipal, situated in the Centro Social, by the bridge that takes you in the direction of Novelda. The museum is housed in a 19th-century nobleman's house and has displays of oil and wine-making processes (original to the house) as well as depictions of life in a small town.

To leave Aspe, cross the bridge in front of the Museo Municipal on Avenida de la Constitución and stay on this road for five kilometres until you reach Novelda. When you reach the traffic lights at Novelda just after the Renault garage, turn right following the signs for the tourist information office and the Santuario and Castillo. Follow the road to the roundabout at the bottom and turn left in the direction of Elda then left again when you see the sign for Centro Urbano in front of the Citroen garage. Park where you see a sign for the tourist office to your right because there is no parking near the office itself, and parking in the small square beside it is reserved for official vehicles (you will also be leaving by this road.)

Novelda owes its existence to marble, saffron and grapes, but what sets the town apart from others are the splendid examples of *modernista* architecture, with its characteristic curved and spiralling arabesques, more widely known as Art Nouveau.

The Plaza del Ayuntamiento has one of the prettiest Cruz Roja (Red Cross) offices in Spain, with its gaily turreted and balconied exterior looking down on the ambulances below. Opposite, across the peaceful tree-filled square, the restored façade of what is now the town hall, is a lovely example of 17th-century Valencia civic architecture. Set in the cool arcaded entrance are large tiled murals depicting the main industries of the area.

Woven palms used in Easter parades

Take Calle Mayor, to the left of the town hall, and at number 24 enjoy a glimpse of how the "other half" lived at the turn of the 20th-century. The house, now known as the Casa Museo Modernista, was originally a grand family home in the centre of the developing town.

It was built by one Antonia Navarro, a widow of formidable business prowess and well supported by an extensive fortune inherited from her father. To get an idea of just how affluent she was, take a look at the row of tiles set in the walls surrounding the delightful internal patio. Each tile, and there are an awful lot of them, bears an image of one of the properties she owned.

No expense was spared in the building of the house, which was inaugurated in 1905 to coincide with the wedding of one of Antonia's daughters. The house fell into near-ruin after the Civil War but fortunately, in 1977, a bank restored it, furnishing it with period pieces from auction houses throughout Spain. The museum also houses an exhibition in honour of Jorge Juan, son of Novelda and one of Spain's most famous mariners.

On Calle Emilio Castellar in the Parque de F. Rodríguez de la Fuente, is the splendid Casino, founded in 1888 and beautifully restored a century later. To the rear of the building, amid tree-shaded gardens full of birdsong stands a superb Victorian bandstand, complete with an angelic harp on its roof.

Leaving Novelda, go straight ahead until you come to a square with a church in front of you. To the right of the church is a sign directing you to Monóvar. At the next major junction you will see, just across the road to your left, the ornate entrance to the Parque del Oeste, a pleasant picnic spot.

The park is a delightful Gaudiesque respite from the bustling town. Passing through the gaudily tiled and luxuriously entwirled wrought-iron entrance, the first thing you spot is an undulating, mosaic seat encircling a pond, from the centre of which spouts a bubbling fountain. It is pleasant to saunter along footpaths and over bridges made from disused railway sleepers that cross over ponds filled with goldfish.

There is a picnic area set aside with wooden tables below shady conifers and, on weekends, the neat little fake ruins bedecked with bougainvillea provide an idyllic backdrop for the constant stream of newlyweds who come here to have their photographs taken.

From the Parque del Oeste head back into town and follow the signs for Alicante. They will take you to the N330 and a quick 25-kilometre drive back to the coast.

Casa Mueso dining room

WHAT TO SEE

ELCHE:

Huerto del Cura, Carrer Porta de la Morera, s/n. Open daily
9am-6pm (summer 9am-8.30pm). Tel. 96 545 27 47.
Entry €2.50

Basílica de Santa María, Plaza de Santa Isabel. Open daily
7am-1.30pm and 5.30-9pm.

Museu de la Festa, Carrer Major de la Vila, 25. Tel. 96 545
34 64. Open Tues-Sat 10am-1pm and 4.30-8.30pm (summer
5-9pm).
Entry €3. (Fiesta museum including costumes and items used
in the Mystery play. Video show of the play daily 10.30am,
11.30am, 12.15pm, 5pm, 6pm, 7pm.)

ASPE:

Plaza Mayor, attractive tree-shaded square with interesting
buildings including the Ayuntamiento, Nuestra Señora del
Socorro church and the Casino Primitivo.

Museo Histórico de Aspe, Avda. Constitución, 42.
Tel. 96 549 34 63. Entry free. Open 6-8pm Wed, Thurs, Fri,
and 10.30am-1.30pm Sat, Sun and Fiesta days.

Mercado de Abastos, Parc Dr. Calatayub. Open 8am-2pm
Mon-Sat. Closed Sun.

Grand stairway in Novelda´s Casa Museo

NOVELDA:
Casa-Museo Modernista, Calle Mayor, 24.
Tel. 96 560 02 37. Open 9.30am-2pm and 4-7pm Mon-Fri
(6pm on Fri), 11am-2pm Sat. Closed August. Free entry.
Casino/Parque F. Rodríguez, Calle Emilio Castelar.
The park open to public but only certain rooms in the
Casino have public access although the caretaker is usually
amenable to visitors seeing the upper rooms if asked
politely.
Parque del Oeste, Avenida Ingeniero Enrique Santo.
On the edge of town in the direction of Monóvar. Open
10am-7pm.

Castillo La Mola, the only castle in Europe with a triangular tower.

Santuario de Santa María Magdalena, a bizarre-looking sanctuary beside the castle.
Note: A visit to the castle and sanctuary outside town is a must. See "Trip 20: Route of the Castles" for details and how to get there.

WHERE TO STAY

ELCHE:
Hotel Faro, Cami dels Magros, 24. Tel. 96 546 00 76.
One of the best of the economy-priced hotels. €
Hotel Milenio, Prolongación Curtidores, s/n. Tel. 96 661 20 33. Elegant modern hotel 10 minutes from city centre, with a restaurant specialising in Mediterranean cuisine.
€€€- €€€€
Hotel Huerto del Cura, Porta de la Morera.
Tel. 96 661 20 50. The place to stay if you are treating yourself. Set in palm gardens with tennis courts, gym, kidney-shaped swimming pool, sauna and solarium.
An oasis in the heart of the city centre. Good value at weekends. Els Capallans is the name of the hotel restaurant and specialises in local cuisine. €€€- €€€€
ASPE:
Hostal Ya, Avenida 3 Agosto, 40. Tel. 96 549 50 51.
Modern hotel offering clean and simple accommodation. €€

WHERE TO EAT

ELCHE:
Restaurante Parque Municipal, Parque Municipal, s/n.
Tel. 96 545 34 15. Open daily 9am-11pm. An enormous restaurant that can appear quite daunting but is one of the best places to try the local cuisine at affordable prices. The daily menu at €9.85 is good value or you can try their speciality menu at €15.65. €- €€
La Masía de Elche, Km62 on the Murcia-Alicante road.
Tel. 96 545 97 47. Highly regarded restaurant outside the city. Try the baby goat cutlets. €€- €€€
Carrer Mare de Déu del Carmé (Calle Nuestra Señora del Carmen) has a good selection of reasonably priced restaurants.

ASPE:
El Montadito, Plaza Mayor, 8. Modern café/restaurant serving regional food. Good-value *menú del día*.
€– €€
Hermanos Amorrich, Avenida de Navarra, 47. Traditional Castilian food. €- €€

NOVELDA:
L'Alarich, Calle San Roque, 22. Tel. 96 560 75 82. Highly inventive chef who changes the menu regularly. Expensive, but recommended.
Azafrán, Av. Alfonso X El Sabio, 24. Tel. 96 560 62 98. Mediterranean cuisine and chef's own recipes. €€–€€€

MORE INFORMATION

ELCHE:
Tourist Information Office, Parque Municipal, s/n. Tel. 96 545 27 47. Open Mon-Fri 10am-7pm, Sat 10am-2.30pm, Sun 10am-2pm.

ASPE:
Ayuntamiento, Plaza Mayor. Tel. 96 691 99 00. Open Mon-Fri 8.30am-2.30pm.

NOVELDA:
Information Office, Calle Mayor, 6. Tel. 96 560 92 28

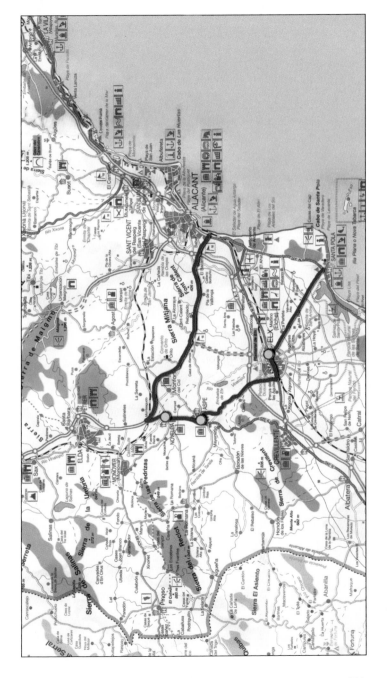

Participant in the famous Moors and Christians fiesta

TRIP 22
BUTTERFLY MAIDS AND PAINTED PIGEONS

AREA: West of Torrevieja.
ROUTE: Torrevieja – Orihuela – Murcia – Archena – Abanilla
DISTANCE: 119 kilometres

Visit a fabulously decorated old-time casino to see the butterfly maidens and dance a polka, then drive through the arid south to wallow in medicinal mud.

You leave Torrevieja on the CV95, in the direction of San Miguel de Salinas and Orihuela, an inland road that takes you 21 kilometres through extensive orange groves, past the Embalse de la Pedrera and on to Bigastro. Leaving this town, you will see a sign just after a roundabout indicating Orihuela four kilometres further on. After a few minutes on this straight road, you will see the great edifice of the Seminario looming on the hillside above Orihuela.

Cross over the next roundabout and at the one after that, in front of the Hipermercado Eroski, turn left where the road becomes the CV925. Moments later, at the next roundabout, turn right to go through an underpass that brings you out at yet another roundabout, this one with a large sculpture of radiating metal bars. Take the left exit (passing to the right of Automóbiles Joyper) for the Centro Urbano and at the end of this street there is a set of traffic lights (with a Benetton sign in front of you). Turn left and almost immediately you enter the town centre with a very pretty park, the Glorieta Gabriel Miró.

Orihuela is a tricky town to drive around and it's best to leave the car somewhere near the park because this is the way you will be leaving to continue the excursion. This is the modern part of the city but it is only a few minutes' walk to the old town.

Orihuela sits on the banks of the meandering Segura, a river that supplies a complex irrigation system dating back to Arab times and feeds the abundant orange and lemon groves that form such an intrinsic part of the regional scenery. The capital of the Vega Baja, Orihuela has no less than five national monuments and more than a scattering of museums, parks and galleries to keep the visitor entertained for hours.

It is a city of grand buildings. The most impressive of these is the 16th-century Colegio de Santo Domingo. Originally a convent with a small school, it was recognised by papal bull in 1569 and became a university. It taught theology, grammar, arts and the law until it was closed in 1824 as part of the suppression of religious orders. Almost two centuries later, it fulfils an educational role once more, housing a secondary school and part of the tourism department of Alicante University.

The Renaissance convent cloister was built in the early 17th-century and the baroque university cloister was built between 1727 and 1737. The latter has two levels of Romanesque arches, slender Corinthian columns and heraldic logos among which are the coats of arms of Spain, Calatrava and a number of popes.

Between the cloisters is the original refectory, decorated in 18th-century Valencia tiles depicting pastoral scenes, said to be one of the most important examples of this kind of decoration in the region.

The interior of the church is an outrageous confection of ornate stuccowork and rich decoration dating back to the end of the 17th and beginning of the 18th centuries. The altarpiece by Juan de Juanes looks out of proportion, hardly surprising as its former home was in a side chapel and replaces the original altar destroyed during the Civil War.

San Salvador began life as a parish church but, in a series of ecclesiastical promotions, worked its way upwards until, in the 14th-century, it became a cathedral. Its main structure is Catalan Gothic and two of its main entrances, the Puerta de las Cadenas and Puerta de Loreto, are from this period while a third, the Puerta de la Anunciación, is of Renaissance origin.

At the rear of the church is the Museo Diocesano, which boasts Velázquez's *The Temptation of Saint Thomas* among its collection of religious art.

For a change from imposing architecture, you could venture underground at the Museo de la Muralla, where a guided tour leads you through the underground remains of the city walls, Arab baths

The picturesque church in the Balneario de Archena

and domestic buildings. The Museo de Semana Santa houses most of the processional thrones and sculptures used in the Easter processions, while the Museo de La Reconquista is dedicated to the folklore of the Moors and Christians fiesta. Here you will see costumes, arms, musical instruments, photographs and publicity material relating to this fiesta.

For the next stop on our excursion, we step over the Valencia border into Murcia and visit the capital of the region. As Murcia is a city, it is strictly speaking outside the realms of this book, but no visit to this area would be complete without a visit to one of the most beguiling buildings you could hope to see.

To leave Orihuela, take the road that runs along the left-hand side of the Glorieta Gabriel Miró (Calle San Gregorio) and turn left at the end, heading for the N340/E15 to Alicante and Murcia. This street brings you back to the roundabout with the metal sculpture, but this time you go straight across. Moments later you come to a small roundabout where you take the exit to the left.

Follow the signs for Murcia and, after two kilometres, it joins the N340. Just after this junction the road rises and to your left you see the Palmeral, Orihuela's palm garden, second in size to Elche, which is itself the largest palm garden in Spain.

The road from Orihuela could never be described as beautiful, running as it does through a number of small industrial areas, but the rugged hills of the Sierra de Orihuela, dotted with patches of pine woods, do have a certain grandeur.

Stay on this road, ignoring the first sign for the A7 and Alicante, until you see a sign directing you to the E15/A7, just in front of the Café Bar Casa Augusto, Cano Muebles to your right. Your map will tell you that this is a longer route to Murcia but it will get you more easily into the city centre. When you reach Murcia, take the exit for Juan de Borbón and Ronda de Levante and follow the signs into the city until you come to a T-junction with MAPFRE offices directly in front of you.

Turn right. At the second roundabout, where there are a number of direction signs take the right for Albacete. You can either park here and walk into the centre, ten minutes or so, as this is the direction you will leave Murcia, or drive to the centre by taking the exit to the left and following the signs for the cathedral.

A stone's throw from the cathedral, down the Calle Trapería, is the Casino, not a bit like a glitzy, high-rolling modern-day casino but more a gentlemen's club where the solid citizens of the town used to socialise, discuss business and play dominoes or cards for small stakes.

The butterfly maids Of Murcia Casino

It's true that these old-time casinos can be found in many towns and villages in Spain but few of them are as grand as Murcia's. If the magnificent entrance with its rose marble pillars and heroic allegorical bas-reliefs isn't enough to convince you that you are entering a building of grandeur and significance, then the Islamic splendour of the Patio Arabe will. Exuberant, multicoloured intricate designs with horseshoe arches radiating fantails of blue and gold arabesques fill the entrance hall, proclaiming its importance to the city's business and cultural life of years gone by.

The Casino of Murcia was founded in 1847 and over the following decades the magnificent palace-like building was expanded and embellished. It was recognised as an Historic National Monument in 1983 and, though a sepulchral calm pervades its halls, it now attracts more than 150,000 visitors annually.

As you stand awed in the Patio Arabé, bright daylight filters through the coloured glass canopy overhead, casting complex shadows and dancing rainbow illuminations over the walls of the upper level, around which runs a wrought-iron balustrade.

An arched glass roof over a marble-floored corridor stretches before you, awash with diffused daylight and leading to a semi-circle of deep armchairs, raised five steps above floor level and surrounding a copy of the famous statue of the Dama de Elche.

Pass through the Arab arch, with its marble columns and intricate plasterwork, and into the room to the left, where you enter an elegant Edwardian library. In the centre of the room, deep maroon and brass-studded chairs surround the two enormous library tables with their brass-hooded lamps. In one corner, a wrought-iron spiral staircase twists its way up to a narrow balcony where leather-bound tomes rest in glazed bookcases. The balcony and bookcases are born aloft on the wings of a flight of herons which great cast-iron brackets.

To lighten the mood, return to the corridor and visit the last room on the left, the *Tocador Señoras* (ladies' powder room), a tiny but delightful room where these days the gentlemen are allowed in, too. Gilded chairs line the walls but it is the painted ceiling that draws the eyes and the gasps. Youthful maidens with bright butterfly wings skitter across a deep blue sky. You think they are ascending heavenward to the centre of the domed ceiling until you realise they are reaching out to a flaxen-haired maid as she tumbles to earth, her wings on fire.

Before you leave the room, stand in front of one of the tall oval mirrors and see yourself reflected into infinity in the mirror opposite as you travel down an Alice-in-Wonderland hole in the wall.

The casino's *pièce de résistance* is the Salón de Baile Regio, inspired by the French palaces of Luis XV and completed in 1876. As you approach the room at the side of the Patio Pompeyano, all is in darkness. Drop a one euro coin into the box to the side of the door and a rousing Parisian polka strikes up as the room bursts into brilliant light.

The ballroom is an incredible confection of gilding and gold moquette. From its stunning painted silk ceiling, now suffering from damp, hang five huge chandeliers, the light from their 326 bulbs reflected in a hundred directions from the rococo, gilt-framed mirrors. Heavenly scenes and Greek rural idylls fill panels in the frieze and a group of maidens floats on clouds.

If you get carried away by all the splendour and can't resist a twirl beneath the candelabras, don't wait too long because, just as the first strains of a waltz fill the ballroom, the lights suddenly go out and you are plunged back into near-total darkness.

Murcia is a pleasant city and you could happily spend a couple of hours wandering its streets. When you are ready to continue the excursion, leave the city by going back to the roundabout mentioned earlier and following the signs for Albacete (A301) and Molina de Segura, Madrid and Alicante (A7). You will pass the large Ikea store near the exit from the motorway you came in on. Keep following the sign for Albacete.

The painted pigeons of Murcia

When the Arabs settled in Spain in 711, they brought with them a culture that was to permeate almost the whole of the Iberian peninsula. They also brought with them the pigeon. The bird was valued for its meat, its plumage and for providing *palomina*, a high-quality natural fertiliser. Documents dating from 1268 tell of a vast population of pigeons living in the 97 towers of the city of Murcia and in the surrounding countryside.

The people of the city had taken the bird to their hearts and specially bred pigeons, often the descendants of those left behind when the Arabs were expelled or fled, were trained by professional *colombaires*. Two hundred years later there was so much bird manure building up on the bridge above the Segura that travellers and tradesmen were unable to cross it.

In 1773, the first pigeon sports club was started in Murcia, but it wasn't until more than 200 years later, in 1994, that pigeon-breeding was finally officially recognised as a national sport, when the Federación Española de Columbicultura was set up. If, on your travels, you see flocks of garishly painted birds flapping around, these are the painted pigeons that make up the singularly Spanish sport of Columbicultura.

Pass Molina de Segura, Ceuti and Lorqui and take exit 375 for Fortuna and Archena, following the road as it loops under the A30 in the direction of Archena (MU554). Take a right at the third roundabout, that looks like the roof of a sunken house, complete with weather vane, and at the next roundabout follow the signs for the Balneario de Archena. At this roundabout look to your left. At the top of a small rise is an unusual building that looks like a small fortress. This novel little structure is known as the Castillo de Don Mario in honour of the owner, Mario Spreáfico, referred to in the local tourism brochures as a *"magnífico médico y excelente persona"*, a magnificent doctor and excellent person. Despite its grand title, this amusing edifice with its round towers and arched windows was, in fact, a pigeon loft (see side bar).

Fiestas, especially costumed affairs, are popular in Valencia

Keep following the signs for the Balneario and a few minutes later you come to the entrance to the spa with a car park to the left.

The Balneario de Archena was built in the middle of the 19th-century and much of its decoration was in the hands of Manuel Castaños, the same man who decorated the Casino in Murcia. This spa actually has its own casino, its elegant green and white façade topped by a pediment of prancing cherubim and its entrance guarded by a pair of caryatid (a sculptured female figure serving as an ornamental support in place of a column or pilaster). Its palm-shaded garden is a haven of peace and quiet where you can enjoy a cool drink or use the enormous marble board and man-size pieces for a game of chess. There is also a delightful little church whose narrow Gothic style and imperial stairway make it look like the home of a fairytale princess.

"Taking the waters" has always been part of the Spanish approach to health and vitality, even to the extent that the Spanish government subsidises pensioners unable to afford the spa fees. Each spa has its own specialities. That of the Balneario de Archena is mud, but not your common-or-garden type. The thermal mud here allows the chemical properties of the hot spring water to enter the body, and is especially soothing as an anti-inflammatory treatment. The spa offers a range of thermal treatments as well as hot-spring bathing.

To leave the Balneario (there's little else to see in Archena), retrace the route to the A301 and go straight across, heading for Fortuna (14km MU411). At last you leave the busy roads behind as you pass through orange groves with beige, barren mountains in the distance, a landscape far removed from the green mountainscapes only an hour's drive north. The barrenness isn't total because here and there small pockets of almond groves dot the hillsides. Even so, this land has a rugged beauty all its own.

At the T-junction in Fortuna, turn left for Pinoso and then right at the traffic lights for Abanilla (eight kilometres). As you arrive at Abanilla, follow the signs for Murcia and Orihuela. (If you want to stop at Abanilla, you can get more information about the town by reading excursion 16: Alicante's Lunar Landscape.) You soon enter large areas of orange and lemon groves with frequent vineyards.

Keep following the signs for Orihuela and, just after Benferri, you reach the A7/E15 autovia, which is the quickest way back to Alicante. For Torrevieja and south, continue on the C4140/CV870 to Orihuela until it reaches the junction of the N340

WHAT TO SEE

ORIHUELA:

Afternoon open and closing hours for the historic buildings of the old town are one hour earlier between Oct and May.

Convento de Santo Domingo, Calle Adolfo Clavarana, s/n. 16th-century university. Tel. 96 530 02 49. Open Tue-Sat 9.30am-1.30pm & 5-8pm, Sun 10am-2pm.

San Salvador, Calle Doctor Sarget. Cathedral mainly in the Catalan Gothic style. Tel. 96 530 06 38. Open Mon-Fri 10am-1.30pm and4-7pm (June-Sept 5-7.30pm) Sat 10am-1.30pm.

Museo Diocesano, museum of religious art at the rear of the catheral. Same opening hours as cathedral. Entry €1.

Museo de la Muralla, Calle del Río, s/n. Remains of city walls, Arab baths and domestic buildings. Tel. 96 674 31 54. Open Tue-Sat 10am-2pm & 4-7pm, (June-Sept 5-8pm) Sun 10am-2pm. Free entry.

Museo de Semana Santa, Plaza de la Merced, 1. Holy Week museum with displays of floats and sculptures from Easter processions. Tel. 96 674 40 89. Open Tues-Sat 10am-1pm & 5-7pm. Entry €1.

Museo de la Reconquista, Calle Francisco Die. Open Mon-Fri 11am-1pm & 5-7pm. Free entry.

MURCIA:

Casino, Calle Trapería. The city's grand old casino. Tel. 96 821 53 99. Open 10am-9pm. Entry €1.20.

Murcia has spectacular Holy Week processions when amazingly realistic religious carvings by famed sculptor Francisco Salzillo are paraded on floats. Also worth seeing are the **Museo Salzillo** and the **Cathedral** with its dazzling Baroque façade, fine views from the tower.

ABANILLA:

San José, a beautiful church with a gilded and marbled altarpiece.

La Fuente, Calle Mayor. Fountain decorated with 12 metres of ceramic imagery telling the folkloric history of the area.

Sagrado Corazón, 10-metre high statue of Christ overlooking the Plaza de la Constitución.

WHERE TO STAY:

ORIHUELA:

Hotel Palacio de Tudemir, Calle Alfonso XIII. Tel. 96 673

8010. Beautifully renovated 18th-century palace. Has good-value weekend offers. €€€- €€€€
Hostal-Residencia Rey Teodomiro, Avenida Teodomiro, 10. Tel. 96 674 33 48. Good-standard hostal in modern part of the city. All rooms have TV, air-con and heating. €- €€

MURCIA:
El Churra, Avenida Marqués de los Vélez, 12. Tel. 96 823 84 00. Pleasant hotel close to city centre. €€€
Rincón de Pepe, Plaza Apóstoles, 34. Tel 96 821 22 39. Large modern hotel tastefully furnished and decorated. You are even given your choice of pillows. Special weekend rates. €€€-€€€€

ABANILLA:
La Posada, Carretera Salzillo, 22. Tel 96 868 00 06. Basic rooms with shared bathroom. €

WHERE TO EAT:

ORIHUELA:
Restaurante Sorzano de Tejeda, Calle Doctor Sarget, 4. Tel. 96 674 51 03. Open for lunch and dinner daily except Mon. Open Sun for lunch only. Elegant restaurant in former palace, famous for its rice dishes. €€-€€€
Bar Cafetería Europa, Plaza Europa, s/n. Tel. 96 674 26 78. Open lunch and dinner. Good basic food with matching prices. €-€€
Hotel Palacio de Tudemir, Calle Alfonso XIII. Tel. 96 673 80 10. Restaurant of recently opened four-star hotel in renovated 18th-century palace. Weekly-changing menu of regional specialities. €€-€€€

MURCIA:
Restaurante El Churra, Calle Obispo Sancho Dávila, 13 bajo. Tel. 96 827 15 22. Highly recommended, 10-minute walk from the Casino. Open daily for lunch and dinner. Beautiful hotel restaurant serving regional specialities and chef's own creations. Dine in one of the elegant dining rooms or in the large open bar. Excellent range of tapas. €€-€€€
Casino de Murcia, Calle Trapería. Tel. 96 821 53 99. Stylish restaurant with a menú del día for €10. Open daily 1.45-5pm except Mondays. €-€€
Murcia has numerous good bars and restaurants.

ABANILLA:
Restaurante La Posada, Carretera Salzillo, 22. Tel 96 868 00 06.
Old coaching house serving regional dishes with large sit-in fireplace. Good value hearty meals. €–€€

MORE INFORMATION

ORIHUELA:
Tourist Office, Calle Francisco Die, 25 (on ground floor of Palacio de Rubalcava). Tel. 96 530 27 47. Open Tue-Sat 10am-2pm & 5-8pm. Sun/Mon 10am-2pm.

MURCIA:
Oficina de Turismo, Plaza Julián Romea, 4. Tel. 902 10 10 70.
Mon-Sat 10am-2pm & 5.30-7.30pm, Sun 10am-2pm. Email: turismo@ayto-murcia.es. Web page www.murciaciudad.com
Information Point, Calle Santa Clara. Behind the Teatro Romea.
Tel. 96 822 06 59. Same opening hours as Ayuntamiento tourist office.

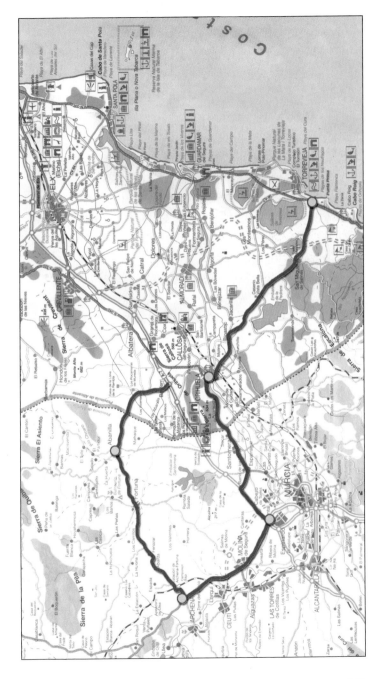

315

VOCABULARY

abierto: open
aficionado: fan, ardent supporter
aguardiente: raw alcoholic spirit
ajo: garlic
alambique: alcohol still
almendras: almonds
arroyo: gulley
asado   : roast, or roast dish
bacalao: cod
barranco: gorge, ravine
becerrada: bullfight with young bulls
berrocal: craggy or rocky area
bodega: wine cellar
calamar: squid
callos: tripe
camino: road, path, way
carta: menu, letter, map
casera: home-style *(eg comida casera* - home cooking)
castillo: castle
cercanías: neighbourhood; suburban railway line
cerrado: closed
cervecería: beer saloon
chaparro: evergreen oak
chispazo: small tot (especially of spirits like *anís*)
chopo: poplar tree
chuleta: chop, cutlet
churrasco: braised steak
ciudad: city
collado: hill, small rise
comida: meal
copa: glass or drink
corrida: bullfight
cueva: cave
dulce: sweet

embalse: reservoir
encierro: driving of bulls from an enclosure to main corral of bullring
encinar: oak forest
estanque: pond
fallas: ceremony of burning effigies and bonfires which originated in Valencia
fiesta, festa: holiday or feast day usually associated with a saint
fuente: fountain
fogón: hearth, fireside; cooking area (in open)
fonda: inn
gambas: prawns
gruta: cave
hoguera: bonfire
jardín: garden
jota: Aragonese dance
madrileño: native of Madrid
menú del día: set meal
merluza: hake
meseta: plateau, tableland
mesón: inn, hostelry
mirador: viewpoint
molino: mill
murallas: walls of a town
museo: museum
olmo: elm tree
pantano: pool, reservoir
paraje: place, spot
pasarela: small pedestrian bridge
paseo: stroll, outing
patronales: fiesta of local patron saint
peña: large rock; club (e.g. *peña taurina*)
pico: peak
pinar: pine forest
plaza: square
plaza mayor: main square
polígono: industrial estate
postre: dessert
pradera: meadow

pueblo: small town or village, populace
ración: ration, helping (of a dish)
requesón: cottage cheese
romería: pilgrimage, picnic excursion
rosquillas: sweet fritters
seco: dry
seguidilla: lively Spanish tune and dance
senda: path
sierra: mountain chain; saw
silla: chair
tapa: tidbit, snack; lid
tasca: tavern
tertulia: club, coterie usually involved in literary
conversations
tinaja: large earthenware jar
tinto: red (wine), dark, dyed
torero: bullfighter
toro: bull
torre: tower
trabuco: blunderbuss
vega: fertile plain, meadow
vendimia: wine vintage
veraneante: summer holidaymaker
verbena: night celebration marking a saint's day:
vereda: path, footpath

ARCHITECTURE

alcazaba: castle
alcázar: fortress, royal palace
artesonado: Moorish-style coffered ceiling
azulejo: glazed tile
barroco: baroque, ornate style
capilla mayor: chapel with high altar
claustro: cloister
churrigueresco: Churrigueresque, highly ornate Baroque art
coro: chancel with choir-stalls
ermita: hermitage
isabelino: Isabelline, Gothic style from era of Queen Isabel

mihrab: prayer niche in a mosque
mozárabe: Mozarab, art developed by Christians under Moslem rule
mudéjar: Moslem art in Christian-occupied territory
murallas: walls, ramparts
neo-clásico: Neo-classical, imitating sober Greek and Roman styles
plateresco: Plateresque, finely carved early Renaissance style
qibla: mosque wall orientated towards Mecca
reja: iron grille
retablo: decorated altarpiece
torre del homenaje: keep

USEFUL PHRASES

ON THE ROAD:

Is there a petrol station near here?: *¿Hay una gasolinera (or estación de servicio) por aquí?*
Fill her up, please: *Lleno, por favor*
Where is the road to Seville?: *¿Dónde está la carretera para Sevilla?*
How do I get to the airport, the market?: *¿Como se puede ir al aeropuerto, al mercado?*
left: *izquierda*
right: *derecha*
straight on: *todo recto*
first right/second left: *la primera a la derecha, la segunda a la izquierda*
to turn left: *girar a la izquierda*
crossroads: *cruce*
traffic lights: *semáforos*
diesel: *gasoil*
driving licence: *carnet de conducir*
insurance certificate: *certificado de seguro*
logbook: *cartilla de propiedad*
mechanic: *mecánico*
oil: *aceite*
petrol: *gasolina* (lead-free: *sin plomo*)
petrol station: *gasolinera*

puncture: *pinchazo*
repair shop: *taller de reparaciones* or *garaje*

ROAD SIGNS
Aparcamiento: parking
Autovía: four-lane highway
Autopista: motorway, turnpike (toll may be payable)
Carga o descarga: Loading and unloading zone, no parking
Carretera cortada: road blocked
Ceda el paso: give way
Centro urbano: town centre
Circunvalación: ronda: bypass
Entrada: entrance
Firme en mal estado: poor road surface
Llamamos grúa: We call the tow-truck (i.e. no parking)
Peaje: toll to pay
Peatones: pedestrians
Peligro: danger
Prohibido aparcar, no aparcar: parking forbidden
Prohibido el paso: no entry
Salida: exit
Tramo en obras: road works
Vado permanente: entrance always in use
Vado inundable: subject to flooding
Vía única: one way

BREAKDOWNS
I have run out of petrol: *Me he quedado sin gasolina*
I have a puncture (flat battery): *Tengo un neumático pinchado (la batería descargada)*
My car has broken down: *Mi coche está averiado*
The car will not start: *El coche no arranca*
The lights don't work: *No funcionan los faros*
I need a tow-truck: *Necesito la grúa*
Where is the nearest garage?: *¿Dónde está el taller de coches más cerca?*
Can you fix it?: *¿Puede arreglarlo?*
Do you do repairs?: *¿Hace reparaciones?*

CAR PARTS

battery: *batería*
brakes: *frenos*
bulb: *bombilla*
car keys: *llaves del coche*
clutch: *embrague*
distilled water: *agua destilada*
exhaust: *escape*
fan belt: *correa de ventilador*
fuse: *fusible*
gearbox: *caja de cambios*
headlights: *faros*
petrol tank: *depósito de gasolina*
points: *contactos*
radiator: *radiador*
seat-belts: *cinturones de seguridad*
spark plug: *bujía*
tyre: *neumático*
wheel: rueda (spare wheel: *rueda de recambio)*
windscreen: *parabrisas*

EMERGENCIES

Ambulance: *ambulancia*
first aid post: *casa de socorro, puesto de socorro*
police station: *comisaría de policía*
Red Cross: *Cruz Roja*
Civil Guard post: *cuartel de la Guardia Civil*
chemist, pharmacy: *farmacia*
hospital: *sanitario, hospital*
doctor: *médico*
casualty department: *urgencias*
I am lost: *Me he perdido*
There's been an accident: *Ha ocurrido un accidente*
I have been robbed: *He sido robado* or *me han robado*
Call the police: *Llama a la policía*
I have lost my luggage, my passport, the car keys, my wife:
*He perdido mi equipaje, mi pasaporte, las llaves del coche,
mi mujer*
I am ill: *Estoy enfermo* or (if you're a woman) *Estoy enferma*

I need a doctor, a dentist, a lawyer: *Necesito un médico, un dentista, un abogado*
I am diabetic, pregnant: *Soy diabético/a, estoy embarazada*
I have heart trouble: *Estoy del corazón*

USEFUL BASICS

Please: *Por favor*
Thank you: *Gracias*
Good morning: *Buenos días*
Good afternoon: *Buenas tardes*
Good night: *Buenas noches*
Goodbye: *Adiós* or *Hasta luego*
Where is the post office, railway station, police station?: *Dónde está el correos, la estación de ferrocarril, la comisaría?*
Where is the toilet?: *¿Dónde están los servicios* (also "*caballeros*" and "*damas*")?
Where can I buy a film, postcards, cigarettes, stamps, medicine?: *¿Dónde puedo comprar una película, postales, tobaco, sellos, medicina?*
Do you have a room free?: *¿Hay una habitación libre?*
I would like a double (single) room: *Querría una habitación doble (individual)*
Can I see the menu?: *¿Puedo ver la carta?*
Me gusta la comida: I like the food
Breakfast: *Desayuno*
Lunch: *Almuerzo*
Dinner: *Cena*
How much is it?: *¿Cuánto es?*
The bill, please: *La cuenta, por favor*
What time is it?: *¿Qué hora es?*
It is two o'clock, midnight: *Son las dos, es medianoche.*

INDEX